John Seybert and The Evangelical Heritage

Biographical and Personal Reflections on
A Life Touched by Godliness

J. Steven O'Malley

Emeth Press

John Seybert and The Evangelical Heritage:
Biographical and Personal Reflections on
A Life Touched by Godliness

Copyright © 2008 J. Steven O'Malley
Printed in the United States of America on acid-free paper

All rights reserved. No part of this book may be reproduced, or stored in a retrieval system or transmitted in any form or by any means, electronic, mechanical, photocopying, recording, scanning or otherwise, except as permitted by the 1976 United States Copyright Act, or with the prior written permission of Emeth Press. Requests for permission should be addressed to: Emeth Press, P. O. Box 23961, Lexington, KY 40523-3961. www.emethpress.com

Library of Congress Cataloging-in-Publication Data

O'Malley, J. Steven (John Steven), 1942-
 John Seybert and the evangelical heritage : biographical and personal reflections on a life touched by godliness / J. Steven O'Malley.
   p. cm.
 Includes bibliographical references and index.
 ISBN 978-0-9797935-4-7
 1. Seybert, John, 1791-1860. 2. Evangelical Association of North America--Clergy--Biography. 3. United Methodist Church (U.S.)--History. I. Title.
 BX7543.S4O43 2008
 287'.6092--dc22
 [B]
                                                              2008013876

Contents

Preface   7

Part One: Setting the Stage

1. A Shoe Box of Letter   15
2. The Last Trip to Cambridge   19
3. Memories of the German Camp Meetings   23
4. The Mystique of Godliness   31
5. Godliness in the Witness of the Church   37

Part Two: The Image of the Prodigal

6. The Prodigal Revisited   43
7. Of Appetites and Thirsts   49
8. Whatever Became of Our Appetite for Heroes?   53
9. Rekindling a Sense of the Heart   57
10. Moral Uses of This World   65
11. The Keepers' Husks   71
12. The Lure of the Keepers   81
13. Who are the Keepers?   87
14. A Road Dampened by Tears   93
15. Getting Through to God   103
16. Dreams of the Spirit   113
17. Songs of the Spirit   123
18. Surprised by Grace   133

Part Three: Home at Last

19. Mingling with God's Children   147
20. Whither the People of God   157
21. This Your Brother Was Dead, And Is Alive   169
22. I'll See You on Tuesday   177
23. A Summons to Discovery   183

Appendix 1 The Doctrine of Christian Perfection   191
Appendix 2: Case Study from the Life of John Seybert   195
Index   203

Foreword

Professor O'Malley's book on the life and ministry of Bishop John Seybert commends itself to us in many ways. Let me mention several. First, the author lends interest from the start by linking himself, through his great grandparents, the Reverend and Mrs. Monroe Scheidler, with the notable evangelical heritage going back to Jacob Albright (1759-1808) and John Seybert (1791-1860).

Second, this book commends itself because it fills a gap in the story of the United Methodist heritage in America. The stream flowing from The Evangelical Church into The Evangelical United Brethren Church and thence into The United Methodist Church needs to be understood and appreciated. An important contribution toward that end has already been made by Bruce Behney and Paul Eller in *The History of the Evangelical United Brethren Church.*. Professor O'Malley has contributed further by presenting here an account of the ministry of Bishop Seybert which bears directly on the historic resources for theological and spiritual renewal.

More broadly, among all communities of faith there is the recurring need to understand afresh those historic "moments" through which the Spirit of God brought new life into the hearts of believers. The movement in America known as the Great Awakening was such a "moment" in our history. And Bishop Seybert and those around him joined others in celebrating that fresh outpouring of the Spirit.

The times in which we are now living show signs everywhere of moral and spiritual decay. Amid vast wastelands, the spiritually fertile regions are few and small. Therefore this book about a man of God who led others into taking seriously the power of the Holy Spirit, has much to say to our time. Always there is the need for moral and spiritual renewal. This book shows us how one important man led others in that grand pilgrimage toward the city of God.

In addition, this book commends itself because it demonstrates again the power of the Holy Spirit in bringing together a thoroughly consecrated human being and the effective preaching of the gospel. Evident also is the report of the presence of the Spirit in fervent singing and in intercessory prayer. In this narrative, then, true piety, effective preaching, singing, praying and serving come together into a living, developing community of faith. Within the bounds of his churchmanship, Bishop Seybert reflected some of the most important aspects of what we know today as the charismatic reality.

Finally, this book is commendable for its scholarship. Professor O'Malley is not only a deeply dedicated Christian seeking to identify his heritage and evoke its meaning, but he is a scholar who has worked through the available materials with a high degree of competence. And he has brought the work together with a style that flows and is readable.

I have personally derived much benefit and felt a sense of renewal from reading this book which contributes significantly to the United Methodist heritage.

>--Mack B. Stokes, Bishop of the United Methodist Church

Preface

The people called Methodists acknowledged that they were a "connectional society." Not infrequently, this has come to mean being in connection with a transcending clerical hierarchy and bureaucratic structure. What John Wesley intended was to raise up "a company of men having the form and seeking the power of godliness, united in order to pray together, to receive the word of exhortation, and to watch over one another in love that they may help each other to work out their salvation."[1] What does it mean for us to locate our roots as a connectional people in this latter sense — to enter into relation with a living God and with a people living in and through Him?

My plan is to bring to the light of day the life and ministry of John Seybert (1791-1860), the pioneer missionary-bishop of the Evangelical Association. My goal is to discover the spiritual taproots of those who are now called United Methodists by together probing the "United" side of our heritage. Our concern will not be to reproduce a chronological survey of that heritage, for this is a task that has been capably completed in other studies.[2] Instead, we shall focus upon the spirituality of these forebears by probing the devotional life of one of their most influential leaders, Seybert.

If I may speak personally without at the same time creating the sense that I have lost my critical objectivity in writing about Sebyert, my encounter with Seybert changed my own life, deepening my love for God and for those whom God has called me to serve. I trace my encounter with Seybert to the discovery of a shoe box filled with century-old letters whose content can help us get in touch with the hopes and travail of that family of Christians who look to him as their spiritual father. This correspondence is between my great grandfather and his fiancee, whose lives were touched by the ministry of Seybert.

The young man in the letters had a taproot that was nourished in the spring of the Great Awakening among the Germans in America. As the correspondence bears witness, Monroe Lincoln Scheidler (1865-1953), a minister of the Evangelical Association, and his bride, Mina Hall (1866-1933), lived out their years in the light of that heritage. Their generation was also one of transition from the days of rural, frontier religion to the tense, uprooted era of an industrialized world society.[3] They sought to leave their children with the spiritual resources to cope with the new order.

My childhood memories of Monroe Scheidler form my connecting link between those spiritual "giants in the land," the founding fathers of the Evangelical Association, and our generation. His ministry was shaped, often unconsciously, by the guiding hand of Seybert. It is through him that my burden to rediscover our identity as a "connectional people" has come.

This is how we shall proceed. Part 1 will "set the stage " by describing how I made my discovery of the deeper meaning of our United Methodist roots through my contacts with Scheidler. As part of this section, we will consider the significance of sacred places. Part 2 will portray the shape of the godly life and probe its heart. Here the unpublished *Journal* of Bishop John Seybert will direct us. Jesus' parable of the Prodigal Son will provide the guiding metaphor for this portrayal. The chapter titles in Part 2 present images from the parable. This theme is not selected arbitrarily. It was the controlling theme in Seybert's account of his own pilgrimage to faith. Part 3, entitled "Home at Last," will explore the goals of godly living, drawing again upon Seybert's reflections.

An explanatory note is needed. The Evangelical Association, the womb in which this family received its nurture in godliness, was one of two major evangelistic movements raised up by God at the beginning of the 19th century to impart the power of living, vital Christianity to the large numbers of German-Americans who had settled throughout the mid-Atlantic and Midwestern states. Their spirituality was distinctive in their expressions of worship, work, and church order from that of their Anglo-American counterparts. Their founder was Jacob Albright (1759-1808), a Pennsylvania farmer and tilemaker who became in his later years a compellingly anointed witness to the powerful work of divine regeneration that had changed his life. He and his consecrated colaborers in the gospel became beacons of light and hope in regions of spiritual darkness and outright oppression. They balanced their boundless ardor for God and their burden for the "lost" and oppressed with an ordered personal and social discipline, including a system of episcopal supervision, to enhance their growth in grace. They developed indigenous and distinctive patterns of hymnody and worship set in a German idiom that disappeared when they began to trade German for English in the latter 1800's.

For three decades after Albright's untimely death in 1808, the Evangelicals remained without a bishop to succeed their revered founder. Evidently no one felt called to step into Albright's shoes until finally, in 1839, in an act of popular acclamation by the brethren in conference, a promising young circuit preacher named John Seybert was made the first "constitutional" bishop of the Evangelicals.[4] More than anyone else he carried the witness of the heirs of Albright into the states of the American Midwest and Canada. This devoted bachelor-bishop traveled by horse 175,000 miles, preached about 9,850 times, made about 46,000 pastoral visits, held about 8,000 prayer and class meetings, besides visiting a least 10,000 of those who were sick and afflicted.[5]

Having drawn freely from the patterns of Methodism, as well as their own heritage of German Pietism, Evangelicals in the twentieth century first united in 1946 with their long-time counterparts in the German-American revival movement, the Church of the United Brethren in Christ. Whereas Albright had been a Lutheran, the United Brethren founders, Philip William Otterbein (1726-1813) and Martin Boehm (1725-1812), brought together the revivalist wings of the German Reformed and Mennonite churches, respectively.[6] Then, in 1968, the unified church, known as the Evangelical United Brethren Church, joined its three quarter million members to the 10,000,000 member Methodist Church, forming the United Methodist Church. When referring to "United" Methodist roots, our principal concern here will be with the Evangelical side of the E.U.B. heritage, which John Seybert represented.

As a diverse and pluralistic church, United Methodism can learn from the communal caring and affirmative witness to Christ that marked life in the primeval days of our Evangelical forebears. Yet, this is not a call for a nostalgic return to a bygone era. Besides being impossible, that would also be contrary to the forward movement of Christ and his Spirit in our world. What is called for is a new willingness for us to see ourselves as we have been conditioned by our history, so that what we are and what we aspire to become in God's grace is viewed against the backdrop of the people from whose bosoms we emerged and yet whose legacy we so easily ignore.

This evaluation of Seybert contains critical observations, such as his bias against the Roman Catholic hierarchy (Chapter 13) and his occasionally censorious spirit (Chapter 20). There is also the tendency of his zeal for conversions to outweigh the need for equipping the laity for effective discipleship on their part (Chapter 20). However, his chief shortcoming enhances rather than detracts from his character. I refer to his awareness of his human capacity for "godless appetites and thirsts" (Chapter 7). He speaks with power because his spirituality is not divorced from his humanness but is rooted in a probing awareness of its reality. Although Seybert's cultural setting was far different from our own, it is quite probable that we shall discover within his witness insights that are critical for our spiritual formation.

A note on sources is in order. I have relied on the unpublished, typewritten manuscript of Seybert's *Journal* that was translated from the German into English by J. G. Eller, of Naperville, Illinois, in 1952.

In addition, Bishop Samuel Spreng, Seybert's nineteenth-century biographer, had access to certain records from Seybert not contained in Seybert's unpublished *Journal*. In several instances, I have cited Spreng rather than the Eller transcript. Denominational historians of the Evangelical Association (known later as the Evangelical Church) whose works have been consulted include Miller, Orwig, Yeakel, and Raymond Albright. Other citations include the denominational periodical *Der Christliche Botschafter*, the German-American religious journal with the greatest longevity (1836-1946), and local historians of the Evangelical Association in Indiana (Baumgartner and Wissler). A final source, never previously used, is the unpublished correspondence of the Reverend Monroe L. Scheidler, that was bequeathed to me.

An earlier version of this spiritual biography was reproduced in a booklet in 1984 in typewritten form. I am grateful to the following persons at that time who read and offered helpful suggestions and encouragement: Professor Paul H. Eller, eminent historian of the former Evangelical United Brethren Church; the late Bishop Reuben H. Mueller, a senior bishop of the United Methodist (and also a former bishop of the Evangelical United Brethren) Church; the Rev. James Buskirk, United Methodist Bishop Mack Stokes; Professor Robert Tuttle; Mr. Lynn Nichols, an experienced editorial critic; Mrs. Janet Bitely, typist; and especially my wife, Angie, for her patience and her numerous helpful insights.

Notes

1. General Rules of the Methodist Church, in *The Book of Discipline of the United Methodist Church*, 1980, par. 69, Section II.

2. See Bruce Behney and Paul Eller, *The History of the Evangelical United Brethren Church* (Nashvilles Abingdon Press, 1979).

3. Cf. Behney and Eller.

4. When Albright was elected to be the first bishop in 1807, the Evangelicals' *Book of Discipline* was not yet written. This occurred in 1809 under the direction of George Miller, one of Albright's first assistants. Hence, Albright had been made a bishop *de facto*.

5. Seybert's detailed *Journal* remains unpublished. The only book length biography in English is S. P. Spreng's *The Life of Bishop Seybert* (Cleveland, 1888), which contains extracts from the *Journal*. This *Journal* is handwritten in Seybert's quaint German script. Several years ago an unpublished translation was made by R. G. Eller, the father of Dr. Paul Eller, President-emeritus of the former Evangelical Theological Seminary, Naperville, Illinois.

6. See my study of Otterbein entitled *Pilgrimage of Faith; The Legacy of the Otterbeins;* AMA Monograph Series 3 (Metuchen, New Jersey: Scarecrow, 1973).

Part One

Setting the Stage

Chapter 1

A Shoe Box of Letters

"There, by that well," wrote Seybert, "the Lord converted me deep into eternal life, and I shall not forget it to all eternity." The Journal *of Bishop Seybert (June 21, 1810).*

"Since we are surrounded by so great a cloud of witnesses," counsels Hebrews 12:1, "let us lay aside every weight...and sin...and run with perseverance the race before us, looking only to Jesus, the pioneer and perfecter of our faith." In the Bible, the people of God are frequently reminded of their legacy of faith, from the Old Testament invocations unto the God of Abraham, Isaac, and Jacob to Paul's reminder to Timothy that he has been nurtured in a family of believers and so should "rekindle the gift of God" (II Timothy 1:5-6). The "heavenly host of witnesses" of Hebrews surely now includes a Luther, a Wesley, and an Albright, as well as a host of forgotten names of persons of faith who dared to "look only to Jesus" in life and in death. John Seybert was of that stature, among the German-American Evangelicals. Included in that sanctified lineage are others who touch our lives quietly yet decisively with the grace of God, and in so doing serve as a connecting link with heroic days when giants of faith were abroad in the land. Our task in this chapter is to discover a young couple, engaged to be married, who will help direct us to those roots. We shall also have to consider the importance of those "places" where sacred and decisive meetings of God and humans occur. It was in such a place that my inquiry began.

In undertaking a quest for spiritual roots, one finds that God often places treasure in very earthen vessels, like an old shoe box. So it was in this quest. Inside the box was found a neatly tied stack of sixty-four handwritten letters, each it its original envelope, from a young preacher to his fiancee. The fading postmarks indicated that their correspondence began on March 4, 1889, and concluded on June 21, 1890, the week before their wedding. Next to these was another neatly bound stack of letters from her to him, written with a markedly more artistic penmanship. My great grandfather Monroe Scheidler (1865-1953) was then a 23-year-old itinerant preacher. He was ordained an elder in the Indiana Conference of the old Evangelical Association in the Spring of 1889. He was completing his service on his first appointment, the Noblesville Circuit. Recently, he had been invited to conduct a revival in the distant Portland church, where he met Mina Hall (1866-1933), a young Methodist woman who had come to hear the youthful, bearded singing evangelist, and soon their correspondence began.

They treasured the privacy of their correspondence, which afforded both of them a freedom of expression concerning matters spiritual and temporal. We hope it will not violate their sacred trust for their descendant to disclose portions of their missives to public view. Our motivation is not idle curiosity; rather, it is our quest to discern how their lives were touched by the spirituality of Seybert. Our goal is to enter into a fuller relationship with the God they and we are called to serve. The tenor of the letters proceeds from discretion and propriety to beautiful and intimate expressions of ardor for each other and for their Lord who brought them together. Woven into their messages are gleanings from their 19th-century Midwestern culture, from the dynamics of church life among early Evangelicals and, most significant, there are insights into the living of the Christian faith that can in turn help us get in touch with the vital witness of Seybert, one of our early spiritual forebears in the lineage of United Methodism.

Before exploring the content of these letters, let us relate the special significance of the place where they were found. The veneration of a physical locality that is symbolic of some transcending spiritual meaning may be either perverse or redemptive for Christian faith. Place veneration of itself may expose an idolatrous preoccupation with finite gods, as in the case of the Baal worship of the ancient Canaanites that sorely tempted the Israelites. The Israelites sought fertility for their crops and were unsure whether their God of deliverance whom they had known as a nomadic people was competent to guide and prosper them in their new agrarian habitat. However, there were sacred shrines erected by the Israelites, as the pillar of Jacob at Bethel (Gen. 28) and the 12 stones set up in Gilgal by the Jordan (Joshua 4), that were marks of God's blessing and served to enhance their covenant life with Him.

Where are our sacred shrines that would evoke for us the presence of God? The busy, mobile quality of American life today, which had its inception in the westward migrations of our frontier era, has brought an unsettled sense of rootlessness to many of our present generation. As the breakdown of families escalates, a primal human need appears, crying for fulfillment; the truth is that many of us want roots and moisture, the "feeling of locality and home and customary love."[1] From St. Augustine to Horace Bushnell, wise theologians have recognized that "the roots that nourish a man's life are in his love—local love, family love, love of old friends and familiar scenes—and he who has no roots of locality, is not a living man."[2] People are probably unable to identify the lack of roots as a cause of their restlessness unless they harbor warm and vital memories from childhood.

The imagery of home and ancestral roots beckons when I consider how it was through their touch that God's presence was first made real to me. They stand out above all the hucksters' claims, which follow one another in our restless age by "such kind of accident as governs wandering stars."[3] More than all others, those founders of church and home can evoke for us the sense of sacred obligation to God and neighbor. They may be forgotten in the clamor of life, only to be recalled with longing in our dying hours.

What elevated our spiritual forebears above the ordinary was the fact that they did remember their sacred meeting places with their God. Their lives were lived out in recognition of those decisive encounters. In his letters to Mina, Monroe Scheidler recalled the country church where his Savior had won over his heart for a lifetime. In Spreng's selections from Bishop Seybert's *Journal*, which I found on Monroe's bookshelf, a horse trough is remembered as the place where he had met Christ's cleansing power as he washed his face. "There by that well," he would exclaim to many a stranger, "the Lord converted me deep into eternal life."[4] This place of God's blessing was holy ground, "and I will not forget it to all eternity." In place of his heaviness and sorrow of heart, he recalled, "I was full of the Holy Ghost, Hallelujah!"[5] Seybert wrote letter upon letter to young preachers, sharing this testimony with them and admonishing them to find constant access to the grace of God.

We have moments in our lives when we sense that we are viewing familiar scenes for the last time, and we are especially attentive to the visible details of the event. Such a time was my latest trip to Cambridge City, the small Indiana town where the taproots of my family and my faith are to be found. It was here, in the dusty attic of the old family home, that I found the shoe box with its forgotten contents.

Notes

1. Horace Bushnell, "Agriculture at the East." An address delivered in 1846, (New York, 1864), 253.

2. Bushnell, 253. Augustine acknowledged that love (*caritas*) is the driving force behind the two cities — the City of God and the City of the Earth. Though the love of God transcends all earthly attachments, it is also recognized that the City of God must find tangible expression in the institutional church. G. G. Walsh, et al., *St. Augustine; The City of God* (New York: Doubleday, 1958), Part III, Book XIV.

3. Bushnell, 251.

4. From Seybert's *Journal*, entry of June 21, 1810. His key statement, as underlined above, was originally uttered in the German words "tief ins ewige Leben hinein bekehrt."

5. From Seybert's *Journal*, entry of June 21, 1810.

Chapter 2

The Last Trip to Cambridge

"I started out for Cambridge, but I reached that place too late for the canal boat. So I had to follow along the rough towpath, carryng my saddlebags, until I finally overtook the boat. Rest was sweet that night." The Journal of John Seybert, June 10, 1846

More than a century after Bishop John Seybert made his midnight rendezvous in our hometown in search of passage and rest, we made our pilgrimage to the old family homestead there. We hoped to find clues that would give access to his life. These clues, perhaps, could best, be located among the letters of those who knew him.

The trip was a hurried one, as have been all of them these last several years. The old homestead was now closed. Its last occupant, the only surviving daughter of great grandfather Scheidler, was living in a retirement home. She had been the first to encourage me to consider becoming a minister, "like great grandpa."

Become a preacher? I hardly knew what the word meant, except for the model provided by great grandfather who, in his eighties, continued to visit and pray for the sick and distressed among his neighbors, often leaving them a gift of produce from his garden. In viewing his countenance, I gained my first awareness of the meaning of worship as that devotion to God embracing the whole of life. I had become a youthful observer of the details of his daily life-style and found in identifying with him that I was sharing in the transcendent power of divine life. Only later would I discover those unseen fathers of the faith, especially John Seybert, whose redeemed life had touched his.

We arrived at dusk at the white frame house that had been his retirement home. Throughout his ministry, he and his Mina had regularly set aside five dollars a month for the house. She died before my birth, but his ardor for God and the church remained vibrantly alive. Here his daughter had cared for him in his later years and now with her departure, the home was ready to be rented to strangers. In the twin attics, family members had deposited mementos over the years, such as hand-carved bedposts and old books and documents removed from the original homestead of his parents many years earlier. It was here that we made our discovery.

Nudging open the stubbornly jammed back door, we found the lights and proceeded immediately to the crates in the north attic, which were the last remaining items to be removed from the home. We took them down to the kitchen, dusted them, and then began to relive the memories of our pioneering forebears who had homesteaded in the country north of Cambridge.[1] In these boxes were government deeds that had been issued to the first Scheidlers who arrived from Pennsylvania in the 1830's. There were worn German hymnals and schoolbooks. Here was that shoe box containing the two stacks of yellowed letters from 1889 and 1890 that bore rich testimony of the struggles and aspirations of that young Evangelical preacher and his bride-to-be. And, yes, there too was great grandfather's annotated copy of Spreng's *Life of Seybert*. It seemed as if Seybert's *Journal* had been left intentionally unfinished, with his story of faith continuing in great grandfather's letters. The story still remains incomplete, and seems to be awaiting a new chapter, which will be the contribution of our generation.

Before finally leaving the house to return to the city with this treasure of musty finds, I found myself taking one last stroll across the property to try to understand the strangely warm feeling that was tugging at my heart. Walking and meditating, I thought of Abraham, who had to pace out the promised land step-by-step to be able to enter into the covenant God had for him. The question occurred to me, is it mere sentimentality that draws me to this place? Is it not time to put away childish things? Has it been trite for me as a teacher of seminarians to emphasize to my students that we are not merely Methodists, but United Methodists, and to insist upon this as being more than a point of legality? Does not this name convey a sense of wholeness to our people of God that somehow needs to be made real? And what is it about this place that causes these thoughts to stir?

The answer to these searching questions seemed to come in a twofold way. First, I was reminded that the person who delights in God's law and meditates upon Him is "like a tree planted by streams of living water" (Psalm 1:2-3). Although we had witnessed the apparent death of the vision of these founders, the leaf really was not withered. This is due to my awareness of the burning flame of their inexpressible love for the

Lord, and I know that the light that he ignited in their hearts also burns in me. Today we might call this flame God's Spirit-filled presence and power. Surely the seedling God planted in these founders' lives and nourished by the stream of his Word has a season of fruitbearing that is still to come. I thought of those great silent oaks alongside the meandering Symond's Creek in whose shade our homesteading forbears knelt and bowed in spirit "with the thought of boundless Power and inaccessible Majesty." Closely related to this first response to my prayer was a second thought — that God's presence in his Spirit-filled power will visit us, his people, anew as we recover our sense of being a people knitted together "in the unity of the Spirit and in the bond of peace" (Ephesians 4:3), because we have been made aware of our mutual dependence upon one another—including our forebears—in and through Jesus Christ.

Setting out to read the letters, it soon became evident that in their courtship, Monroe and Mina were unconsciously enacting a parable. You see, he was an Evangelical (later an E.U.B.) and she was a Methodist. On page after page, their letters disclose the loving intention of introducing each other to their respective ways of living the gospel with the expressed hope that their coming marriage might be consummated in Christ. As United Methodists, our wedding is past, but much remains to be done if we are to make a marriage after God's heart. Much remains if the latest chapter in this story of faith is to stand alongside those others. We set ourselves to this task remembering, above all, to "be grateful for receiving a kingdom that cannot be shaken, and thus let us offer to God acceptable worship, with reverence and awe; for our God is a consuming fire" (Hebrews 12:28-29).

Notes

1. Cambridge City, Indiana, was for a short era in the 1940's the principal shipping center in Indiana, when it was the intersection of the first federal higheway, the National Road, and the Whitewater Canal, built to connect shipping on the road with Cincinnati and the Ohio River to the South. Seybert joined the throngs of travelers passing through here when he took passage on a canal boat in 1846.

Chapter 3

Memories of the German Camp Meetings

"Now, dear brethren! Let us part;
The Lord has blessed us here,
Our hearts are burning in love,
We feel new pulses of grace;
Our praying is now more earnest,
And brother love burns brighter!"

"Nun, Liebe Bruder! scheiden wir;
Der Herr uns hier gesegnet hat
Die Herzen sind entbrannt in Lieb',
Wir fuhlen neuen Gnadentrieb,
Das Beten ist nun ernstlicher
Die Bruderliebe brunstiger!"

From the old songster of the Evangelical Association (1850), No. 169; in the days of Bishop John Seybert.[1]

The ministry of Seybert, which is recorded in his extensive, unpublished *Journal*, becomes significant for us in two ways. First, he provides our link with the generation of Albright and the inception of the German-American Awakening.[2] A veritable St. Francis of the American frontier, his incessant missionary labors transmitted the influence of that powerful revival from its early centers in Pennsylvania to the new frontiers of the Midwest. Second, the figure of Seybert looms large in our account because of his memorable visits to the Cambridge vicinity, where he guided the course of the revival among the forebears of Monroe Scheidler.[3]

Our location is Wayne County, in east central Indiana, whose gently rolling hills and vales are bisected by the old National Road, the first turnpike built in the early 1800's by the federal Government. Along its route through the county are historic towns, like Richmond, the old Quaker center of the Midwest; Centerville; and Cambridge City. In the secluded countryside away from the road, numbers of Pennsylvanians settled in the early 1800's, including Quakers and German farmers, who brought with them their language, their social customs, and their religion. There were Lutherans and Dunkers (or Dunkards, now called the Church of the Brethren) and some who identified themselves as the "Albright People," the adherents of the Evangelical Association.

The latter were regarded by their more staid neighbors with occasional suspicion and, by the unregenerate adventurers who were filling the towns along the road, they were objects of ridicule and occasional persecution. Why was this? They had experienced in their rustic camp meetings[4] what John Seybert described as "the baptism in the Holy Spirit,"[5] which was then more commonly spoken of as "experimental (or experiential) religion." It is a phrase that circulated within the camp-meeting religion of these early German-American revivalists.[6] Seybert spoke of concluding one camp-meeting service by baptizing seven persons, "three of whom were baptized *under* water, and the other four *with* water." He commented, "The baptism of the Holy Ghost came down upon *all* the subjects of baptism on this occasion, both upon those who were baptized *with* water and upon those who were put *under* the water." He emphasized that "the Lord made no difference between them."[7]

The place where this *Journal* entry took place remains unnamed, but four years later he made his first inspection of the fledgling mission of the Evangelicals in Wayne County. Preaching in the vicinity of Cambridge,[8] he deeply impressed a young farmer named John Dill, reputedly the first Evangelical convert in the state.[9] Dill, who was the grandfather of Monroe Scheidler, then opened his farm as the first camp-meeting site for the Evangelicals in Indiana. A glorious meeting was held on the Dill farm the following spring, in 1840.[10]

Witnesses reported that scores of German-speaking families converged on the place, arranging their campsites in a large beech grove. It was called a "melting time" in the Spirit as many "broke through" from dark bondage to sin into life and light in Christ. Their spirit lives on in the camp-meeting songs that these Evangelicals wrote and sang between 1800 and 1850. One of Seybert's favorites began with the announcement, "Now, dear Brethren! let us part; the Lord has blessed us here; our hearts are burning in love, we feel new pulses of grace; our praying is ne'er more earnest, and brother love burns brighter!"[11]

It may be objected that these persons lacked a vital heritage of church and sacraments upon which their evangelical experience of grace could be built. However, evidence indicates that a large number of those attracted to the camp meetings at Dill's had migrated from Pennsylvania as members of the German Baptist (or "Dunker") sect. In this tradition, now known as the Church of the Brethren, there was a distinct sacramental heritage associated with believers' baptism, foot washing (based upon John 13), and love feasts. The Dunkers, like other Old World church groups, often resisted the camp-meeting revivals. Their leaders viewed the revivals as incursions upon their way of life. They increasingly relied upon their rituals as a way of protecting their integrity as a group. Seybert thought that this attitude constricted the free operation of the Holy Spirit in bringing persons into the experience of regeneration in Christ.

Those Dunkers who experienced saving grace in their "new birth" on the Dill farm brought their tradition of community life and personal discipline into their new lives as adherents of the Evangelical Association. They were fond of concluding their week-long camp meetings with a Sabbath "sacramental service," a love feast for those reborn in Christ. This was the climax of their meeting. Only those who experienced the glorious "breakthrough" into salvation could participate in this sacrament. Unlike the love feasts of the Dunkers, it was open to anyone, the only condition being the experience of the new birth. The sacredness of the moment is reflected in one of Seybert's *Journal* entries during a sacramental service that concluded an 1835 camp meeting. He reports unusual difficulty in preaching the "sacramental sermon." He seemed to lack the "inflowings of the power of the eternal world of light."[13] Despite his anxiety, God's Word was so anointed that several persons in the throng began to weep over their sins during the sermon. The preacher's weakness fitted him to be a yielded vessel of God. He reported such "touching demonstrations of godly sorrow as are seldom witnessed." Conversions resulted, and in the end nearly two hundred joined in the communion of the Lord"s Supper."[14]

Scheidler's memoirs recalled the camp-meeting scenes of his youth.[15] Cabins of small logs were built amid groves of trees on the farm, and they surrounded an arboreal auditorium consisting of pulpit, altar, and pews hewn from nature's raw materials, always abundant and near at hand.. Normally, several preachers were present during the meeting on the platform, which was placed prominently in front of the rows of log pews. Preaching took place in the morning, afternoon, and evening. Rams' horns would call the faithful to worship, and the dominant image was that of a holy conflict with the forces of evil. The goal was for the hold of the demonic to be broken in the lives of the penitent worshipers through the preaching of the Cross of Christ. The intercession of the Holy Spirit to accomplish this "breakthrough" in the hearts of the penitents was the vital work for which the preachers watched and prayed. One preacher would hold forth until the Spirit's anointing power in his message would seem to subside. Then one of his colleagues, seated behind him on the platform, might tug at his coattails to signal that it was his turn to speak. Other preachers would pray with the seekers at the makeshift altars.

Some camp meetings were more memorable than others. These were the ones that went beyond even the salvation of souls to the worship of God for God's own sake. Seybert wrote about one meeting where the people became so blessed during the ministry of the Word that the exaltations of praise and weeping for joy caused him to cease preaching and kneel, "quite oppressed with the weight of the glory."[16] In this moment, silence was more profound than speech. Afterward, he probed the deeper meaning of this moment as he wrote "Let the children of God, who suffer so much persecution for righteousness sake, rejoice."[17] Since their sturdy ranks were being increased with new converts, also "let those who have been led to Gethsemane and Calvary march down Olive with shouts and songs and hosannas to their King."[18]

Anyone who is searching for a deeper purpose in living may be helped by the testimony of these United Methodist forebears. Their camp meetings provided them with a powerful bond of community in the days when frontier life kept them isolated and endangered by the prey of man and beast. Today, more subtle but no less dangerous social forces keep people isolated and endanger human community, characterized by family breakdown and the secularism of mass society. Their testimony has appeal because it presents their spirituality without divorcing it from their humanity. They even remembered their meetings as being places of physical and spiritual danger as well as worship and celebration.

All of these dimensions were remembered at the camp meetings held on the Dill farm. They remained vivid in the memory of Monroe Scheidler, who was himself converted at a later-day meeting on the farm in 1885. The earliest and most noteworthy meetings there were held in the 1840's by Absalom Schaefer and other preachers sent to this field of labor by Bishop Seybert. Old Ben Wissler, great grandfather's country schoolmaster, left accounts of these early encampments that recalled some of their more ordinary, human aspects. Whereas Bishop Seybert and Preacher Schaefer remembered the spiritual feasts that occurred during the sacramental service, schoolmaster Wissler remembered the sumptuous meal that followed the service, "served at times to as many as two hundred persons" and complete with a menu of "corn bread, pork, beef, chicken, large kettles of soup, potatoes, and pies in great stacks."[19]

One of the preachers remembered the moments of danger when the worshipers were attacked by ruffians, such as the episode that took place at Dill's farm in August 1845. On a Tuesday night, while many were seeking salvation, "The hordes of Satan gathered without the camp, all armed with clubs and knives." This foreshadowed trouble. "During preaching, a sham battle was played, hoping to lure us out, but when this failed, the horde rushed in upon us as we surrounded the altar and were praying with the penitents." The scene is appalling. "For an hour or more, we had a serious and rough time." God's people fell on their knees, "praying earnestly for victory," and "sinners cried mightily to God for pardon while the hoodlums mocked and filled the air with their profanity." A postscript notes that "The ringleader called himself an orthodox Lutheran."[20]

Their rural isolation notwithstanding, these folks were aware that they were living in the midst of a vital work of God that could not be stopped. In their eyes a perverse collusion prevailed between denominations opposed to revival and the lawless adventurers who populated the frontier. Both seemed to have one thing in common; namely, they were scandalized by that convulsive, life-transforming work of grace called the new birth.

Camp meetings were widespread in frontier American Christianity. What, then, was distinctive about those conducted by the early German Evangelicals at places like the John Dill farm? It was the German idiom in which they were conducted. Many of these brethren had fled persecution in the European state churches, particularly those who had been associated with sects like the Dunkers or the Mennonites. Others, including Seybert, had come from Lutheran parentage, which had frequently been the church of the persecutors. Now they found a way to lay aside this tragic chronicle of man's inhumanity to man by finding a common point of meeting in Jesus Christ. What they discovered in common was their intense experience of regeneration which they were fond of describing as a "renewed" Pentecost.[21] Their newly found identity in Christ was expressed in a medly of animated, German camp meeting choruses. Among Seybert's favorites were "O Happy Life" ("O Seliges

Leben") and "O Yonder Is Joy" ("O Droben ist Freude").

United Methodists today cannot return to the frontier, ethnic setting that produced these extraordinary camp meetings. However, we can probe the lively faith of those whom God touched in that setting. In doing so, we shall get in touch with some of our most vital spiritual roots. What surfaces is the portrait of the godly life, whose mystique we shall explore.

Notes

1. *Evamelisches Gesangbuch and Geistliches Viole* (Cleveland, 1855), 169 (Viole). (Author's translation)

2. Albright himself left no journal, but only a brief autobiography dictated to his assistant, George Miller. See George Miller, *Jacob Albrecht* (Reading, Pa.: Johann Ritter, 1811).

3. Seybert made his first visit here in 1839, a year before the first Evangelical camp meeting in the State was held nearby.

4. They were first called *"grosse Versammlungen"*, or "big meetings." See the recent study of camp-meeting spirituals by Ellen Jane Lorenz, *Glory, Hallelujah!* (Nashville: Abingdon, 1980).

5. The *Journal* of Seybert, entry for September 18, 1835.

6. Charles Finney was an English-speaking evangelist and contemporary of Seybert who also used this phrase, although no links between the two have been established. Their fields of labor were quite dissimilar.

7. Seybert's *Journal*, entry for September 18, 1835.

8. He made this trip as the newly elected bishop of the Evangelical Association in December 1839. See S. H. Baumgartner, *Historical Data and Life Sketches of the Deceased Ministers of the Indiana Conference of the Evangelical Association* (Cleveland: C. Hauser, 1915), 11.

9. Noted in "The Evangelical Church Centennial and Homecoming" (pamphlet), Pershing, Indiana, October 18-23, 1938.

10. Reported by A. B. Schaefer in *Der Christliche Botschafter*, V (October 15, 1840), 158. He reports *"unsre Lagerversammlung...gehalten auf dem Lande von Bruder John Dill, welche die erste war, die wir in jenem Staate hielten."* ("Our camp meeting was held on the land of brother John Dill, which was the first that we have held in that state.")

11. Seybert's *Journal*, entry for September 18, 1835.

12. Seybert's *Journal*, entry for August 14, 1835.

13. Seybert's *Journal*, entry for August 14, 1835.

14. These descriptions are found in his letters to Mina and in an essay written by his Dunker schoolmaster, B. F. Wissler (n.d.).

15. Seybert's *Journal*, entry for August 14, 1835.

16. Seybert's *Journal*, entry for August 14, 1835

17. Seybert's *Journal*, entry for August 14, 1835.

18. Benjamin F. Wissler, quoted in S. H. Baumgartner, *Historical Sketches of Circuits, Missions, and Stations of the Indiana Conference of the Evangelical Association 1835-1922* (n.p., 1924), II, 68.

19. G. G. Platz, quoted in Baumngartner, 312.

20. The United Brethren in Christ (who joined in 1946 with the Evangelicals to form the E. U. B. Church) traced their birth to a meeting of a Reformed Church pastor and a Mennonite lay preacher, whose traditions were enemies in the Old World, on Pentecost Sunday, 1767. I refer to the meeting between William Otterbein and Martin Boehm at the Long barn "big meeting." See Behney and Eller, Chapter 1.

21. From a tribute to Seybert by Bishop J. J. Esher, quoted in Spreng, 361.

Chapter 4

The Mystique of Godliness

"And as Jacob Albright, by the grace of God, was the instrument of their solemn union and holy zeal in the exercise of godliness, [their followers] were at first frequently called 'The Albrights.' But in the year 1816, they formally adopted the name, 'The Evangelical Association,'...a union of such persons as desire to have not merely the form of godliness, but strive to possess the substance and power thereof." The Doctrine and Discipline of the Evangelical Association, 905, v.

The last time I saw great grandfather was on a Spring Sunday in 1953 when he attended a service commemorating the twenty-fifth anniversary of Broadway E.U.B. Church in Indianapolis, my home church. The preacher for the service was the venerable Bishop J. Balmer Showers, then retired from active service in the episcopacy of the Evangelical United Brethren Church. Toward the end of his sermon, the bishop surprised us by taking notice of our family patriarch who was sitting next to me on the pew. He asked him to stand for recognition, remarking that here was "Brother Scheidler, the oldest member of the Indiana Conference and one of the most godly men I have ever known." This was to me an unfamiliar description of the man I knew in my childhood as a very human figure, who enjoyed washing dishes, eating popcorn with us younger children, and taking us fishing out to Symonds Creek. I still have a photo of the bishop and "Brother Scheidler" standing arm-in-arm after the service. After he stopped by our home to visit my ailing younger brother, great grandfather left with his daughter to check into a clinic for a physical examination. Here, five days later, while still in apparently vigorous health at the age of 87, he peacefully fell asleep for a last time in the presence of his God.

As the news of his homegoing shattered the normal routine of our household, my thoughts returned to the event of the preceding Sabbath. My mind began to ponder the meaning of that startling term used by the bishop that seemed to grasp the core of what great grandfather had been to me — a man of godliness. I recalled driving home with him from the service on that Sunday and being aware of a sense of reverence and thoughtfulness that shone on his face. In a momentary gaze, as my young eyes met his, it was as though his mind was sweeping back across the years of a ministry that had been called "godly." He had always been simply "great grandpa" to me. Recalling how the bishop had addressed him as "Brother Scheidler," I now began to see him in a different light. He was not only our family patriarch—as important as that is in a day when such durable models are so rare among American families—but one who was also esteemed as a colleague in a larger company of the committed.[1] He was part of a greater cloud of witnesses who bear testimony to their Lord through a life of godly service.

What is the final meaning of great grandfather and the heritage of spirituality that his life embodied for me? First, this means that we are a connectional people. We all live within some sphere of influence, such as our family, place of work, church, or neighborhood. Each of us has some context for ministry unlike that of anyone else. Not even a John Wesley or a Jacob Albright could "hold a candle" within our sphere, nor could we hold one within theirs! Our problem is that we often fail to live with the conscious intention of transforming that unique sphere of influence—for no two are alike—for Christ and his kingdom. Our failure may in part be due to the fact we have sought God apart from the history of God's dealings with His people. His covenant is not just with us as individuals. We have not really placed ourselves in that larger connection which would enable us to see and act from the perspective of God's will for His people.[2] As a consequence, loneliness and the lack of significant purpose have emerged as chief causes of the social problems in current American society. Individualistic, private religion is not only far afield from Biblical faith; if believers are not vitally connected to the lives of others, neither are they accountable to others. As Jesus reminded both his disciples (Matt. 4:21-26) and the Pharisees (Mark 7:9-13), there is no way to be rightly related to God without entering into right relation with others.

Second, the heritage that great grandfather embodied has taken hold of me because of its Spirit-filled character. In introducing this term (with which some present-day United Methodists would identify themselves)[3], we must differentiate its usage here from two opposing ones. On the one hand, we do not refer to the "Hollywood" version of charisma with its romanticism. On the other hand, neither do we refer to the particular doctrines that characterize the theology of Pentecostalism. These include the doctrine of the two baptisms—the one that comes at conversion when we are baptized into Christ, and the one that must follow conversion, when we are baptized by Christ into the Spirit. Pentecostal emphasis is upon the second baptism, and this experience is introduced by speaking in tongues.[4] By contrast to these divergent usages, Spirit-filled here refers to the "believers who openly acknowledge the gifts (charismata) of the Holy Spirit at work within them."[5] Moreover, in Wesleyan terms, Spirit-filled refers to the work of sanctification that begins with their justification but reaches its climax in higher states of grace that is a life empowered by the Spirit for fruitful ministry.[6] The Wesleyan emphasis upon entire sanctification as subsequent to regeneration and instantaneously received was a prominent aspect of Seybert's preaching.[7] Unlike Pentecostals, he did not insist that Spirit baptism is to be accompanied by speaking in tongues. Instead, those from the Evangelical tradition would choose to interpret their encounter with the Holy Spirit in the light of their own traditions. For us to introduce the term Spirit-filled to describe this heritage is to embrace this outlook, but there is more. It is also to affirm our continuity with grace-saturated believers of other generations whose lives have touched our own, and to appreciate the rich psychic depths available to men and women of biblical faith. This is the heritage of godliness.

To be rightly related to God and our neighbor is to be "godly," and to be godly is to be anointed with the charismatic power of God's Spirit.[8] Seeking to attain individualistic, private godliness runs the risk of making a person a god unto oneself, which is idolatry. There is a transcendent power to godliness that is not so much taught as it is caught, especially as it is modeled in the formative years of a child's life. It certainly cannot be bought like merchandise; we must ascend into its transforming power, which is the mystery of "Christ in you, the hope of glory" (Col. 1:27). Paul writes that there is glory in the mystery of being caught up beyond ourselves in Christ. When we live in this power of godliness, our spheres of influence are transformed because they have been placed in vital contact with Christ, our transcendent head.[9] The task before us is to consider how we may ascend into this mystique of godliness. My proposal is that we include among the means of grace that God has entrusted to the church, the gift of the biographies of our spiritual forebears. By attending to their lives, we find that Christian beliefs are not merely "propositions to be catalogued or juggled like truth functions in a computer.[10] Rather, they are "living convictions which give shape to actual lives and actual communities."[11] What can an awareness of these lives do for those of us who aspire to be more faithful and more effective in our

Christian witness? This awareness can do more than illustrate and embellish a doctrinal precept, e.g., the doctrine of "godliness." It can direct us to ways of reforming and renewing our faith by making it more true, more faithful to its ancient vision, and more adequate to the newborn age of 2008 and beyond.

Over the years, great grandfather gave his children, down to the fourth generation, the choice of "which will it be tonight, a Bible story or a story from when I was a boy?" By alternating between the two, we became aware of a dynamic continuity between the Word of God as revealed in Scripture and as lived out in human tradition through the Spirit's witness. Tradition, as intended here, was surely no graveyard of dissected creeds or bankrupt promises; it was the record of sacred symbols that evoked for us a vision, that told us truth about the Biblical faith because the image-bearing lives we heard about gave witness to that faith. Let us call this vision the mystique of godliness. What relevance might this have for the church today? We are not simply concerned with whether their vision was a faithful witness to the gospel in light of their times. Much more, our concern is with the challenge they pose to the depth of our spirituality and to the justification of our present way of life when held against theirs.

Notes

1. See Elton Trueblood's important study under this title.

2. Jonathan Edwards long ago reminded us that the nature of true virtue is in mortal "being's consent to Being-in-general" (God). See William K. Frankena, ed., *Jonathan Edwards's The Nature of Time Virtue* (Ann Arbors The University of Michigan Press, 1961), Chapter 1.

3. The chief agency for the charismatic renewal in United Methodism is the United Methodist Renewal Services Fellowship (UMRSF), with offices in Nashville, Tenn.

4. See the discussion of Pentecostalism in Robert G. Tuttle, Jr., *Wind and Flame; Our Living Faith Series* (Student book), (The United Methodist Publishing House, 1978), 64f.

5. Tuttle, 73.

6. This is the difference betweeen "Christ for us" and "Christ in us." Cf. Laurence W. Wood, *The Meaning of Pentecost in Early Methodism, Rediscovering John Fletcher as Wesley's Vindicator and Designated Successor* (Lanham, Maryland: Scarecrow Press, 2002).

7. Spring, 360.

8. The Greek word *"charisma"* may be translated gift.

9. It is significant that the Albright people adopted the name *"Evangelische Gemeinschaft"* (Association or Community), not *"Gesellschaft,"* (Society).

10. James William McClendon, Jr., *Biography as Theology* (Nashville, Tenn., 1974), 37.
11. McClendon, 37.

Chapter 5

Godliness in the Witness of the Church

"Our meeting was a blessed time...the forests were vocal with prayer and praise before daybreak . . . there were sudden and powerful conversions. . . . I was reminded of those delectable times when Albright, Miller, and Walter were yet among us and blew the gospel trumpet." From the Journal of John Seybert *(July 8, 1842).*

In February, 1889, Monroe Scheidler, then twenty-three years old, had been serving for seven months as a traveling preacher on the Noblesville Circuit when he was invited to conduct revival services in a distant town. Here a Methodist young woman named Mina Hall, twenty-two years old, came forward as a seeker of salvation. Monroe began his correspondence with her the next week. In April, he visited her again, en route to his new charge in northern Ohio. The day after his arrival, he wrote to her, describing his "lonely as well as long journey" that followed their parting. "Marvelous," he remarked, "how we were ever brought together by His own hand." He requests her prayers as he prepares to depart the next day for his first preaching appointment on the new charge. He has chosen for his text Titus 2:11-12, "For the grace of God has appeared for the salvation of all men, training us to renounce irreligion and worldly passions, and to live sober, upright, and godly lives in this world."[1] In the springtime of his ministry and in his season of courtship, here was the image of the godly life, beckoning him. In the late autumn of life, as the bishop's final tribute was given to him, this image was again uplifted to convey the ultimate meaning of his life to us.

How deeply within our Christian heritage can we trace this concern for godliness, which reverberates from the "United" side of our United Methodist heritage? It has its roots in the apostolic witness of the early church. Paul repeatedly instructed Timothy in this doctrine, writing "great is the mystery of godliness," and "exercise thyself unto godliness" (I Tim. 3:16a and 4:7b). However, as Christianity became increasingly accommodated to secular culture in the Middle Ages, the concern for godliness became the domain of monastic life, as reflected in the Rule of St. Benedict and his "counsels of perfection." These counsels, based upon the Beatitudes, were not binding upon the entire church. They were normative only for those who consecrated themselves to poverty, chastity, and obedience as monks and nuns. The church had preserved a place for extraordinary spirituality in a day when she had made her peace with the world, which is now called in rather triumphal terms "the body of Christendom" (*corpus Christianum*).

New impulses of spirituality were unleashed in the later Middle Ages as the new class of mendicant or traveling friars emerged. Men such as St. Francis in the thirteenth century and the Brethren of the Common Life in the fourteenth century promoted a practical godliness. This has to be an uncompromising love for God and neighbor that could be exercised by the lay person in the sphere of daily living. These practitioners of the "modern devotion" (*devotio moderna*) emphasized direct, unmediated access to God through devotional prayer in a way that threatened to undermine the sacerdotal authority of the Catholic priesthood and the sacramental system of grace.

The Protestant Reformation of the sixteenth century gave promise of offering a new lease on life for godliness with Luther's concern for personal faith and the priesthood of all believers. However, in his struggle with the Roman Catholics and with such "spiritual Reformers" as Carlstadt and Schwenkfeld,[2] Luther gave greater emphasis to forensic righteousness (Christ *for* us) than any real, direct change within the believer (Christ *in* us). To be sure, justification is the completed gift of Christ's sacrifice that is immediately received by faith through the proclaimed Word of God, but sanctification for Luther is always secondary, subordinate, and gradual. It is the "overflow of faith into love" (*quellende Liebe*), and as such it is not the cause of our salvation but is among its effects.

For Luther, faith is always identified as personal trust, but in the generations of Protestant scholasticism that followed, faith becomes mental assent in the stated propositions of the faith. A condition of sterility and acrid polemicism now beset the churches of the Reformers in the late sixteenth and early seventeenth centuries. As a consequence, a counter theme began to be heard: the clarion call for a renewal of personal godliness among the confessors of Christianity was first clearly sounded by

Johann Arndt (1555-1621), a Lutheran pastor whose classic of Christian devotion, called *True Christianity*, was appreciatively read by John Wesley and was the prized favorite of our early Evangelical forebears. In this work, which nurtured generations of German Pietists from Spener to Albright, Otterbein, and Seybert,[3] Arndt's chief interest was in the miracle of the new birth. He described this conscious renewal of the life of God as the gracious, holy second birth of a Christian "that comes out of Christ, by which the seed of God and the heavenly, *godly* man is perpetuated in a spiritual manner."[4]

Since George Cell first rekindled the interest of Methodists in the heritage of Wesley in 1935,[5] a host of studies have sought to locate the genius of Methodism in one emphasis of Wesley's or another. Our proposal is that "godliness" be considered as an essential resource in our heritage that strikes to the core of what God is calling us to become, if we are to be his "United" people in the twenty first century.

While visiting great grandfather's retirement home at Cambridge in the years following his death, a favorite boyhood haunt of mine was an old bookcase, concealed behind a drawn, blue curtain that harbored the books he had studied during sixty years of ministry. The one that intrigued me most was a worn, black volume that contained segments from Seybert's *Journal*. In this forgotten volume, filled with the reader's annotations, is a treasury of testimonies to the outpouring of God's Spirit in the pioneer days of the Evangelical Association. Seybert also was aware that he was ministering within the heritage of the living church. He is said to have owned the finest library of Christian devotional classics of any Evangelical in his day. His insights into the Word of God were informed by the witness of à Kempis, Tauler, Luther, Tersteegen, Runyan, Arnold, Rambach, and Schwenkfeld.[6] When the Spirit of God was poured forth with converting power in his meetings, filling the forests with praise, he was conscious of the abiding influence of the late Jacob Albright and his stalwart colaborers in the gospel, George Miller (1774-1816) and the hymn writer John Walter (1781-1818). He knew that he was not ministering God's grace in a vacuum.

My first awareness of the power of godliness came from great grandfather Scheidler's impact upon me as a child. Although years passed before due attention was given to the meaning of this word, its impact had sunk deeply into my being. What becomes apparent is that the alluring mystique of godliness joins us to the connectional and Spirit-filled dimensions of our faith and that in doing so we are empowered by Christ for our present mission through sharing in the vision of our spiritual forebears. By taking up this concern as our own, we join in pilgrimage with Christians from other places and times whose tasks have remained unfinished.

Notes

1. This account has been constructed by correlating his letter of April 25, 1889, with his pastoral record book, which lists the texts of all of his sermons and the dates and places where they were preached.

2. Andreas Carlstadt, a disciple of Luther at Wittenberg in the early 1520's, advocated the "Spirit without the letter," insisting upon the violent overthrow of monasteries and masses in that they serve to bind the Spirit. Caspar Schwenkfeld (1487-1541) also began to differ with Luther on the issue of spiritual authority, although his approach was more inward and quietistic. He became noted for his suspension of the Eucharist, preferring instead a "celestial Eucharist" where the sacrament is interiorized and spiritualized..

3. Pietism may be defined as that effort to renew the Protestant churches between 1675 and 1750 by an emphasis upon a personal, disciplined life of faith grounded in the new birth and frequently fostered by the use of conventicles (the *collegia pietatis*), where the exercise of godliness could be incubated. It also had a deep influence upon 19th century theology in Europe and America. Philipp Jakob Spener (1635-1705), the author of *Pia Desideria* (1675) was a pastor and the principal theologian of Lutheran Pietism in Germany. Under his disciple, August Herman Francke, founder of a new university at Halle, Pietism became interested in ministering to total human needs, involving education, missions, orphanages, and hospitals. Rhineland Reformed mystics provided the most lasting impact on the German-Americans of our study, especially Gerhard Tersteegen (1697-1769), whose works were often quoted in the Christliche Botschafter. As an American Lutheran, Jacob Albright (1759-1808), founder of the Evangelical Association, was deeply influenced by Pietism, as was the chief founder of the Church of the United Brethren in Christ, William Otterbein (1726-1813), and the first regular bishop of the Evangelicals, John Seybert, whom we will meet later. For a recent study of Otterbein, see my *Pilgrimage of Faith: The Legacy of the Otterbeins* (Scarecrow, 1973), ATLA monograph Series, No. 3.

4. Peter Erb, editor, *Johann Arndt: True Christianity; The Classics of Western Spirituality* (Paulist Press, 1979), Book I, Chapter 3, 37.

5. George Cell, *The Rediscovery of John Wesley* (New York, 1935).

6. W. Orwig, *History of the Evangelical Association*, II; (Cleveland, 1895), 91. à Kempis and Tauler were pre-Reformation German mystics, Bunyan was a Puritan, Luther and Schwenkfeld were Protestant Reformers, and the rest were mostly Rhineland Pietists of the seventeenth and eighteenth centuries. Tersteegen's address on "The Outpouring of the Holy Spirit" (ca. 1752), was a prototype for the Spirit baptism emphasis of the Evangelicals.

Part Two

The Image of the Prodigal

Chapter 6

The Prodigal Revisited

"I found it easier to proceed on the road to Hell plastered with good resolutions. With armor I was made strong, my heart having yielded to Satan's influence, to hold it from the Palace of the Prince of Peace." From John Seybert's Preface to his Journal.

A common theme runs through the letters of the young engaged couple and through the *Journal* of the pioneer bishop who was their model and spiritual benefactor, John Seybert. It is the theme of the errant life finding the way back to its true home. It is the struggle and ultimate victory of the godly life over the godless life. Here the parable of the Prodigal Son (Luke 15:11-31) is vividly recalled as Monroe and Mina describe what their lives had been before meeting their Savior. This was a dominant image in the spirituality of our early Evangelical forebears. Its richest expression is to be found in the *Journal* of Seybert, where the parable becomes the key to disclosing the vital facets in the life of godliness. In the pages that follow, our focus centers upon Seybert. At crucial points we will note the impact of others in the stream of the Evangelical tradition in which he stands, including Albright before him and Scheidler after him. Seybert's extensive *Journal* provides our most definitive source of insight into the faith of these founders. What are those major facets that can be gleaned from their lives for the renewal of ours?

The first evident but unspoken premise that pervades their character can be stated simply: genuine godliness does not draw attention to itself or count the cost. This is the caliber of serving God and neighbor that rendered our spiritual forebears persons of uncommon faith. This is the outlook that has always been so rare in the church, and especially among her leaders.

Second, the pattern of godly living is not born overnight. The foundation of godly roots often goes back for generations. Becoming aware of the shape of this pattern is essential for us if we are to learn our place in God's plan for His people on earth (the *ecclesia*). This awareness is crucial in guiding the way we order our talents and resources for ministry.

Third, godly living is concerned with more than facts and feelings. Its focus is upon the sense of the heart. This is a Biblical theme that denotes the way of acting of the whole person (see Psalm 51:10). This means that godly living is that which tests the head by the heart redeemed by Christ. The heart is exercised to really see the compassion of our Savior, for me and for others. The result is a character that is both gentle and sensitive, yet tough-minded and realistic in its grasp of evil. Such a person also finds that it is hard to sin when he becomes aware of God's presence.

Fourth, godly living is not passive piety. Instead, it involves courage and determination to live in the conscious awareness of the presence of God. The kind of persevering prayer that achieves this result "opens you up" to God, until you begin to see with spiritual perception other circumstances of your world as God sees them.. Seybert's graphic expression for this state of grace is "being preached through."[1] It is the condition of being fully saturated with divine energy until this is reflected in our very countenances.

Fifth, the highest motivation for godliness emerges not as the desire to have needs gratified, nor to be blessed, nor even to be liberated from forms of oppression. Each of these proximate goals is superseded by another: unreserved service to God and neighbor in the now. As the tyranny of the urgent continuously impinges upon us, the godly person cuts through these distractions by discerning what God would have me do this day for others.

Sixth, since godly roots are connectional roots, we will need to consider the testimonies of lesser-heralded saints, such as those of Monroe and Mina. What Seybert wrote is far more than a catalog of precepts. The power lies in the sense of urgent conviction that the narrative as a whole evokes in us. It puts a tremendous load on us, properly chastens us, and surely spurs us to reach beyond our fingertips to the vision God has for us.

Seybert writes that his father arrived in this country in 1776 as a young Hessian soldier, one of 25,000 hired by King George III of England at $100 per man. He was among those captured by General Washington's army that winter. While he was imprisoned at Lancaster, Pennsylvania., after the Revolutionary War, he became indentured to a man who purchased his freedom for him.[2] After completing his indentureship, he became a tailor, married a German girl named Susanne Kreutzer, and had four sons.

John, the eldest son, was born in 1791. His was an ungodly youth, for despite his father's threats, he "determined to do as he pleased." The problem at root was that "neither parent was as yet converted." They were "well-meaning, unconverted, church members (Lutherans), like thousands of others, and...honorable citizens." His mother had a melancholy temper, and, being "terrified when the Spirit of grace moved mightily upon her heart," she resisted God's wooing. His parents regarded John as being "more inclined toward evil than the other children."

When John was about twelve years old, his father sent him for religious instruction to an "ungodly university-educated teacher." He and his "co-confirmants indulged in godlessness and sin before and after study hours." For some forgotten reason, "something happened" that prevented his confirmation. Either the pastor died, or he may have been so unchristian in conduct that "my father took me out, better than being confirmed in an *ungodly* condition." Meanwhile, he began to "realize touches of the Spirit" in his life, though he did not yield to His promptings because "procrastination was planted in my heart by the devil. With armor, I was made strong, my heart having yielded to Satan's influence, to hold it from the palace of the Prince of Peace." Being "more godless at school," he wrote that "the temptations to do evil, to commit sins of all types, and to participate in games[3] was so strong in me like as a *dreadful appetite or thirst*." He lived on in this enjoyment of sin until thirteen years of age.[4]

At that point, he noticed a change in his parents. His mother, deeply convinced of her lost condition, "became more enlightened by the glorious gospel" until "there was awakened in her a hunger and thirst so predominant that *the husks given to the swine by their keepers* were loathsome, disgusting, and nauseating to her."[5] "So also were the unwholesome waters of Samaria, and the dead, dark confused reasoning of the learned and their teaching, and at last she finally resolved as did the Prodigal Son to return to her heavenly Father and be converted." Thus did she enter into "the fellowship of God's people where God's Word is taught in purity and power." Soon John noticed that the change in his mother's life "touched the heart of my father, and he no longer found pleasure in sin and wickedness." (Inference: The godly discover that it is hard to sin when we become aware of God's presence.) As a consequence, he "opened the doors of his, home for religious services," and so were his parents persuaded "by the mercies of God, despite self-denial and persecution, to follow Jesus Christ the Lord."

Young John's life was now decisively touched by the hand of God. His parents' change "broke my heart and moved me to tears." He now began attending a "protracted meeting"[6] of the Albright people where "the Spirit of grace touched me so mightily that tears as from a fountain gushed over my cheeks." He recalled one meeting where "I was so *thoroughly preached through* and became so penitent that on the way home …I left the company of my associates and followed on behind far in the rear…to conceal my many tears. I could have dampened the road going home."[7]

Seybert now found that "good and evil were continuously in contest within me." As his penitential struggle continued,[8] he confessed that "at times I resolved to go with God's people, and live a holy and *godly* life; and then again at other times, the temptations raged so furiously within, since I was not yet born again, and (was) unable as a very ruined young man to overcome sin." Why was he so helpless? "Because the Son of God had not yet set me free." The society of the ungodly now became clearly distinguished from that of the godly. "When I *mingled* in the company of youth, I was frequently led by them into sin, which caused my conscience to condemn me when I came into *the society of the righteous*, whose services I visited near and far." Next he visited a protracted meeting of the United Brethren where he came under such a conviction by the Holy Spirit that "warm tears ran down my cheeks" and, weeping openly without shame, "the people of God who noticed it came to and prayed with me, *yet I did not get through*."[9] "I did not get far enough.…I began attending prayer meetings and volunteered to pray." "There came to me also a strong impulse and desire to read and commit gospel songs to memory."[10] In contrast with his former ungodly delight in wickedness, "my pleasure now was in the service of the Lord."

Seybert concludes his account still on the precipice. He had not yet fully "broken through" to saving grace. However, this moment does come for him, and when it does, a power of godliness is released through his life that ripples over the far-flung settlements and across the generations of the Evangelical people in this land.

Notes

1. Spreng, 361.

2. In this instance, an indentured servant is one who is obligated to serve a person who bought the servant's freedom from slavery or imprisonment.

3. In early 19th-century America, "games" normally referred to such baser

sports as cockfighting or gambling.

4. See Chapter 7.

5. See Chapter 8.

6. A protracted meeting was, in later days, a revival series conducted in a local church; at this early date (ca. 1810), it most likely refers to a "big meeting" (*grosse Versammlung*) conducted by traveling preachers in a neighborhood barn. The United Brethren trace their origin to a "big meeting" held in the Isaac Long barn of Lancaster County, Pennsylvania on Pentecost, 1767.

7. See Chapter 9

8. The German Pietists, reflecting A. H. Francke of Halle, called the "penitential struggle" *der Busskampf*; it was the necessary precondition of the miracle of the new birth, which they called *der Wiedergeburt*. However, it, too, was the gracious work of the Holy Spirit and could not be induced by human effort.

9. The climax of the experience of the new birth (*Wiedergeburt*) was the moment of "breakthrough" (called *Durchbrech*) when grace began at last to prevail over the enemy in the battleground of the soul.

10. These were the native German folk hymns, whose content we will presently examine.

Chapter 7

Of Appetites and Thirsts

"The temptations to do evil...were so strong in me, like as a dreadful appetite or thirst." From John Seybert's Preface to his Journal

What are those appetites and thirsts that propel the godly on the one side, and the godless on the other? When Seybert wrote these words, "a dreadful appetite or thirst," he was mindful of the prodigal son's journey into that far country (Luke 15:13). He believed that the way we are motivated to respond to God's world is the clue to godly living. He knew from personal and pastoral experience that the result of organizing the world around ourselves and our desires leads inevitably to the perversion of nature, beginning with ourselves. By contrast, the godly person does not draw attention to himself because his thirsts and appetites are God directed and God fulfilled. Seybert speaks with power on this theme because he is aware of his human capacity for "godless appetite and thirsts." This means that his spirituality is not divorced from his humanness but is rooted in a probing awareness of its reality.

St. Augustine powerfully reminded us that our God-given capacity for affection (*caritas*) can be turned in a demonic or a redemptive direction, as "God-denying love of self" or as "self-denying love of God."[1] In making that judgment, he was reflecting upon personal experience, under the guidance of the Spirit. His insight is helpful in probing the memoirs of our Evangelical forebears, including the Bishop's *Journal* and the letters of his spiritual heir, Pastor Monroe Scheidler.

Perhaps nothing brings old love letters to life so much as recapturing the sense of pleasure and desire that is being expressed. Young Monroe Scheidler, writng to his fiance in that long past spring of 1889,[2] spoke of such primal joys as catching a full bucket of fresh fish in the creek on the old farm, or planning a rendezvous with his Mina during his forthcoming move from the Noblesville to the Hicksville charge. These were still pioneer days in rural Indiana, when life was often physically harsh and its pleasures were modest. By contrast with the insatiable passion for self-satisfaction that abounds in our day, Monroe and Mina wrote with a deep, unexpressed conviction that these fleeting pleasures do not define the purpose of life. Their lives were being guided by a pervading sense of sacred order that was their legacy from Albright and Seybert.

Monroe concluded this letter by saying that he will preach his farewell message Sunday. "Can not think of it without tears," he said, since "I have so many warm friends, especially children." Balancing pleasure and duty with a reverent regard for sacred order and for the sacred worth of others, he closed saying, "I ask that your prayers may accompany me especially when I go out into the strange world. May Jesus be your constant friend—is the earnest desire of your True Friend."[3]

It is a giant leap to move from his world to the desacralized and radically secularized ethos that envelops our present-day Western society, even immobilizing large segments of evangelical Christianity.[4] Much has been spoken about the symptoms of this condition—blatant immorality (the defiance of sacred order), aggressive amorality (the concerted effort to destroy sacred order), and the widespread acceptability of nonobservance (the repudiation of sacred symbols).[5] Even more anxiety has been registered about such tangible dangers as the exploitation of the world's poor and the threat of nuclear attack. If we are to locate the spiritual roots of our social malaise, we will need to reclaim what Albert Outler has called a vivid sense of the Sacred Milieu, the environment of grace surrounding human life, and of the Sacred Order, the framework of moral life by which we are obliged to respond to God's grace. Our strategy for reclaiming these prerogatives is to seek to understand how our godly forebears were sensitized to the wooing of the Holy Spirit in their lives and motivated to respond in faith to God's saving presence. This sensitivity is the key to their stature as spiritual heroes.

Bishop John Seybert, that spiritual father of so many early Evangelicals, including Monroe and Mina, mirrored in his *Journal* two contrasting faces in the progress of the godly life. The first of these, which was cited at the beginning of this chapter, describes a life in bondage to demonic forces that finds expression in illicit passions. The second is the glimpse we have of the weary but joyful preacher who pauses in midlife, about to embark on another mission, to pray "O God! What shall I render unto Thee...for all the goodness Thou hast shown me? Thou hast caused me to experience Thy great love all the years, months, days, hours, minutes and seconds of my life." His boundless desire was to serve God and not merely petition divine blessings for himself. "O God!" he prayed, "I am pained at the thought of having done so little for Thy glory and for Thy kingdom." His petition was a selfless one, asking only, "Oh give grace and strength that I may dedicate my future life wholly to Thee, and that I may spend all my future days joyfully in Thy service, through Jesus Christ, Amen."[6] It is this appetite for pleasing God that elevated the humble Seybert to the rank of a spiritual hero in the annals of United Methodism.

What intrigues me is not the great chasm that separates his pre-Christian life from his later life of grace. This is readily apparent. Even more remarkable is the way his witness functioned to motivate his spiritual heirs, including great grandfather Scheidler, and then almost entirely ceased to continue as a living source of faith in our day.

If United Methodists today are to recover the appetite for godly living that marked these fathers in our "United" heritage, we will need to examine these questions. What has happened to our appetite for spiritual heroes? What are the consequences of failing to distinguish between appetites that are God-honoring and those that are God-denying? What happens to our appetite for nature, or the way we use the world around us, when a vivid sense of God's presence is discovered? In probing these questions, the *Journal* of John Seybert will he our chief resource.

Notes

1. V. J. Bourke, ed., *St. Augustine: The City of God* (Garden City, NJ: Doubleday, 1958), Book XIV.

2. Letter from Monroe L. Scheidler to Miss Mina Hall, April 12, 1889.

3. Letter from Monroe L. Scheidler to Miss Mina Hall, April 12, 1889.

4. This desacralization was referred to by Martin Buber as the "eclipse of God" and by Philip Rieff as "a world of spent sacred forces—a world made easy for profanations, all grievances sticking out and every sense of limit challenged." A radical and inevitable secularism has been propounded by such contemporary prophets of doom as Heilbronner and Toffler as well as by such utopians as Reich and Rozak. Cf. Martin Buber, *The Eclipse of God* (New York: Harper, 1957); Philip Rieff, *Triumph of the Therapeutic; Uses of Faith after Freud* (New York: Harper and Row, 1968); and Charles Reich, *The Greening of America* (New York: Random House, 1971). Richard Dawkins, *The God Delusion* (New York: Houghton MIfflin Company, 2006, 2008), further develops this secular attitude that ridicules in a militant fashion the notion of God as as an intelligent idea.

5. Professor Albert Outler elaborated on these symptoms and their apparent causes in a discussion in which the author participated entitled "A Colloquy on the Loss and Recovery of the Sacred" held at the University of Notre Dame in November 1979.

6. This is Seybert's *Journal* entry for July 7, 1842, after arriving in Chicago on horseback, when he was holding the first German camp meetings in Illinois. He reports that no preaching could be held on the first evening due to a heavy thunderstorm, but that already there was "weeping and praying among penitents" in several tents.

Chapter 8

Whatever Became of Our Appetite for Heroes?

"John Seybert lived for the unseen world, and therefore this present world has largely forgotten him." Tribute to Bishop Seybert by Bishop Samuel P. Spreng, 1888.

Seybert has been little remembered outside the surviving remnant of the former Evangelical Church, despite the noble life he lived for God and humanity. He demonstrates the wisdom of Alexander Pope's dictum, "Who builds a church to God and not to fame, will never mark the marble with his name."[1] He is an instance where history has left the best buried in obscurity because the world was blinded by one whose goodness outshone his greatness. Yet, did not our Lord reverse the priorities of this world in the parable of the prodigal, which was Seybert's model for living? The lost son is really a non-hero in the parable, for it is the father's compassion that is the focus. Here, in their compassion for the lost, is also where the secret for Albright's and Seybert's anointed ministries lay.

Whatever has become of heroes and heroines in our day? They seem to be scarce. The absence of an appetite for solid heroes, especially among the young, is often apparent. It may be that there is a correlation between our lack of innocence, "a commodity in short supply these days," writes one commentator,[2] and the absence of heroes. This premise is recognized by secular observers as well as by church historians, and it is seen as a recent turn of affairs. In our electronic era, too many demands clamor for attention. There seemed to be no shortage of heroes when I was growing up—figures who put a challenging burden upon us, properly chastening us, and inciting us to reach beyond our grasp. Who was a hero? This was a person "just over life size, painted with broader stokes, made of something immeasurably broader, stronger, more resistant than ordinary people."[3] The mystery and the appeal were enhanced by all of this.

At one vital point such nostalgia is mistaken. If our concern with heroes, especially spiritual heroes, is to be more than wistful nostalgia, then we need candor without sentimentality. Only then can the memory of our godly heroes become an incentive for mortifying our old nature and bringing to life "Christ in us, the hope of glory" (Colossians 1:27). It is simply untrue that our heroes and our childlike lovers of heroes were "almost untouched" by sin, as Downing surmised. Seybert's appetite for God and his loathing of sinful passions were so intense precisely because he had known the weight of sin and so could grasp the greater reality of God's grace! It was out of this Christian realism, not out of naivete, that Charles Wesley penned the verse, "I want a principle within, of jealous, godly fear; a "sensibility of sin, a pain to feel it near.[4] It was because the godly had felt the "kindling fire" of sinful appetite that they were so intent not to "grieve God's love." The awareness of sin was not be glossed over and made to seem inconsequential. Its only use for the godly was to "drive me to the blood again, which makes the wounded whole."[5]

Why did we not smirk when our childhood books introduced the sturdy young protagonist as "our hero"? It was not simply some disposition to be properly respectful of elders who did things that were apparently beyond our reach. No, a deeper motive was that they kindled within us a sense of the free, ascending human spirit. Because the spirits of our designated godly heroes bore witness to God's Spirit (Romans 8:16), their vision reached the highest ascent and wooed more appealingly than did all other childhood heroes. The fact that it is more fashionable to worship at the feet of non-heroes and to "depreciate rather than openly to admire or seek to emulate"[6] indicates that the dearth of godly vision has run its full course to cynicism. When this cynicism touches our churches, the infection has run its full course. We may then rightly suspect that tomorrow's heroes will be merely survivors.

The heroic qualities in Seybert's life were recognized by his nineteenth-century biographer who wrote that "John Seybert lived for the unseen world, and therefore this present world (1888) has largely forgotten him."[7] He was not forgotten by his Evangelical heir, Monroe Scheidler, who began his ministry in the year these words were written and who took the account of Seybert's life to heart. Seybert belongs to the heroic age of United Methodism—to those days when there were giants, and he was among them.

Spreng enumerates Seybert's character and features so as to portray him as a godly hero to be emulated. He embodied the soul of the early Evangelicals, especially their mission to "firing the gospel where no other church would go."[8] A nonconformist in his age, the bachelor-bishop was remembered for his restless zeal, his robust yet small frame, his penetrating eyes expressing earnestness and the luster of Christian joy, and his plain, homespun garb.[9] Grounded in the Scripture and well read in German devotional literature, he was earnest in preaching and in conversation, endued with an "unction of the Holy One," being "full of the Holy Ghost and mighty in the Scriptures."[10]

Above all, he possessed an untiring vision for fashioning the German people of America, in their farflung settlements like Cambridge, into a people of God.

The contrast between this posthumous assessment of the Evangelicals' hero and his own account of his trials of faith is striking. There is a basic truth that eulogies tend to overlook, as well as those in our day who have become heroless. It is that the godly were capable of reaching others with the Christian gospel because they knew firsthand both the enslaving appetites that torment folk and the liberating thirst for righteousness that come when one is awakened by the gospel. Could it be, in this rootless age, that our appetites for their living faith might be rekindled? A more direct question is, what is the price we pay as a church for failing to do so?

Notes

1. Alexander Pope, cited by S. P. Spreng, 371.
2. 'Fallen Heroes: Has the loss of innocence robbed us of something precious?" by Jim Downing, in *The Tulsa Tribune* (Wednesday, June 25, 1980), 48.
3. *The Tulsa Tribune*, 48.
4. Charles Wesley, "I want a Principle Within," *The Methodist Hymnal* (New York and Cincinnati: Methodist Publishing House, 1905), No. 320.
5. Charles Wesley, "I want a Principle Within."
6. *The Tulsa Tribune*, 48.
7. Spreng, 371.
8. Spreng, p. 372. The early Evangelical missionaries often ministered in lonely fields, among the German people who were long overlooked by the English-speaking denominations, including the Methodists (until the coming of William Nast, who was inspired by Seybert and the Evangelicals in founding his German Methodist work). See R. W. Albright, *History of the Evangelical Church* (Harrisburg: The Evangelical Press, 1956), 286.
9. Spreng reported that Seybert "wore a broad-brimmed, stiff felt hat after

the manner of itinerants fifty years ago (the 1830's); his coat, closing up to the neck, was adorned with a thick row of large buttons; his trousers were of corduroy; his feet were covered with common leather shoes tied with strings." Although his appearance was unique in his day, it was not "affected," nor did he ask anyone to imitate "the cut of his coat, nor to comb his hair as he did, straight down." Spreng, 374.

10. Spreng, 376.

Chapter 9

Rekindling a Sense of the Heart

"His utterances came evidently from the heart, and made such an impression that the whole conference was melted to tears." Seybert's response to his election as bishop at the General Conference of 1839, as reported by the Reverend Absalom Schaefer.

Our Evangelical forebears did not disparage a sound intellect or healthy emotions, but when it came to describing that faculty whereby they related to God in a personal way, they chose to speak of the "sense of the heart." Like the prodigal, the young Seybert was inwardly stirred to return to his Father's presence. For him, it was not sufficient that a sermon be delivered with sound Biblical exegesis or polished rhetoric, as important as he knew these factors to be. A message was of no avail if it remained cold to its listeners' ears. Above all, it must breathe the "unction of the Spirit." Here was a precept that all Evangelicals who were his spiritual heirs observed.[1] Seybert once complained that a given preacher whom he heard "may have been a messenger from God, but he lacked one thing: an unction of the Holy One."[2]

He took quite seriously the Psalmist's declaration that "The precepts of the Lord are right, rejoicing the heart" (Psalm 19:8a). Penetrating the heart of the hearer was the real test of a preacher's effectiveness. He was convinced that the heart was what God in His Word was seeking to probe. Following one camp meeting, he wrote that "the quick and powerful Word of God cut deep wounds into many hearts, which only Jesus Christ could heal with the blood of His atonement."[3] The heart was the scene of a twofold divine work: the crucifying of the old nature, which is the work of the law, and the quickening of the new nature, which is Christ's saving work.[4] In short, this "sense of the heart" is where the action is in godly living.

The attention our forefathers gave to this theme has much to do with why their work was so productive of spiritual fruit. What are the consequences of failing to distinguish between hearts that are atune to appetities that are God-honoring and those that are God-denying? Seybert possessed a fervent passion for the former and a holy hatred of the latter. This is because he knew firsthand what happens to a person and his world when an appetite that should be God-directed gets perverted to himself.

One consequence is to be unable to distinguish between serving the Creator and God's creation (Romans 1:25), which is idolatry. Recalling his youthful struggles with carnality Seybert wrote, "When the opportunity came to sin, I was glad over it, that in its commitment I could have shouted and jumped for joy."[5] Let us not miss his point. It was not that the God he worshiped despised human pleasure. Like Augustine in his *Confessions*, he saw the deeper problem whereby small things can become the occasion for the swelling of pride, which the classical authors called "hubris." The problem with those appetites that he called sinful is that they are perverted by being self-serving. The enjoyment of God's creation is good, but evil resides in the self-serving reasons the mind gives for liking or disliking what is perceived, and the self-serving actions that inevitably follow. When Seybert spoke of "a sense of the heart" or "a revulsion of the heart," he was expressing with Biblical insight the conviction that we perceive with our senses and provide reasons for giving or withholding approval with our minds.[6] To be sure, he did not leave us with an exposition of the inner working of the mind and the heart. He was a practical man of faith, impelled by a burden to reach the lost for Christ. In the tradition of the great Pietists, he knew that "true Christianity" was a matter of visible words and deeds and not empty professions and platitudes.[7] Yet, his meditative reflections show that this was the way his practical theology functioned, rooted as it was in Scripture and tested by his lived experience and confirmed by the tradition of the German devotional theology that he had internalized.[8]

Another consequence of a deadened heart is that it subtly opens our lives to the influence of the demonic, which can be overcome only by the greater power of the Holy Spirit. Seybert once recorded that "an extremely wicked man" named Kahler was converted to God. Enraged by his conversion, his wife began to persecute him mercilessly. Suddenly, and without warning, her swearing and scolding ceased, and she appeared entirely "calm and peaceable." Amazed by her transformation, her family and friends repeatedly asked her for an explanation. She finally spoke, explaining that a "form in gray" had appeared before her the preceding night. The spirit offered her a bag filled with gold and silver if only she would continue to persecute and abuse her husband. Seybert commented, "The dream so shocked her that she resolved to cease from her shameful conduct." Her demonic thirsts were now vanquished by the power of godly affection. "She soon afterward requested worship services in their house, and sought the Lord without delay."[9] In the heat of the revival among these German Americans, where God's grace was operating, the forces of spiritual regeneration and repression were often locked in deadly combat. As sacred order was being forged in this heat, wise shepherds of souls like Seybert plumbed the wisdom of Jesus' admonition that "where your treasure is, there will your heart be also" (Luke 12:34).

A more subtle consequence of the heart that is unresponsive to God is the cloud of dull apathy that engulfs and deadens a person or a church who is its victim. Jacob Albright, the founder of the Evangelicals in whose steps Seybert followed, left no recorded journal of his brief but dynamic career as .a field preacher and counselor of souls, which lasted from 1796 to his death in 1808. However, in a brief autobiographical account that he dictated to his traveling companion, George Miller, Albright described how he had been awakened from the sleep of cold-hearted, spiritual apathy. "I travelled the path of life with frivolous and trifling desregard, was happy with the pleasure-bent and thought little about the purpose of human existence." Having little regard for the welfare of others, he lived as though his "little span of duration would last eternally." He marvelled that in such a reprobate condition of heart "most persons seem to be happy—perhaps many so regarded me since I seemed contented and cheerfulness smiled on my countenance. Yet," he continued, "I was not really happy, and I do not believe that a person in such a condition can ever be entirely happy." Once the pleasures of this world have been tasted by the prodigal, "there remains a void, an uneasiness in the back of the heart, which awakens a painful feeling." The "mystical voice of conscience" was stirring within him, to "embitter all forbidden pleasures," and his "conscience forcibly opposed it."[10]

Albright's account reveals his capacity for sensitive and penetrating self-analysis, despite his limited opportunities for formal education in colonial Pennsylvania. He had learned the rudiments of "reading, writing and ciphering" in the German language, and the few books accessible to him were the Luther Bible, the Small Catechism and hymnal.[11] In an early chronicle of Albright's travels that I found on great grandfather's bookshelf, Titus 2:11 and 12 appears as the text that was instrumental in

Albright's awakening. It admonishes that saving grace teaches us to deny "ungodliness and worldly lusts." This was also the text with which Monroe Scheidler opened his ministry after his ordination as an elder by the Evangelical Association in 1889.[12] By the providence of God, this theme endured in the witness of the "Albright people" long enough for it to touch my life.

The failure to distinguish between God-honoring and God-denying appetites has serious implications for human societies, as well as for individuals. The triumph of godly appetites in Albright (ca. 1791), Seybert (ca. 1810), and again in Monroe Scheidler (ca. 1885), describes a normative pattern that was expected of all Evangelicals, according to the standards for members outlined in their *Book of Discipline*.[13] These leaders knew nothing of the so-called "counsels of perfection" that relegated the higher disciplined life to members of monastic orders.

The purpose of their Association (*Gemeinschaft*) was to form a "friendly union of such persons as wish to have not merely the form of godliness, but strive also to possess its substance and power."[14] This could be accomplished only if every member became activated by an appetite for godliness. As Wesley had done with the English Methodists, Albright brought together in 1800 several persons deeply convinced of their sinful condition and earnestly sighing for "deliverance" to intercede for another and "properly to commence and accomplish this important work."[15]

This was the beginning of their new society in Christ. However, a subtle but telling shift can be detected among these brethren as we move beyond the vision of the founders. Albright's heart had grown heavy with the lost condition of his spiritually neglected neighbors. He had been led to witness to them convincingly, directly, and "only in the power and spirit of God whom he honored in all his utterances," knowing "that which comes from the heart reaches hearts."[16]

At Albright's death in 1808, George Miller, his early colaborer in the gospel, reminded his fellow ministers, "For you know full well that God was mighty in him among us" and "we must be exceedingly watchful for ourselves, that we do not lose this grace, nor receive it in vain." Therefore, "Let none detain you in the way you have begun" "mid all worldliness, pride and self-exaltation."[17] The witnesses whom God raised up around Jacob Albright knew that genuine godly living does not draw attention to itself, and that salvation would come to the German people in America only to the extent that "all of us together do those necessary firs works in the secret closets of our hearts."[18]

In reading these church fathers one readily notes that their piety was genuine, and this was in large measure because they knew just how frail their humanity was. They had a heart for God because they knew only too painfully the depth of sin, which they remembered as "godless appetities and thirsts." They required ongoing, day-by-day cleansing under the discipline of the Spirit if they expected their society to be equipped to advance the gospel. Their piety does not seem stale and ingrown to us. This is because they did not permit themselves to think that their cause was so righteous that they could forget how prone they were to be unrighteous toward God.

By the end of the century, in the era of Monroe Scheidler, Evangelicals were no longer a small, persecuted sect and it was becoming possible for them to believe that they, like the nation in which they prospered, had been elevated to a measure of glory and honor for their successes.[19] Traces of this theme appear in the *Book of Discipline* of the Evangelical Association for 1897, where we read that, despite the contempt that has been suffered by "carnally-minded worldly Christians," the people of this society "have not suffered themselves to be deterred or confounded in their internal or external improvement, nor in the progress of the great work which the Lord has given them to do." "Therefore," their statement concludes, "success to the undertaking! Success to the Edifice! Amen."[20]

Undoubtedly some are drawn to the church by being impressed with the outward edifice. For me, it was because the church was represented by a man who was in touch with God. Youthful fascination with great grandfather was due to the way he drew my attention to his God and also to the way he put the needs of others first. Memories linger of his praying in a secluded attic bedroom in the old home, and there he was, washing dishes, caring for the children while staying in others' homes, and delivering his garden vegetables as gifts to the sick and the poor in Cambridge. That was surely what Bishop Showers meant when he called him "godly"—he simply let others see God through him. This was the image that impelled me to probe his heritage. I came to see that he had assimilated, through a heritage of godly forebears, something durable and authentic, something of Christ, that had first been kindled among the German Evangelicals by Jacob Albright. John Seybert was the intermediary link. He modeled for the second and third generations of the Evangelicals the rare disposition.of godly living that is the foremost gift of the Evangelical people to Methodism.

An element of paradox lies in this story. Seybert's unquestioned heart for God made him a winsome and effective witness to his hearers. This then secured the outward success of the denomination and the attending temptation to succumb to an ungodly, institutional pride. We are reminded of the dictum that mankind's pitfalls are often the byproducts of his greatest achievements. As folk began lauding the construction of the denominational edifice, there stood Seybert, long the sole elected bishop of the church, who kept bearing witness to the insight that "God gives grace to the humble" (James 4:6). And why is this? His humility gave others access to God, and they could see that his unashamed ardor for God was not contrived for the approval of others.

Seybert evoked this sense of God's holy presence for his fellow ministers when he was unexpectedly and unanimously elected to the office of bishop at the General Conference of 1839. Remembering this event in his *Journal*, he wrote that "this important office unexpectedly fell to my lot, which oppressed me, and on account of the importance of the office, caused me to shed tears."

Constantly in touch with his feelings, he recalled that "My appetite failed, and sleep left me for a season." Only gradually did he feel relief, and then he "felt disposed to submit myself to God and to my brethren."[21] A delegate named Absalom Schaefer wrote in his diary that as the news was announced, Seybert turned and walked to one of the back pews where he bowed and wept. When he at last arose, he came forward and said, "I have promised God to be obedient.... I will acquiesce.... You must pray for me and have patience with me." Schaefer concluded that Seybert's "heartfelt utterances" made such an impression that "the whole conference was melted to tears." Here is a rare instance where a godly man is entrusted with institutional power and authority. Schaefer, who was to conduct the first Indiana camp meeting on the Dill farm the next year, wisely recorded these words: "At this episcopal election I saw how necessary it is that the office seek the man and not the man the office."[22]

Notes

1. My recollections of the ministry of Great Grandfather Scheidler attest to that.

2. Seybert's *Journal*, entry for Monday, June 28, 1824.

3. This meeting was held in the Mahantango Valley of Pennsylvania, which Seybert entered on April 21, 1837, as cited in Spreng, 175.

4. Seybert makes no general claims that Christ's atoning death avails for the healing of all physical disease, although he knew from experience that it some-

times did. In most cases, he reserved complete bodily healing for the resurrection life. However, he had no doubt that the cross availed for salvation in the now.

5. From the Preface to Seybert's *Journal*.

6. This insight is most clearly formulated in Jonathan Edwards' *Freedom of the Will* (New Haven: Yale University Press, 1957), although with an anti-Arminian polemic.

7. This theme was developed by the Lutheran Pietist Johann Arndt. See the new edition of Arndt's *True Christianity* edited by Peter Erb in *The Classics of Western Spirituality* series (New York: Paulist Press, 1979).

8. Seybert's *modus operandi*, it may be argued, closely reflected the exposition of the will that Edwards had presented in the days of the Great Awakening among the Puritans in New England. Neither asked people to make a "rational decision" for Christ (as, for example, the Campbellites) but to open themselves to the wooing influences of the Holy Spirit, who accompanies the ministry of the Word.

9. Seybert's *Journal*, from Tuesday, January 1, 1822.

10. George Miller, *Leben Erfahrung and Amtsfuhrung Zweyer Evangelischer Prediger, Jakob Albrecht und Georg Miller* (New Berlin, Pa., 1834); my translation.

11. This account is given by Albright's nineteenth-century biographer, Reuben Yeakel, in his *Albrecht und sein Mitarbeiter* (Cleveland, 1883), 18f. (translated: *Albright and His Colaborers*).

12. Yeakel, 22; and the pastor's records of the Reverend Monroe L. Scheidler.

13. See *The Doctrines and Discipline of the Evangelical Association* (Cleveland, 1893 ed.), Part I, Chapter II. This more closely follows the sequence of the Methodist Episcopal *Discipline* than did the *Discipline* of the early United Brethren, which reflected more the Reformed and Mennonite roots of Otterbein and Boehm.

14. *The Doctrines and Discipline of the Evangelical Association*, Part I, Chapter I. This parallels the *General Rules* of John Wesley (1739), that were translated into German by Ignatius Roemer and adapted for the use of the Evangelical Association by George Miller in their first *Discipline* of 1809.

15. *The Doctrines and Discipline of the Evangelical Association*, Part I, Chapter I. These are likely the words of George Miller, who had been commissioned to prepare the first *Discipline* after Albright's untimely death in 1808.

16. George Miller, *Jacob Albright* (Reading, Pe., 1811), trans. in 1959 by G. E. Epp for the Historical Society of the Evangelical United Brethren Church, 11.

17. Miller, 13.

18. Miller, 13.

19. They were approaching 200,000 members by the year 1900 and they had largely ceased to use German in worship. The name "The Evangelical Church" was adopted in 1922 when a schism within the denomination between the original Evangelical Association and the United Evangelical

Church (that erupted 1891-94) was healed. For a discussion of the "success" syndrome that influences American denominationalism see Conrad Cherry, *God's New Israel* (Englewood Cliffs, N. J., 1971), 82-92.

20. *The Doctrines and Discipline of the Evangelical Association* (Cleveland, 1897), 9f.

21. Seybert's *Journal*, cited in Spreng, 196. Albright had been acclaimed bishop by his brethren in the conference of 1807, but there was then no printed church discipline to formalize the action. No one succeeded Albright as bishop, possibly out of deference to the founder, until Seybert's election more than thirty years later. See Raymond Albright, 178ff.

22. *The Journal of Absalom Schaefer* (unpublished), quoted by Reuben Yeakel in his *History of the Evangelical Association*, Vol. I, (Cleveland, 1894), 289. Schaefer is buried in the Evangelical cemetery at East Germantown, Indiana, which is one miles east of Cambridge City on the old National Road.

Chapter 10

Moral Uses of This World

"These beautiful groves with their wealth of flowers, and their grassy slopes, shall no longer belong to the father of lies, but to the Lord Jesus, to whom belongs the riches of the Gentiles. Let these groves and prairies be consecrated unto Him, for the truth has already triumphed." From the Journal *of John Seybert, entry from the Spring of 1844.*

What happens to our appetite for nature, or the way we use the world around us, when a vivid sense of God's presence is kindled in our hearts? Seybert lived closer to nature than do most present-day United Methodists. In his old age, iron foundries and locomotives were making their appearance, although he never traded his buckboard for a train ticket. The "bush country Dutch," as the early Evangelicals and United Brethren have been called,[1] often settled in more remote country than the English settlers who were evangelized by the Methodists, Baptists, Presbyterians, or Campbellites. Living close to nature, Seybert and his flock knew firsthand the many faces of God's holy presence in His creation.

The virgin wilderness was often viewed by pioneers as a prize to be conquered as well as a dreaded place of disease and hardship,[2] but the Spirit-led Seybert saw it as the sanctuary of his Creator and Redeemer God. Viewing its splendor enhanced his appetite for the presence of God. One April day in 1838, as Seybert was in a buoyant mood, he was overtaken by a fearful storm. He recorded his impressions in a manner quite unlike that of the trembling young Martin Luther, who had cried out in panic to St. Ann when caught in the storm of the Thuringian forest.[3] Gazing upward, Seybert noticed the massive clouds gathering overhead, filled with darkness and wrathful commotion. The leaping lightening brightening the landscape reminded him of the gleam of Jehovah's "glittering sword." He tracked the hollow roar of its approach as it rushed through the ravines. As the storm threatened to loose its torrents, Seybert rode calmly on until he reached a human dwelling just as the rain began. Permitted to enter, he greeted the family and took a place by a window, where he became absorbed with delight at this evidence of the majesty and power of his God. With every crashing thunderbolt, he inwardly responded "Amen!" His host became suspicious that this uninvited guest might be one of those "hated preachers of repentance." He began to question Seybert, asking, "What are you after, anyhow?" "Why," he replied, "I am an itinerant preacher, and my business is to proclaim the Word cf God to all who will hear it."

His host, now feeling convicted, raged, "You don't need to come to our neighborhood.... Such cursed tramps as you are, may just keep out of our houses."

Sensing his rage, Seybert politely withdrew from the house, thinking that he would rather "endure the wrath of the elements than the storm of anger that was brewing in this man."[4]

Some new contours in our emerging portrait of the godly person are appearing in this dramatic episode. In place of his former self-centered appetites and desires, he is gifted by grace with a new appetite for the wonder of creation. He is not a pantheist, worshipping nature itself. The crateful response of his renewed heart has led him to worship His Lord as Creator as well as Personal Redeemer. His cleansed appetites, being redirected from self to God, are also directed toward God's world and all life that inhabits it. Nature, as well as nature's God, is no longer his enemy. Even amid its violent displays, he would rather trust his life to God in the great outdoors than remain in a human shelter dominated by wrathful, God-denying appetites.

Nature provided a great variety of images for the itinerating Seybert, but in each of them he found some compelling moral purpose that became instructive for his life. There were times when nature signaled life in the absence of God, as when he became lost on wilderness trails. On August 15, 1822, he was overcome by the darkness of night in one of the great primeval forests of Ohio. Determined not to give up and neglect his appointment, he spent the night finding the way. Sorely tried in spirit, it seemed at times that his little ark of faith (*Glaubensschifflein*) would sink beneath the troubling waves. He wrote how he wept and prayed much that night, often stopping in the shadowy depths of that great forest to plead with God, wrestling until he was blessed.[5]

One anonymous "bush country Dutchman," to use Yoder's phrase, expressed in song his somber mood when he ceased to be able to find

God in nature. "How long and difficult time becomes when Jesus is absent so long—the flowers, the birds, and the joys lose their beauty to me." The state of his soul was reflected in the face of nature. "The sun shines dimly to me, the fields are mournful too; O, when I am happy in Him, December is as lovely as May!"[6]

Sometimes Seybert found the settlers in the most remote sections to be also the most morally depraved. In one of his longest journeys from his native Pennsylvania, he crossed the Mississippi River into Iowa, and then across the Wisconsin River where many Indians were living. Writing in his characteristic poetic fashion, he described these outskirts of white civilization as the place where "twilight struggles with gloom."[7] His remarks were not directed toward the Indians, whom he admired for their apparently natural reverencing for God and for all places where humans worship.[8] Instead, he was describing the morally deplorable condition of the German settlers in this region. He wrote that many were skeptical of his ministry and nearly all were "extremely wicked," thereby making that mission a most difficult field of labor. Even here, he remained convinced of the ultimate triumph of grace, pending his obedience in his calling. He saw with realism the way things were, but he also envisioned by faith the way things would be when the new order of God's Kingdom would break forth. Despite their efforts to the contrary, he believed that "these beautiful groves with their wealth of flowers, and their grassy slopes, shall no longer belong to the father of lies, but to the Lord Jesus, to whom belong the riches of the Gentiles." Claiming the land for God, he declared, "Let these groves and prairies be consecrated unto Him, for the truth has already triumphed."[9]

We live in a day when many Americans appear to have a renewed appetite for "returning to nature," as an alternative to their weariness with a "plastic," technological age. A different hazard lurks here, which might be called the myth of "ecology romanticism," as expressed in the saying, "nature never hurts anyone."[10] Seybert was opposing that frontier attitude that regarded nature as only an enemy to be feared or conquered. He countered by upholding nature, as well as history, as part of the arena where God's glory was being displayed for the redemption of humankind. Unlike many present-day nature lovers, he did not worship nature as our "Mother." He received her, as did St. Francis before him,[11] as our fellow-creature, fashioned for the glory of our Creator God. Since we have the same Creator God, the Father of our Lord Jesus Christ, in common with her, we can admire her beauty as a brother or sister would, but without worshipping her. Because of the fall, we know that she, like us at birth, is subject to the "bondage of decay" (Romans 8:21).

Like St. Francis, Seybert offers us a sanctified view of nature. This is in contrast to every pagan form of nature worship. With the prostitution of nature by the ancient fertility cults, all nature became soaked with sexual imagery. It ceased to be our servant and became instead our tyrant. As Chesterton reminded us, the modern talk about the body being "free like any tree or flower" is "either a description of the Garden of Eden or a piece of thoroughly bad psychology, of which the world grew weary nearly two thousand years ago."[12]

The ancients needed a new heaven and a new earth, for they had defiled their own. They could not look skyward for salvation, nor to the birds and flowers, without seeing erotic images from their cultic practices scrawled upon them. Only faith in a personal God who transcended nature could purge man's obsession with these ugly appetites. Finally, with the piety of people like St. Francis and our own John Seybert, nature again began to look clean. Fire and water were felt worthy to be the brother and sister—though not the god—of a saint. As Seybert rode through those virgin American forests and mountain trails, it was to him as though all these things were newly made and awaiting new—and godly—names.

Is there wisdom here far us? If our appetites are to be safely and profitably directed toward nature, they must first be directed to nature's God, whose Word alone can point us to its proper use and enjoyment.

How do we measure the stature of these Evangelical forebears, whose lives became dominated by God-centered appetites and thirsts? From them there comes to us a "whole awakening of the world" and a "dawn in which all shapes and colors could be seen anew."[13]

Notes

1. See the excellent discussion of this culture in Don Yoder, *Pennsylvania Spirituals* (Lancaster, Pa.: Pennsylvania Folklife Society, 1961), 43f.

2. See Sidney Mead, *The Lively Experiment* (New York: Harper & Row, 1963), Ch. 1. He identifies "space" (i.e., nature) as the basic category for American theology, analogous to the centrality of "time" in European theology.

3. Roland Bainton, *Here I Stand* (Nashville: Mentor, 1950), 25.

4. The host also charged, "You are a Methodist, and nothing else." Seybert responded, "I would not be ashamed of being a Methodist, if I were one; but I am not a Methodist." From Seybert's *Journal*, entry for the first week of April 1838.

5. Seybert's *Journal*, entry for August 15, 1822, here we see an allusion to

Genesis 32:24.

6. Recorded by Yoder from Valeria Gable, 254, as translated from the Pennsylvania Dutch: "*Ve longi oon shvair vott de tseit Von Yaisoos so longi nicht heer, De blooma, de feggel oon freid Farleera eer shain-heit tsoo meer. De soon-na de sheinet meer dreeb, De fel-der shtain drou-rich dapei, Och, yen ich bin sailich in eem Detsember iss leeblich vee Moil*" Monroe Sheidler shows a similar reverence for creation as he writes to Mina of his love of the outdoors on his rural circuit.

7. Seybert's *Journal*, entry for the spring of 1844.

8. After an Indian came to hear him in Marietta, Ohio, he remarked, "A great many, who have all their religion in their mouth, could learn from this Indian how to behave in the house of God, in a manner becoming a civilized and enlightened race." *Journal.*, entry for May 12, 1821.

9. *Journal.*, entry for May 12, 1821.

10. See A. V. Hoover, "Nature Has No Children," in *Christianity Today*, XXIV, No. 13 (July 18, 1980): 807.

11. See the analysis of St. Francis in G. K. Chesterton, *St. Francis of Assisi* (Garden City, N.J.: Doubleday, 1957).

12. *St. Francis of Assisi,* 29.

13. *St. Francis of Assisi,* 157.

Chapter 11

The Keeper's Husks

"There was awakened in her a hunger and thirst so predominant that the husks given to the swine by their keepers were loathsome, disgusting, and nauseating to her."

Seybert used the expression "the keeper's husks" to describe his mother's growing dissatisfaction with the ministry of the Lutheran clergy in whose care she was rearing her family. Her discovery of the new birth (*der Wiedergeburt*) as announced by the early "Albright" preachers was not appreciated in her home church, where the emphasis was upon liturgical form that was not coupled with vital, godly living. Seybert likened her attitude, as well as his own, to that of the prodigal, coming to his spiritual senses and vowing to lay aside the husks that the swine ate (Luke 15:16-17).

Three religious groupings were among these early nineteenth century Pennsylvania Germans (and their Midwestern descendants). The "church Dutch," from whom the Seyberts came, were primarily Lutheran and Reformed. The "plain Dutch," from whom the early Scheidlers came, included the Mennonites, Amish, and Dunkers. Finally, the "bush meeting Dutch" included the followers of the revivalist sects, primarily the Evangelicals and United Brethren,[1] who arose during the Second Great Awakening (ca. 1800), primarily under Methodist influence. Most of their members were attracted from the first two groups.

It is not our intent to assess the rightness of the secession of the early Evangelicals and United Brethren from their parent church bodies. Because they had embraced revivalism, many were forced out of their churches while a few, like Otterbein of the United Brethrn, tried to maintain dual adherence to both groups.[2] At the least it can be said that the "bush meeting religion" met the religious need of large numbers of Pennsylvania Germans more effectively than did the older church bodies, which were long more resistant to adapting their ministry to the American ethos. Furthermore, many saw that the preachers of the revival were living the message of the godly life, while the clergy of the older churches tended to give only occasional lip service to this theme. This was certainly the motivation in the case of Seybert and later, in the case of my forebears in Indiana, the Scheidlers.

Our intent is to identify the pitfall that subtly traps the "keepers" of religion, lest we fall prey to their peril today. In reading these accounts in Seybert, it becomes apparent that this pitfall was their effort to keep the "religious life" going until they were thrown into a "religious spirit." By the "religious life" I mean that life that is devoted to standards more than to God, whether it be the standards of creed and catechism, as in the "church Dutch," or the standards of precept and discipline, as in the "plain Dutch." By a "religious spirit" I mean the binding spirit of human striving under law rather than the freeing power of the Holy Spirit. It is the outlook that Jesus identified as "Pharisaic" (see Matthew 16:11).

The godly can distinguish by the Spirit between chaff and kernels, but Seybert was convinced that the godless are in the precarious position of becoming the ready prey for religious pretenders. His family had shunned the "unwholesome waters of Samaria" and the "dead, dark, confused reasoning of the learned and their teaching." In setting an example for him, his mother had "finally, resolved as did the Prodigal Son to return to her heavenly Father and be converted."[3] He also refers to the religious pretenders as "hirelings," whose ministry is not motivated by love for their flocks (John 10:12-13).

For years to come, those Evangelical ministers who looked to Seybert as their model gave emphasis to the pastoral dimension of their calling. For example, after arriving at his new charge in Ohio, the youthful Monroe Scheidler wrote his beloved Mina in a moment of loneliness, saying that he had become so discouraged he "felt like going home." Despite "large congregations" and "many kind friends" on his circuit, he felt at that moment overwhelmed and "far from God." "So many souls are committed to my trust, the responsibility is so great, my weakness and inability still greater. Oh, the burden at times seems more than I can bear. —Your prayers."[4] Here is a moment of truth faced at some time by every Christian worker who has the heart of a shepherd for God's people, and not that of a "hireling" who "leaves the sheep and flees" when the wolf comes, since he "cares nothing for the sheep." Here is a picture of a young minister far from home who has begun to feel the weight of his calling. In the years that followed, he, like his Master, did lay down his life for his sheep.

Seybert and his ministers knew from painful experience the tragedy that results when the care of the flock is entrusted to a "hireling." He was also convinced that Christians are often ineffective in their witness and in the vitality of their faith because they have settled for husks—a cheap substitute for the reality of the faith. Kierkegaard, the great 19th-century Danish theologian, spoke of this unfortunate condition with contempt when he wrote that we have at hand "a complete crew of bishops, deans and priests; learned men,...talented,...humanly well-meaning." Further, they all preach—"doing it well, very well, eminently well, or tolerably well, or badly." However, not one of them is "in the character of the Christianity of the New Testament." The existence of this "Christian crew" is no advantage, he believed. Instead, it is a peril, "because it is so infinitely likely to give rise to a false impression and the false inference that when we have such a complete crew we must of course have Christianity too."[5] The seductive appeal of false religion has always been great, although the forms it has taken have been different from one era to another.

One disarming ploy of the false keepers that our United forebears discerned was for pastors to comfort and assuage people in their state of apathy and neglect concerning the claims of God. This was to desire the "easy yoke," which our Lord promised, without bearing the burden of our cross.[6] It is to accept the gospel's promise of salvation but to refuse the responsibility of witness and serving that accompany it. Philip William Otterbein, the German Reformed missionary to America who was the guiding light in forming the United Brethren in Christ, linked this problem to a false reading of the Heidelberg Catechism, the valued standard of faith of his mother church.[7] Its opening question asks, "What is your only comfort in life and in death?" The answer, "That I belong to my faithful Savior Jesus Christ" is the solid foundation for all else that it teaches about the Christian life.[8] It seemed to these United Methodist forebears that this teaching could be misunderstood to mean that "everything, including our salvation, is in God's hands and we can do nothing more than quietly await the triumph of good over evil." This seemed to them to be its practical impact, although the intent of the Catechism was to encourage believers to disciple their lives to Christ out of gratitude for their redemption. For this reason, Pietists such as Otterbein insisted that people should not be comforted while they still were slumbering in a condition of sinful deadness to God.

Among the Evangelicals, this was also a major pastoral concern for

John Seybert. In a conversation he once held with a Lutheran clergyman, Seybert inquired about the spiritual condition of the town of Womelsdorf, Pennsylvania. To Seybert's dismay, the parson replied that everything was "all right." "This preacher," he wrote, "calls everything all right, while at the same time the masses of the people there live like veritable heathen." To illustrate, he recollected that "two church members had a heated quarrel at a dance." After fighting, they professed to make peace. One of the combatants, who was a fiddler, resumed his music, while the other man returned with a knife and murdered the fiddler. Seybert reported that this parson declared at the fiddler's funeral that "this brother had fallen asleep in Jesus....This preacher calls this getting along well in religion!" Seybert concluded, "Surely, this is the prosperity of the wicked," and "no wonder that such a state of affairs exists when the spiritual leader cry 'peace, peace,' when there is no peace."[9]

Opposing these purveyors of "cheap grace," to borrow Bonhoeffer's expression, Seybert insisted that the Word of God is not first heard as a word of peace that would gloss over and legitimatize unrighteousness. This is the seductive ploy of the hireling. George Miller, one of Albright's first assistants, spoke with sensitivity on this issue in his manifesto on godly living. He advised, if "faith does not fill the heart of a preacher with godly peace...it is not easy for one to (speak) of peace"; further, "if it is done, peace is generally preached where there is no peace, where instead the conscience should be awaken to godly sorrow, true penitence and conversion."[10]

These persons knew firsthand that the gospel must at times afflict the comfortable, as well as comfort the afflicted, if we are to discover the meaning of the consecrated life. Miller continued, "A minister is in duty bound to attack the kingdom of Satan...in every possible way," but the price he will pay in doing this is clearly indicated. "It will be impossible for him to live at peace with the world, and the devil."[11] Here are hard words, spoken in love for the brethren, that continue to call us to accountability as United Methodists. If one ministers so as "to tickle the ears...so that he can live at peace with (the wicked who are around him),...no wonder that such escape persecution, and are considered wise, and are honored by the world." "Wherein," he asks, "consists the cross of such preachers?" He concludes, "I am convinced that general applause and worldly ease are not good signs in a minister.[12] The keepers of the flock, it follows, reason that "shunning the cross" is "prudence," and by this means they endear themselves to the people. He found repugnant the idea that "only some of the servants of Christ must suffer reproach," and that God will "exalt Christians to honor and renown in the world," maintaining them there until death.[13] These early Albright brethren doubtless would be distressed by present-day Christians who would covet prosperity as their right without understanding that Christian faith demands cross bearing.

The message of these Evangelical fathers is clear. Our search for solace and comfort in our faith may be either demonic or redemptive, God-denying or Godlike. To seek comfort on our own terms is to play into the hands of "false keepers" who are only too glad to buy our souls for a price. Seybert reflected upon this from firsthand experience in his Journal entries for May 1839. He was visiting a newly established Evangelical mission among the "neglected" German population of New York City when he found "rationalism" and "skepticism" rampant among nominal Lutherans and Catholics. He then preached to a large audience in Allentown, Pennsylvania, where many became convinced of the need for conversion but were unwilling to "bear the reproach of Christ." "Though they became aware of the decay of their churches," he was disappointed that they were unwilling to "come out from the world for Jesus' sake." Nevertheless, "When a rationalistic freethinker invaded the town, they left their churches to follow after him." Seybert observed that this is what results when persons "stifle their best convictions," reject "vital godliness," and become practicing "infidels."[14]

Our perception of this bold style of witness is further highlighted by noting the inflamed wrath of his clerical opponents. This occurred despite the fact that Seybert followed the lead of Albright in seeking to "reverence every place where God was worshipped, regardless of manner and place."[15] The antagonism directed against them appeared to result from the convicting power of their message, plus the fact that they, like the apostolic church, were drawing folk from all walks of life to their preaching. Like Rachel of old their cry was "Give me children or I die." John Wesley carried out his evangelistic mission from within his native Church of England, and Phillip William Otterbein of the United Brethren remained a pastor in good standing in his German Reformed Church. Unlike these leaders, the Albright brethren were not called to their evangelistic mission from the ranks of the existing clergy and so they had no sense of official accountability to the parent church bodies of the German immigrants.

The brethren did feel a spiritual bond with the founders of those churches, as Albright stated on at least one occasion, saying, "You Lutherans, of course, think you have Luther, and that he was a converted man. You think you have the Catechism. However," he concluded, "your sinful lives prove that you are not Lutherans, for you live contrary to God's Word and Luther's teaching." Continuing, he asks: "And you, German Reformed—what does it mean to be Reformed? It means to be restored, to be converted from sin and the world to God." Again, he tests their confession by the fruit of their lives, which "prove that you have turned from God toward the world." Finally he shifts his attention from the "church Dutch" to the "plain Dutch," saying "You Dunkards and Mennonites, with your peculiar dress and outward plainness, by which you comfort yourselves, you will be lost without the new birth, despite the fact you have large farms and earthly possessions." He concludes by citing his authority: "Be not astonished that I said unto you, 'You must be born again,'for these are the words of your Savior and Judge."[16] One observer who heard Albright that day declared that he saw "in the Spirit" the earth open and swallow his adversaries "in their wickedness."[17]

Lest we misjudge this zeal, let it be noted, first, that these Evangelical fathers also gave credit to those clergy who were trying to preach the gospel and lead their people into righteousness. Second, they never adopted the self-righteous position that theirs was the "only" Christian fellowship. There is considerable correspondence between the early Evangelicals and other church leaders committed to the preaching of the new birth and "true godliness, including Otterbein and the United Brethren, Winebrenner and the Church of God, sympathetic pastors among the church Dutch", and, above all, Francis Asbury and the "people called Methodists."[18]

The early Evangelicals were clearly not disposed to the concept of a pluralistic church, with which we identify United Methodism today. Neither did they impose a confessional standard as a test for church membership, as did the Lutherans, yet they did recognize that the Spirit is creative and operates in a unlimited variety of ways to effect His saving work among persons. However, they were less willing to compromise with lukewarm, apathetic, or nominal Christianity than is the church in our day. Seybert described those "keepers" who withheld the message of personal regeneration and godly living by the term "hirelings," and "wolves in sheep's clothing."[19] Why do they set up such a "fearful howl," saying that we have "invaded the land" to deceive the people? Why, he wondered, do they suddenly become so protective of their people when the Evangelical missionaries arrive in their vicinity? It is not because they care for the sheep but because, in his judgment, they care "only for their wool." Not only do they warn the public against us, writes Seybert, they also seek to lure away the "praying people" into their fold. They chided, "This movement will soon collapse; before long you can pen all the Albrights together into a corn crib."[20]

To his surprise, Seybert discovered that the "false keepers" often took pride in the pretense that they were the protectors of a sacralized society. They were the protectors of their communities and their civil religion against the incursions of the revivalist preachers. History is filled with precedents for this behavior, from the Egypt of the pharaohs, to the Rome of Innocent III, to the religious wars of the Protestant era in Europe—from which many German immigrants had fled to America, to the theocracy of Khomeini. In each of them, there was a perverse partnership between theocracy and persecution, and between orthodoxy and affluence.

These tendencies were demonstrated in the frenzied attacks of several of the regular pastors of the German churches, who saw their comfortable hegemony being threatened and replied with the slander of person and doctrine. Seybert was once charged with moral unchastity so that, he said, "I found it necessary to confront them with living witnesses in my favor, thus putting the adversary to shame."[21] Soon afterward, a "so-called Reformed pastor," searching for a way to undermine Seybert's influence, circulated the rumor that the latter had left a wife and children back East, and, reported Seybert, "it was necessary for the cause of the church which I represented to vindicate the integrity of my character in this strange land."[22] The doctrinal attacks were also frequent. In the years after Albright's death, a "certain Synod in Pennsylvania" resolved that "the Evangelical Association with her ministry was not a part of the (universal) church because she was not in apostolic succession," since Albright had not been ordained by a minister from a recognized church body.

Despite persecution and hostile resolutions from the keepers of the church establishment, the verdict of history is that Albright's solemn prophecy did prevail. He said, "If it is God's will that you should become a church, then men will appear among you who will be able to accomplish what I have been unable to do."[23] These men did appear—Miller, Seybert, Scheidler, and a host of others—ensuring that this was in fact a work for which God would provide, because they were meeting deeply felt spiritual needs.

Notes

1. These groupings are discussed in Don Yoder, *Pennsylvania Spirituals* (Lancaster, Pa.: Pennsylvania Folklife Society, 1961), Chapter 2. Other smaller revivalist groups include the Church of God (Wineurennarian), The United Missionary Church, the Evangelical Congregational Church, the United Brethren (Old Constitution), the United Christians, and the Holiness Christian Church.
2. On Otterbein see my discussion of his ministry in *Pilgrimage of Faith; The Legacy of the Otterbeins*.
3. From the preface of Seybert's *Journal*.
4. Letter from the Reverend Monroe Scheidler (age 23) to miss Mina Hall (age 22), written on may 20, 1889.
5. Søren Kierkegaard, *Attack upon Christendom*, tr. by Walter Lowrie (Princeton, 1944), 29f.
6. The yoke is the Hebrew phrase for entering into submission to another, as to the law; the word "easy" is in Greek *chrestos*, which can mean "well-fitting." To paraphrase, coming into submission to Jesus is to accept a task that is measured to fit our needs and abilities exactly. See William Barclay, *The Daily Study Bible: Matthew*, II (Philadelphia: Westminster, 1958), 19f.
7. Written in 1563 by Caspar Olevianus and Zacharias Ursinus for the Elector III of the Palatinate, this conciliatory textbook of the faith was designed to mediate between Lutheranism and Calvinism without departing from the presecribed, official doctrine of the German state church, which was the Lutheran Augsburg Confession. See my *Pilgrimage of Faith*, Chapters 1 and 2.
8. Question 1, *The Heidelberg Catechism* (Philadelphia: United Church Press, 1962), 9.
9. Seybert's *Journal*, entry for April 28, 1828.
10. George Miller, *Practical Christianity*, 60.
11. Miller, *Practical Christianity*, 73f.
12. Miller, *Practical Christianity*, 74f. On one occasion (February 9, 1823), Seybert complained because the people praised him for his preaching, saying he "wished they knew how poverty-stricken" he felt because he was out of touch with the Spirit. Seybert's *Journal* for February 9, 1823.
13. Miller, *Practical Christianity*, 76.
14. Seybert's *Journal*, entry for May 6, 1839.
15. George Miller, *Jacob Albrecht*, p. 2.
16. Our source here is "father" Henry Spayth, the primitive historian of the United Brethren, cited by Yeakel, 71f.
17. Yeakel, 71f.
18. It is reported that John Dreisbach, the first presiding elder among the Evangelicals, once met with Bishop Asbury with the intention of uniting the two denominations. He wrote, "The bishop made me a very liberal and respectable offer, on certain conditions to unite with his church. I was to withdraw from the

Evangelical Association and go with them to Baltimore...yet I could not determine in my mind to take such a treacherous step toward the Evangelical Association....He replied that the German language could not exist much longer in this country....I made him the following offer: 'If you will give us German circuits, districts and conferences, we are willing to be one people with you." "This cannot be—it would not be expedient,' was the bishop's reply." Dreisbach's *Journal*, quoted in W. W. Orwig, *History of the Association* (Cleveland, 1858), 26. See also K. James Stein, "Church Unity Movements in the Church of the United Brethren in Christ until 1946," Unpublished Th. D. dissertation, Union Theological Seminary, 1965.

19. Seybert's *Journal* for February 21, 1821.
20. Seybert's *Journal* for February 21, 1821.
21. Seybert's report of the Erie mission, May, 1833, cited by Spreng, 140.
22. Seybert's report of the Erie mission, May, 1833, cited by Spreng, 140.
23. Yeakel, *Albright and His Co-Laborers*, 103.

Chapter 12

The Lure of the Keepers

"It seemed to me the German theologians were flying very low, they even teach the beginning of regeneration in infant baptism, that conversion commences in the cradle and is continued to the grave, that the Christian must always sin again, but in the Lord's supper he would eat and drink Christ and thus have the forgiveness of sins. I can see nothing of their lofty soaring, they fly along quite low over the marshes of sin and crime." Bishop Seybert's remarks to Reuben Yeakel in the fall of 1857.[1]

In Chapter 11 we explored Seybert's distinction between true and false shepherds, noting how a religious spirit is often at odds with a life of genuine godliness. The theological issue that surfaced in this controversy was the interpretation given to the doctrine of salvation. The doctrine of those German theologians whom Seybert critiqued in the above quotation was, he believed, the underlying problem to be faced. Many persons had been beguiled by this teaching in Europe and in America. Seybert was convinced that one of the chief reasons why the "Albright people" were called into being was to counter the lure of that doctrine with the demanding and narrow way of Christian perfection. Seybert's teaching of this "new way" was broadly Wesleyan in outline, yet tinged with strong overtones of German mysticism that formed a distinctive style of spirituality in the Evangelical Association.

Although Seybert first encountered this "German theology," as he called it, among the "church Dutch" of Pennsylvania, especially the Lutherans and German Reformed, his most careful reflections on the subject were given when this theology unexpectedly made its appearance from within the ranks of the Albright people. The remarks recorded above were in response to a pamphlet questioning Christian perfection that was written in 1857 by a popular Evangelical presiding elder from Pennsylvania named Solomon Neitz.[2]

It is significant that the Wesleyan doctrine of holiness generated little controversy among the Evangelicals so long as it was a subject of practice and not debate. That Albright sought and realized this state of grace with all his heart is the unanimous testimony of those "fathers and mothers in Israel" who personally knew and heard him. The doctrine, stating that conversion would normally lead to entire sanctification, was more convincing when observed in practice (as a life lived in unmitigated love for God and neighbor) than when debated in polemics. However, an article appeared in 1856 in *Der Christliche Botschafter*, the church paper, which concluded that those who die without entire sanctification would be wholly lost. It was simply signed, "An Old Evangelical."

Neitz's pamphlet, entitled "Christian Sanctification in Accordance with the Apostolic Doctrine," appeared in response to this polemical piece. From Seybert's standpoint, Neitz's pamphlet also engaged in polemical excess. He asserted that "justification and sanctification are one indivisible work."[3] Neitz rightly sensed that "The apostles had no such idea that there was only here and there a 'sanctified one' among believers," for "they are the holy people (1 Peter 2:9)."[4] However, he went too far for Seybert by suggesting that entire sanctification in this life is in opposition to the teaching of the apostles. Curiously, Neitz had argued that "the English or Wesleyan theology is shallow" whereas "the German Theology is pithy and profound." The German theology "soars high" and "will in a few years outstrip the English and drive it from the field."[5]

He pointed out that Wesley had traveled to Germany to consult Zinzendorf, the leader of the Moravians, and that after his return to England, he "established his extra sanctification doctrine, but it will not endure very long." He likened Wesley to the wren (*Zaunkoenig*) in the fable, which hid itself in the feathers of the eagle on his flight into the upper regions. "When the king of birds was soaring above all the other birds the little rogue shot out from his hiding place, flew a little higher yet and sang his *Zitteritterattadat*."[6]

Seybert, who had little appetite for polemics, remarked to one of his preachers, "Oh, brother, there ought to be no strife about sanctification –it ought to be earnestly sought."[7] He added that he had written to Neitz, stating that "it seemed to me the German theologians were flying very low, they even teach the beginning of regeneration in infant baptism, that conversion commences in the cradle and is continued to the grave, (and) that the Christian must always sin again." However, he added that they are assured their sins are forgiven by perfunctorily receiving the Lord's Supper. "I can see nothing of their lofty soaring," concluded Seybert, "they fly along quite low over the marshes of sin and crime."[8]

These remarks are hardly descriptive of the theology of Zinzendorf, but they do describe the typical views of the "church Dutch" pastors who seemed to be opposing Seybert's mission at every turn of the road. Aside from the question of which theology is shallow or profound, he was more interested in the practical religious consequences of a faith that did not expect God's grace to triumph victoriously over evil. Such a faith makes one susceptible to the seductive lure of those pastors who offer the comforts of Christian faith without cross bearing and self-denial. They are oblivious of the kind of agonizing in "faith, prayer and tears until...hearts are cleansed from all sin and cured from moral evil, ...being enabled like Enoch to walk with God and lead a chaste, righteous and godly life in this present world."[9] Apart from the theological issues at stake, Seybert is here fighting a battle with those who are lured by an easy, accommodating faith. It is religion without godliness. Addressing a group of his ministers, he once said, "Most Christians in our day regard (our doctrine of Entire Sanctification) as excessive and hope to get to heaven without it." He believed this is the reason that "so few of the fruits of godliness appear in many so-called converts" and that "the Church swarms with worldly minded and backslidden professors of religion." He does not object so much that such faith is quiet and undemonstrative as that it makes no real impact on the world. "These people are (hardly) an obstacle to many worldly men."[10]

Doctrinal orthodoxy among either the "church Dutch" or the "bush meeting Dutch" could be wrong-headed when it was used in defense of a self-serving cause. Its error was its tendency to espouse only rational, propositional belief and to suppress the free operation of the Holy Spirit, who is to make God's Word operational in the lives of God's people. Seybert's *Journal* is a veritable casebook that documents for us this Spirit-led theology in praxis. His repeated insistence was that doctrinal truth, if it is worth holding, must be proved in life. From this conviction he continually held his Evangelical people accountable to God, so much so that his penetrating witness has been described as a time when "Jerusalem was searched through with lanterns."[11] Rather than arguing with the doctrinal aspects of his adversaries' positions, he chose to address their practical implications. His ground of defense against the so-called "German theology" was that it undermined the very foundation of the mission to which his people had consecrated themselves, which was to herald the call to godliness and to live fully yielded to its power.

Another reason fueled Seybert's resistance to the lure of the keepers of the religious establishment of his day. Many of the early Evangelicals had been either immigrants from Germany or the children of immigrants, and they carried the memories of established church systems that had stifled the free worship of God.[12] In North America it was the protection of religious liberty by American civil law, combined with the protection of divine Providence, that helped minimize the number of Evangelical itinerants who were stoned or shot from their horses, which did occur as late as 1840.[13] Albright and Seybert encountered conditions of fearful drunkenness, lewdness, and child abuse among many "nominal" German church members, and their calls for repentance unleashed angry counterattacks from their clergy. "Humph!" retorted an old card player, "the whole thing (meaning the Evangelical Association) is going down faster then it came up. Our parson told us last Sunday we should be careful, maybe they give the people some kind of poison so as to deceive them the easier!"[14] One of Seybert's tent meetings in 1825 was attacked by a parson named Boyer, who armed his "sheep" with clubs and pitchforks for an attack that wounded several.[15] Sensing their loss of influence in their communities, such clergymen abandoned the appeal of reason and resorted to brute intimidation. They strained every nerve to defeat what appeared to many to be a work of God, much as Demetrius the silversmith incited attacks upon Paul at Ephesus (Acts 19:23-41).

Because of the lack of governmental protection in Germany, the oppression of Evangelical missionaries there was even more serious. John Seybert helped motivate his brethren to establish a missionary work in the "Fatherland" in 1848. The first missionaries experienced severe trials during the chaotic revolutionary era of 1848, when there was sentiment in Germany for abolishing the church altogether in a reign of terror akin to the French Revolution of 1789. After one missionary and his band of praying penitents were brutally clubbed, he wrote back to his brethren in America the "we still have courage, for with our God we can leap over a wall."[16]

These missionaries testified that the attack upon Christianity by the civil and professional leaders was rooted in ungodly appetites for power, which led to a restless departure from the stable moorings of family, church, and community values. Even one state church pastor, who had come to see the feared Albright preachers as "friends of Christ and His church," wrote that most of his countrymen had lost all sense of moral obligation to God and neighbor because "the inordinate desire for enjoyments and the lust of the flesh became very powerful."[17] He reported that no days were more abused than Sundays, as all forms of lustful self-gratification were "postponed until the Lord's Day," with the result that "the people became continually poorer, and a people made poor by sinful indulgence can easily be incited to insurrection."[18]

This pattern is one that present-day Christians can ill afford to ignore. The self-indulgence of the affluent and the oppression of the poor had their origins in attitudes of self-conceit and dominance that were learned in the homes of church members who were orthodox in doctrine but unregenerate in heart. The testimony of Pastor Henhoefer continued, declaring, "The bond of love that previously included all in its embrace ceased, and indifference, coldness and exclusiveness came instead," manifested in pretentious "dress, furnishing of houses, and feasting."[19] Hearts that are not exercised by love for God are unfaithful and their fruit is libertinism, which took the name of "enlightenment" but was in fact "the liberty of the ungodly."[20]

Seybert and his colaborers recognized a truth that is becoming apparent again in our day. They saw that the payoff for godless living is a rootless existence that leaves people open to becoming parasites—the pawns of demagogues who manipulate the unfulfilled needs of their victims. Perhaps the warning of our pioneer Evangelicals can be heard again with clarity. They lived in an age when Americans possessed a land with seemingly limitless frontiers and resources of nature. We are now coming against the limits of our effort to find freedom of self-expression and self-fulfillment. Until now we have known the security, the protection, the time, space, and unencumbered wealth to cushion us from our illusions about human nature. As Seybert discovered among folk in his day, many are also finding in our day that the harvest of their lives is in the enslavement of broken marriages, troubled children and stagnating, uncreative lives lost in tormenting insecurity. The legacy of our Evangelical fathers stands as a judgment upon the folly of cheapened religion allied with avaricious living. Their lives endure as a testimony that "godly life and conduct speak louder than words."[21]

Notes

1. Reuben Yeakel, *History of the Evangelical Association*, II, 64.
2. Yeakel, 61. Seybert represented the doctrinal positon on entire sanctification or Christian perfection (following justification and regeneration) found in the *Doctrines and Discipline of the Evangelcial Association* (New Berlin, 1809). This

text is found in the Appendix).
3. Solomon Neitz, quoted in Yeakel, 62.
4. Solomon Neitz, quoted in Yeakel, 63.
5. Solomon Neitz, quoted in Yeakel, 64.
6. Solomon Neitz, quoted in Yeakel, 64.
7. Solomon Neitz, quoted in Yeakel, 63.
8. Solomon Neitz, quoted in Yeakel, 64.
9 Seybert's address to the East Pennsylvania Conference, *The Evangelical Association*, Winter, 1852, quoted in Yeakel, 29.
10. Seybert's address to the East Pennsylvania Conference, *The Evangelical Association*, Winter, 1852, quoted in Yeakel, 29.
11. Spreng, 140.
12. The major upheaval afflicting the German "Holy Roman Empire," which involved religious issues, was the Thirty Years War of 1618-48. This was followed by further, more mitigated conflicts between rival princes.
13. Spreng, 50.
14. Seybert's *Journal*, entry for February 21, 1821.
15. Seybert's *Journal*, entry for May 19, 1825.
16. Brother Noah Schaefer, quoted in Yeakel, 296f.
17. Pastor Aloys Henhoefer, quoted in Yeakel, 231. Like prophets crying in the wilderness, leaders in the German state church such as Henhoefer and Professor Tholuck of Halle called the church to its duties amid the political and theological unrest of 1848, which was a phase of German struggle for national unification. Tholuck wrote, "If you should ask me whether the religious condition has been growing better or worse since the March revolution of 1848, I am compelled...to answer, decidedly worse. The indifference, yes enmity toward religion has increased very much. The attendance upon public worship is entirely neglected in some Prussian provinces." A. Tholuck, in *Evangelisches Christentum*, May, 1850, quoted by Albright, 416.
18. Albright, 416. The work of the Association in Europe gradually grew to 31,109 members, at the time of Methodist - EUB union in 1968.
19. Albright, 416.
20. Albright, 230.
21. From the church paper of the Evangelicals, *Der Christliche Botschafter* (1850), cited by Yeakel, 15.

Chapter 13

The Marks of the Keepers

"Whenever the devil and the world stay still, there the religion of Jesus is not genuine." -John Seybert's Journal, entry for the first week of August, 1855

The picture of the wayward prodigal eating the "keeper's husks" is a dominant image used by our Albright brethren to portray the condition of moral bondage from which they felt called of God to summon people. In their mission of retrieval, they probed the spiritual roots of that bondage. What are the telltale marks of these false keepers, and of those who become their victims?

1. These include Christians whose communities seem tranquil because there is no ministry of the Word of God in the power of the Spirit. Amorality, if not immorality, is usually flagrant. After one camp meeting in Ohio, John Seybert wrote that "The Lord wrought mightily, but the ungodly raged fearfully." So it goes, that "when the Lord works powerfully, the devil rages horribly." By contrast, "Whenever the devil and the world stay still, there the religion of Jesus is not genuine." Speaking in a metaphor, Seybert declared that "Where Jesus Christ, Peter and John are, there are also Herod, Pilate, Caiaphas, the Pope, Caesar and the devil, together with the whole serpent brood of unbelievers...who make common cause in persecution."[1] Despite his suspicion of Catholicism which we are fortunately putting to rest today, his basic message is clear. If there are no pressures upon the forces of spiritual and moral bondage in our communities, such as the purveyors of narcotics, pornography, child abuse, and the oppression of the poor, here is one indication that God's spokesmen are asleep on the job. Such Christians—Seybert would call them "professors of religion"—do not measure up to our fathers' norm of true godliness, however much they may be preoccupied with the cultivation of their inward piety. They are not giving faithful attention to the Word which they profess if their society is not being called to repentance. There is an element of paradox in

the fact that Seybert opposed those rebels who resisted God, but he was also the rebel, challenging the sterile life of the status quo.

2. Another mark of the "religious keeper" is intemperance. In the 1880's, Bishop Reuben Yeakel of the Evangelicals interviewed an aged patriarch known as "Father Wonder," who recalled from his childhood when Albright visited his father's house. He remembered Albright's speaking with his unconverted family in a "gentle and touching way" about the Saviour. As he prepared to leave, Albright was offered a glass of whiskey, which was a custom among the Pennsylvania Germans. After he firmly yet gently declined, asking that offense not be taken by his refusal, Wonder's astonished family could not help noting the difference between this preacher and their intemperate pastor, who frequently had to be carried to his house in drunken stupors. The father switched to Albright, but not the mother. Above all, Albright's witness made an impact upon the children. They teased their mother, saying, "There is a difference...Father's pastor sings and prays...." Then came the clincher: "Mother's pastor does not pray, but curses and gets drunk—we will stick to Father's pastor."[2]

This model made a greater impact upon the children, who became future leaders of the church in the West, than all the temperance sermons they would ever hear. It helped them understand what later temperance debates often overlooked—that temperance is more than abstinence; it is the total way we order life's resources in response to God's grace. Seybert's *Journal* richly attests to this outlook. What might be the impact for United Methodists if renewed attention were given to this positive view of temperance as an integral part of our spiritual formation?

3. Closely tied to intemperance is softness, or flabby faith. It is widely recognized[3] that anointed, powerful expressions of Christian faith thrive best under conditions of austerity and persecution. The ardor of the church for her mission has traditionally cooled when she has come to be "at ease" in the world, and especially when she takes on the trappings of an affluent society. Seybert once visited a worship service where, in his words, "The preacher belonged to that class who live in kings' houses, to judge from the soft raiment which he wore, rather than to the humble followers of Jesus." He knew that plain dress had no virtue in itself, but he believed there usually was a link between an extravagant life-style and an inability to "endure hardness" as a soldier of Christ and to be carble of "life" and "fire" in the worship of God.[4] That preacher who only occasionally reproves sin, "but at the same time walks in the vani-

ties of this life," causes the powers of this world to rejoice and leaves weak Christians "offended and discouraged."[5] "Hirelings" might like to attract and impress church members by appealing to their taste for opulence and ease.[6] Seybert was looking for workers whose hunger was for the righteousness of God that would be made visible in godly living.

4. A mark of the keeper that is often overlooked is his misdirected humor. This is the "put-off" humor that serves to keep people from knowing who you really are and what you really think, not the kind of humor that draws people to you because it discloses your joy in Christ that is without guile. Such "graceless, superficial preachers can never build up a godly, holy church any more than thorns and thistles can produce grapes and figs." This is because they "spoil far more by their conversation (and) levity...than they can make good by their preaching."[7]. In those summers I spent as a boy at great grandfather Scheidler's, I recall much laughter and joy, but it was never at the expense of other persons' sense of self worth nor was it used as a mask to blunt basic convictions. Sometimes wit was an effective means of discipline. As a young girl, my mother once was heard "sassing" her elders. Great grandfather walked around and around the rooms of the house, cracking a whip against the ground and asking, "Where is she?" He had to step over her, crouched as she was with her head under the draw curtains of the old bookcase, but he kept pretending he could not find her. She recalls that this was far more effective discipline than an actual whipping.

5. Not infrequently, a keeper lays hold to his flock by the seductive appeal of intellectualism. The early church had confronted this threat from the Gnostics, who substituted salvation by faith with salvation by secret knowledge (gnosis) that was imparted by a teacher to his initiates in the cult. This recurrent danger was met "head on" when Seybert was witnessing from house to house in Philadelphia in 1823. He met two budding theological students who insisted to him that "literary, scientific and intellectual training" were the main prerequisites for effective ministry. Seybert, of course, insisted on a "change of heart" and the "gift of the Holy Ghost."[8] He was mindful of Paul's warning to Timothy against that "wrangling among men who are depraved in mind and bereft of the truth, imagining that godliness is a means of gain" (I Tim. 6:5 RSV). For his part, Seybert was well read, although he was self-educated. It was the regenerated mind and heart that these early Albright brethren championed. Through the error of an "unregenerate intellectualism," warned George Miller, "the devil deceives thousands and is himself the watchman of their souls." He continued, "What wonder then that the whole

body of mankind is...approaching the shores of eternity without concern, for as the preacher is, so will be the hearer."[9] Without sacrificing our concern for quality theological education, could not United Methodism ponder with profit the priority that these fathers established? Miller wrote that wisdom secured from God, in accordance with James 1:5, "cannot be obtained in the high schools of learning, or among the dead languages, however useful (this) learning may be in its proper place." Rather, "The blessing to his work must be obtained from on high, through prayer."[10]

6. In present-day America, physical attacks upon the regenerate are less frequent than in the nascent days of the Great Awakening. However, our Evangelical forebears were not strangers to the subtle and indirect attacks that were often instigated by unfriendly clergy. One day in December 1824, Seybert entered a store to purchase some stationery, but he was refused. "The proprietor," he noted, "would not sell any paper to a *strabler* (ranting) preacher."[11] Snubbed, John quietly withdrew with this reminder that he was on alien ground. To his credit, Seybert frequently struggled with the difference between persecution for godliness, where the offense arose as a response to the gospel, and opposition that is incurred by our own offensiveness.

In their best moments, our Evangelical fathers did not stoop to reply in kind to those who vilified them for their witness. Theirs was an overcoming faith, as seen in one prophetic utterance from Seybert's lips. He was responding to a searing attack from some hostile clergy in Ohio concerning the memory of Jacob Albright, his spiritual father. "Notwithstanding all their efforts to the contrary," he proclaimed, "these beautiful groves with their wealth of flowers and their grassy slopes, shall no longer belong to the father of lies." Instead, he said, may they belong to the Lord Jesus! "Let these groves and prairies to consecrad unto Him, for the truth has already triumphed!"[12] Here we catch a glimpse of his vision of a nation saturated and made godly by an outpouring of grace that would overflow to the latest generation.

An important caution accompanies Seybert's vision. Toward the end of his life, he wrote a letter to a young preacher, saying, "With the ministry, the church will stand or fall." he continued, "Even among converted ministers there is a great lack of divine power in our days (1855)." He readily agreed that there was then more learning and eloquent preaching than in the days of Albright, but we had also become "more conformed to the world in our worship, preaching, and entire conduct." His prayer was that God would deal with our ministry "so that the church may not be ruined by us!" He concluded, "There is certainly danger threatening us from this direction—of this there is no doubt."[13] This prophecy was fulfilled in 1891, when a division occurred in the ranks of the Evangelical Association.[14] By then, their total commitment to be a uniquely spiritual people, set apart by godliness, had become far less than total. As the flame of the Spirit burned low, the forces of disintegration prevailed.

To the generations of people down to us who are the latest recipients of their witness, Seybert's words remain an undying hope: that these valleys of our discontent and disinterest and spiritual bondage in every form "shall soon see a great change, and a great work of salvation will ere long break out in this territory, which everybody will see."[15] If this work is to prevail in our day, we need to probe that miracle of regeneration in Christ, the new birth into the godly life, which is the centerpiece of our concern. The recovery of its power and abiding reality is, in the witness of John Seybert, the last, best hope for the church.

Notes

1. Seybert's *Journal*, entry for the first week of August 1855, as cited by Spreng, 324.

2. Cited by Yeakel in *Albright and his Co-Laborers*, 83 f.

3. This is Jonathan Edwards' initial observation in his *Treatise Concerning Religious Affections*.

4. Seybert's *Journal*, entries for June 1821.

5. George Miller, *Practical Christianity*, p. 80f.

6. Seybert found a parallel to this in the public arena when politicians lured votes by promises of bread and circuses—a la ancient Rome. See his *Journal* for the last week of July 1840, where he comments on a political demonstration in Centerville, Indiana.

7. Yeakel, *History of the Evangelical Association*, Vol. I, 15.

8. Spreng, 68.

9. Miller, *Practical Christianity*, 55f.

10. Miller, *Practical Christianity*, 57f.

11. Seybert's *Journal*, entry for first week of December 1824, as citied by Spreng, 86.

12. Written from Long Grove, Ohio, "six miles west of Wheeling."

13. Letter from Bishop Seybert to a young minister in the East Pennsylvania Conference, cited by Yeakel, 51.

14. See Terry M. Heisey, "Immigration as a Factor in the Division of the Evangelical Association," *Methodist History*, XIX (October 1980), 41-57.

15. Seybert's *Journal*, entry for May 11, 1826.

Chapter 14

A Road Dampened by Tears

"I remained behind to conceal my tears, which were many, (for) I could have dampened the road going home." -From the preface of John Seybert's Journal.

Our portrait of the godly person, in the heritage of our Evangelical forebears, has developed from a view of his awakened appetites for God, which is like a trace of brightness on a dark canvas. As the light intensifies, the darkness is thrown into sharper relief. This contrast began to come into perspective when we considered his growing dissatisfaction with the cheap "husks" of his religious keepers, disgusting fare indeed, said Seybert, for a lover of Jesus. Now we give our emerging portrait a personal identity. The godly are repentant persons. Speaking again in metaphor, Seybert captured the mood of his awakening to this vital, heartfelt repentance when he described his return under conviction from a camp meeting of the Albright people in 1810, at the age of nineteen. He withdrew from the company of the youths who followed him and "followed on behind, in the rear." He confessed, "I remained behind to conceal my tears, which were many, (for) I could have dampened the road going home."[1] The image of the prodigal returning to his father's home was clearly in his mind.

This brings us to the heart of the early Evangelicals' quest for the godly life. Their antidote to the debilitating "religious spirit" of the predominating churches of their day was drastic. They gave up the effort to keep that life going, either by means of creed and liturgy (as the "church Dutch") or outward deportment (as the "plain Dutch"). Instead, they took to heart Jesus' words for one to "deny himself and take up his cross daily and follow me" (Luke 9:23). Cross-bearing did not mean shouldering your responsibility in life. It was far more radical than that. It meant asking their Lord to slay them in their inward nature.

Nowhere in John Seybert's extant notes and correspondence did he ask God to help people by improving and strengthening their character.

He resisted the immoral and manipulative actions of ministers who were deemed "false shepherds," and yet his witness began with a call for the utter destruction of the moral life itself. He believed that humankind was too mortally afflicted by sin ever to grow by natural ability into an approved filial relation with the Creator God. No "character formation" could be based upon our fallen, prideful nature. The only possible starting point for vital Christian living was the Cross of Christ. It is not enough that we claim Christ is for us, by His atoning work. For true Christians, who wish to confess Christ "by hand and mouth," there must also be the confession of "Christ in us," by the inward testimony of the Holy Spirit.[2] Our "bush meeting" forebears believed that this living confession required an intense encounter with God's judging and redeeming grace, which Seybert called "deep conversion" (*tiefe Bekehrung*). It began with a soul-searching, penitential struggle (called *der Busskampf*) and ended in a glorious "break-through" (*Durchbruch*) into the new birth (*der Wiedergeburt*).

The Evangelical camp meeting songs captured the ecstasy of the redeemed sinner who has struggled his way through and is now able to give his shout of Hosanna.[3] The gospel of these camp meeting preachers, which was "Jesus Christ and him crucified," was surely orthodox in motif, though hardly churchly in form. From our distant vantage point, it would be easy to become preoccupied with the displays of emotion, as did their detractors, and forget the crucial insight that these forefathers have left for us. It is the recognition that there can be no meaningful progress in the Christian life or in the church unless we first come to the point of full surrender of self in the shadow of the Cross.

How God and humankind are rightly joined is the issue at stake here. The descriptions of conversions were far less stereotyped in Seybert's memoirs than in the later generations of holiness theology, when revivalism became atrophied into formalism. He recognized that the Holy Spirit operates with creativity and diversity. In a few instances he established broad categories to describe the sorts of persons whom he encountered. Ministering among the "Tunkers" of eastern Pennsylvania, he reported finding the "rough and extremely wicked," the "respectable and moral who have never been awakened," those who were "struggling with conviction," and a few who "may have had some genuine knowledge of a genuine Evangelical experience."[4] The early Evangelical author, George Miller, described the diverse workings of the Spirit in reaching persons as follows: God speaks through "the various means of grace" and those "who persistently strive against the operations of the Holy

Spirit, God will not raise to spiritual life; for he will force life and happiness upon no one but offers it unto all through Christ."[5] His summons come in "many and various ways, so that no one can make the excuse that divine grace and eternal life were not offered to him."[6]

Despite this diversity, these Evangelical fathers agreed that there was always a "narrow way" for entry into the godly life. Each of them learned to walk the "way of the cross." Seybert's youthful friends grew weary and gave up the struggle to find mercy, but he "went on," eagerly hearing the "hated preachers of repentance," being "too sin-sick" to care about persecution. His struggle was to grasp the reality of faith in the "sufficient merit of Jesus," and he continued to wrestle "day and night," in prayer and tears, until he finally "broke through" and found himself washed of sin as he bathed his face in the watering trough.[7] The rapturous experience of God's grace grew out of a lively sense of the seriousness with which our holy God views sin. Because he walked the road "dampened by tears," he could be tough-minded when it came to living amid the forces of evil in the world. At the same time, he reflected a gentleness that enabled him to love the sinner, for that was he, save for the grace of God.

Seybert used a constellation of terms to describe this entry into the "narrow way" to life eternal. A drunken fiddler once overheard the gospel being preached in a meeting and he was "*arrested* on the spot by the Spirit of Cod, and the deep of his soul was *broken up*." The pipers and dancers who had accompanied him stopped their music and whispered to one another with consternation, "Look, he's praying."[8] Similarly, a prominent citizen of Warren, Pennsylvania, once came to his meeting to dispute with him. Seybert said he was preaching with such liberty on the love and compassion of God in Christ that "our moral persecutor was struck by the Word of the Lord and began to melt like wax" until he "fell upon his knees in great distress of soul."[9] To those under conviction, the light of his message was called "burning," while to the redeemed it appeared shining."[10]

He also referred to this penitential struggle as a divine "wounding" of the contrite, which is followed by calling salvation a divine healing. In a house meeting where he was preaching, a woman once was so "wrought upon" by the Spirit that "she fled to an adjoining room, threw herself on a bed, and would not permit the arrow of conviction to enter her soul deeper." Seybert remarked, "She is certainly severely wounded, and at least a few arrows of conviction are fast in that soul," and so he prayed that God would "give this woman no rest until she turns unto Him."[11] At a camp meeting in 1834, Seybert reported that "the convicting energy of the Spirit and the Word was manifested to an extraordinary degree as another brother preached." The people cried out, "fairly staggering to the altar," and "even in the outskirts of the audience, the spiritually wounded began to tremble and quake and cry out." A woman with a child in her arms "trembled and wept so sorely in her appalling spiritual grief" that bystanders relieved her of her child until she came to "find peace in the Redeemer."[12] The district that was literally "burned over" with revival by the Evangelical itinerants was the Mahantango Valley of Pennsylvania. Seybert reported conducting a camp meeting here in 1837 where the quick and powerful Word of God "cut deep wounds into many hearts, which only Jesus Christ could heal with the blood of His atonement."[13]

This camp meeting context for conversion is far removed from the experience of most present-day United Methodists. However, they were convinced that there can be no significant growth in Christian living until one is rightly related to God. That relationship does not begin by imploring God's help in our living; it begins by allowing God to "slay" us, in Seybert's terms, or to bring to death the idea that God's love for us is based upon how we perform. For this reason he undertook the work of an evangelist. Seybert once returned to preach in his hometown of Manheim, Pennsylvania, like our Lord returning to Nazareth, and while preaching on "Him that is athirst, come" (Revelation 22:7), "a general power of repentance came upon the people." He reported that "the slain of the Lord were of all ages." There were cases where "parents have beaten their children unmercifully because they wished to lead a godly life and desired to abandon the prayerless ways of their parents." He tersely summed up what he saw happening when he wrote, "Since the Lord is working so mightily in Manheim, there is great uneasiness in the kingdom of darkness."[14] Not infrequently his audiences became convinced of the need for conversion, but they were often not willing to "bear the reproach of Christ" and "to come out from the world for Jesus' sake."[15]

Seybert learned in his pilgrimage of faith that the capacity to forgive was a barometer for determining whether one had experienced the pardoning grace of Christ. The Christian who finds it hard to forgive his persecutors is still walking in the "flesh." The remedy was not to ask Christ to help him forgive: it was to ask Christ to slay him and to love the unreconciled brother through him. He confidently expected God would "work for good with those who love Him" (Romans 8:20). Accordingly, Seybert spoke of "religion" (the saving, heartfelt kind, that is) as a "work." One of his favorite "bush meeting choruses" was entitled "Conversion is the best work."[16] The prayer meeting was for these "Dutch" the pious substitute for the secular work party assembled for barn raisings or threshings.[17] The task now became working out one's salvation with fear and trembling, as the Epistle to the Philippians advises. It is understandable yet ironical that the "high church Dutch" accused the Evangelicals of "Pelagianism," the doctrine that one makes oneself holy through good works,[18] since Seybert insisted upon the supernatural destruction of the old nature and regeneration in Christ as the basis for moral living.

Seybert also learned from his "penitential struggle" the need to contend with his God in times of distress, lest he falter in his warfaring against the powers of darkness. Once during a bout with malaria, he was in agony to reach his appointments. He reported that he "wept and prayed much" on the trail, no longer for himself but for his neglected flock. Often stopping on his journey to plead with God, he wrestled until he was blessed.

We must take care not to think of the "penitential struggle" as a graceless, morbid theme derived from preaching "legal conviction" without the gospel. Jacob Albright clarified this issue when he related his conversion to his assistant George Miller, in the primitive days of our tradition. He traced his prodigal "homecoming" to the moment when he sensed an inner "void, an emptiness that awakens a painful feeling" which he described as the "working together" of the "voice of conscience" and the "voice of the gospel" to produce a sense of "lively repentance."[19] His painful feelings of divine punishment and inward despair were transitory. The voice of God changed from conviction to the dawn of illumination and comfort as he discovered "the merit off my Savior (in) his bitter suffering and death."[20] The key to his recovery was when his deep-felt sense of being crucified for sin was joined to his vision of the cross of the Savior. Then he realized that his suffering, though justified because of his offense against God, need not be prolonged for himself, because he now saw that his old nature was crucified with Christ. After this, his burden of soul was for the salvation of his neighbors.

Unlike those who are "performance oriented" in their religion, these Albright brethren did not look for their center of values "out there" in goals that they set for themselves. Despite their emphasis on a simplified style of dress and consumption, they knew that outward behavior does not itself earn a place of "belonging" for Christians. Their center of value was "right here" in the message of the cross that was proclaimed to them. Their worship was not motivated by tasks to be performed. They had learned from their sojourn with the "keepers" that this approach builds upon the lie that I am loved because I do right rather than because I am God's child and He has dealt with my sin nature for Christ's sake. With tears in their eyes, the bush-meeting converts would tell their erring brother or sister to "look away to Calvary" ("shou-et heen ouf Goalyadaw"), and meditate on the suffering love of the Savior.[21] As signs of conviction began to appear, they pled with him or her, "O come ye to your Jesus—He alone can save you" ("O koomt tsoo eirem Yaisoos").[22]

What is distinctive about the Evangelicals' perception of how God and humankind are rightly to be joined? Each major faith tradition in Christianity has had its own "normative" response to this question. Roman Catholics have been taught in the school of Thomas Aquinas that grace perfects our nature and that it is bestowed sacramentally by the Church as an infused "habit" (Latin, *virtu*), assisting us in negotiating the crucial stages of life from birth to death. The Protestant Reformers of the sixteenth century were convinced from their study of Scripture that grace is God's good will (*beneficium*) to sinners, which is the promise of the gospel. They held that God's law convicts rather than redeems us (Romans 7), and only the righteousness of Christ, to which we remain passive, is saving to us (Romans 1:17). True faith is trust, which relates us to this personal grace of God. To the scholastic theologians, especially among Protestants, we are rightly related to God by means of our intellectual assent to creedal propositions of truth given by God to the church. By the seventeenth century, scholastics like Gomarus had redefined faith as mental assent rather than as personal trust.

By contrast to these options, our Evangelical fathers shared the outlook of the German Pietists (both Lutheran and Reformed), who reinstated the emotion of adoration and wonder and the mystic sense of Christ's presence which the Catholic feels in the Mass. This dimension had been diminished by the attempt of the Protestant scholastics to intellectualize worship. To Seybert it seemed to be singularly lacking in the worship of the "church Dutch" of Pennsylvania in the early nineteenth century.[23] Like the Pietists whom he treasured, especially Arndt,[24] Seybert used portrayals of ecstatic mystical transport to describe experiences of love for God possible for believers during intense prayer. For Seybert, faith as assent to God's Word or even as trust in God's promises is not the highest species of relating to God. The best way, indeed the godly way, was to envision and return the suffering love of the Savior as we conform to His image in our daily living. When he was faced with a problem with his own lethargy early in his ministry, Seybert prayed for deliverance "for the sake of the Redeemer's bitter sufferings."[25] Once when he was chided by a farmer for his fervent mode of worship, he reminded him that the Lord Jesus "Himself prayed with strong crying and tears."[26]

Perhaps the deepest motivation undergirding the "penitential struggle" was not the desire for pardon to escape a dreaded judgment. Deeper than that was the state of being "constrained by love . . . to suffer the loss of all things."[27] Then we see ourselves as the sinful woman who anointed Jesus in the presence of the Pharisees, whose "sins, which are many, are forgiven, for she loved much" (Luke 7:47). This was a pardon that could not be gained by learning a catechism; it had to be "worked through" in the struggle on the bench of the mourner. The struggle was to get self out of the way so the unconditional love of Jesus could be seen and adored. When the penitent saw that the Savior's wounds were for him, his heart began to respond with reverberations of grateful love. Not infrequently, the preacher was assisted in his effort by the pathos of other seekers. Seybert described one sister who so wept in her agony for souls following his preaching that he likened her to Jeremiah of old, who exclaimed, "O that my head were waters, and mine eyes a fountain of tears, that I might weep day and night for the slain of the daughter of my people" (Jeremiah 9:1).[28]

In reading the long-silent record of these early Evangelical testimonies to the "penitential struggle," the best thing about them is that we can hear their very lives, their sufferings, and their longings speaking. At one meeting where a notorious drunkard appeared, Seybert reported that "His penitential struggle was protracted and severe, but God's children wept tears of deep sympathy for the unfortunate man, and ceased not day nor night to pray for his salvation."[29] Concerning another camp meeting, he said, "Already on the first evening we had a good time, but not until Tuesday did we have a perfect breakthrough (*vollkommenen Durchbruch*), when many tears were shed by penitents who wrestled for salvation." On Friday one woman was so "wrought upon by the Spirit" that she began to tremble and weep. Her husband, who was "bitterly opposed" to her going to the altar of prayer, took hold of her to detain her. She then tried to kneel where she was, but he also prevented this. At last she prayed standing, "weeping so bitterly" for mercy until "at last the light of salvation broke in upon her distressed soul." Finally "the stubborn captor himself began to quake. He trembled like an aspen leaf, and tears involuntarily rolled down his hardened face." Though it seemed he would "sink down with his burden" he held out, refusing to surrender himself. As they went home together, Seybert noticed that "he was of sadder countenance than his wife, who was full of joy."[30]

The further we get from these earliest generations of Albright and his brethren, we see less emphasis being placed upon this penitential struggle. Those intermediate generations that stand between them and our own often continued to mediate the heritage of godly living even though their conversions were less "thorough," as Seybert would say, because the penitential struggle was cut short.

In her next letter, Mina Hall reflected upon her own recent conversion. Her words are terse and to the point: "The way is much brighter than ever before. I have no desire whatever to turn back. I find there is nothing to turn back to." Mina Hall and Monroe Scheidler began their correspondence, which was to conclude with their marriage a year later, by discovering their common devotion to their Savior. This first love and their budding romantic love were each described in very nearly the same breath.[31]

The frequent absence of the penitential struggle from the chronicles of conversion of United Methodists of more recent generations probably constitutes one of the major differences between the Christian experience of our Evangelical forebears and our own. They would not permit conversion[32] to be reduced to our assenting to certain facts about Jesus Christ. It also could not be relegated to a formal profession of faith made in the presence of a congregation if there were none who had been witness to some evidence or fruit of that "professor's" conversion. To them, conversion to Christ was distinct from "accession" to class (later church) membership, and Evangelical United Brethren pastors were obliged to list both separately as late as 1968 in some annual conferences.[33]

It is significant that the issue of a valid conversion exercised the thought of the greatest theologians in the history of Christianity, including Jonathan Edwards and the Wesleys in the eighteenth–century Awakenings. And the question at stake in the penitential struggle is just how genuine is our motivation for identifying with the cause of Christ? Here is the question that shall surely prompt each of us to pause in reflection.

Notes

1. Preface to Seybert's *Journal*.
2. This theme is also developed by Philip William Otterbein (United Brethren) in his only full-length, published sermon, *Die Heilbriqende Menschwerdung* (1760), which is found in translation in Arthur Core, *Philip*

William Otterbein: Pastor, Ecumenist, Churchman (Dayton: Board of Publication, 1968), 77-90.

3. For example, the Evangelical camp meeting song by John Driersbach entitled *"Die Nacht des Sunden ist nun fort"* ("The night of sin is over now"), in *Geistliche Viole* (Cleveland, 1855 ed.), no. 41.

4. *Geistliche Viole*, entry for the last week of April, 1829, as cited by Spreng, 110. The "Tunkers" were adherents of the Schwenkfelder sect, among whom the early Albright brethren frequently ministered. One of the early Evangelical catechisms, prepared by W. W. Orwig in 1847, was taken directly for the text of a Schwenkfelder catechism.

5. Miller, 21.

6. Miller, 21. This divine summons that precedes salvation was called "preventing" (or prevenient) grace by John Wesley, who cited John 1:9, "That was the true Light, which lighteth every man that cometh into the world." (KJV) 5ee John Wesley, "The Scripture Way of Salvation," in Albert Outler, *John Wesley*, (Mew York: Oxford, 1964), 273.

7. From the "Preface" of Seybert's *Journal*.

8. From Seybert's report of the Erie mission, May, 1833, cited by Spreng, 137-142.

9. Spreng, 137-142. This citizen was the father of Bishop J. J. Esher of the Evangelical Association, who was converted at this reeting at eight years of age.

10. Spreng, 137-142, Decerber 5, 1821.

11. Spreng, 137-142, February 14, 1821.

12. Seybert's *Journal*, entry for August 14, 1834.

13. Seybert's *Journal*, entry for August 14, 1834. Seybert reports that he arrived in the Valley on April 21, 1837; this remark was cited by Spreng, 175.

14. Seybert's *Journal*, entry for March 2, 1826.

15. Seybert's *Journal*, entry for "the last Sunday in May, 1839."

16. *"Baikairing iss des beshta varrick"* (in the Pennsylvania Dutch dialect), recorded in Yoder, 193 f. Yoder notes (p. 450) *"Varrick"* (High German: Work) suggests the theme of *"Heilsordnung"* (order of salvation), brought to the Pennsylvania Dutch by the Methodists.

17. Yoder, 113.

18. This charge was made by the high church leader, John Williamson Nevin (1803-1886) of Mercersburg Seminary of the German Reformed Church, in a tract, The Anxious Bench (1843), cited by Yoder, p. 460. Seybert's doctrine of divine-human cooperation in salvation is properly called "synergism."

19. George Miller, *Kurze Beschreiunq*, 7.

20. George Miller, 12f.

21. Recorded in Yoder, 300.

22. Yoder, 283.

23. A similar protest against formalism in worship was made by Wesley and the Methodists in England and colonial America. Yoder refers to these developments as the "folk fringe" of the Romantic reaction against Deism in Europe and

America. Yoder, 460.

24. Peter Erb, 10.

25. Seybert's *Journal*, entry for Thursday, May 24, 1821.

26. Seybert's *Journal*, entry for Thursday, June 24, 1824; here Seybert cited Hebrews 5:7.

27. John Seybert, sermon on Solomon 8:5 ("Love Is as Strong as Death") published in Spreng, 405.

28. Seybert's *Journal*, entry for November 15, 1820.

29. From Seybert's camp meeting at Lebanon, Pa., in the winter of 1836, described by Spreng, 177.

30. Seybert's *Journal*, entry for August 26, 1838.

31. There is evidence in the correspondence of Monroe Scheidler and Mina Hall in the 1880's that this experience played a part in their spiritual formation. They met while Monroe was preaching a revival in her hometown of Portland, Indiana. In her first letter that followed, Mina informed the youthful preacher that the meeting was "continuing with interest" and that "there are seekers at the altar almost every night." Two youths, for whom the people had been praying "for quite a long time," came forth and she reported that "there was great joy in seeing them surrender."

32. While the term "conversion" was often used interchangeably with "new birth" among the Evangelicals, the term "salvation" was commonly used to describe a process which is completed in glory. This compares with Wesley's distinctions between salvation begun (justification), salvation continued (sanctification), and salvation completed (glorification).

33. See, for example, the 1968 *Journal of Indiana Conference South*, The E.U.B. Church, 142-201. By this time, the term "accession" was changed to "members gained by (a) confession of faith, (b) certificate of transfer, or (c) certificate of membership." Membership was no longer predicated on conversion alone, and the categories for "conversions" and "reclamations" were the last ones listed, which reversed the priority of early-day Evangelicals and United Brethren, as well as Methodists.

Chapter 15

Getting through to God

"The Spirit of Grace often touched me so mightily . . . that tears as from a fountain gushed over my cheeks. How I remember (such) a meeting where I was so thoroughly preached-through." From the preface of John Seybert's Journal.

In all ages people have been preoccupied with finding the presence of God. Our Evangelical forebears have not been recognized as great theologians, but in reading their long-silent journals and letters we find one very vital insight. They knew how to live in the presence of God. They knew how to enable that vital presence to inform and direct the way they carried out their daily tasks. This was because their "penitential struggle" had led them to "break through" (der Durchbruch) into God's holy presence in such a way that their lives were thereafter profoundly transformed. Bishop Seybert described this experience in the camp meeting idiom as being "preached though," or saturated with divine mercy. In his *Journal* reflections, he likens this breakthrough to the moment when the homeward-bound prodigal son is first greeted by his father, and he is astonished and humbled to discover that he is still loved as a son and not as a hired servant (Luke 15:19-20).

Surely this "breakthrough" experience has some important implications for present-day United Methodists who are intent upon discovering God's presence in their lives. Seybert's testimony casts aside some treasured idols. For one thing, he has brought home to us the easily forgotten premise that behaviour does not earn a place of belonging for us in the presence of God. He helped many see that their hope does not rest in creeds (the "church Dutch") that are not proved by godly living, nor in outward dress and demeanor (the "plain Dutch") that mask hearts that are not alive to God. How many ways have we devised to convey to others that our love for them depends upon their virtues and accomplishments? As a youth, Seybert had rejected the ministry of the pastor who let it be known to his catechetical students that "this is how we believe and you are acceptable if you conform." He found no hint in the man that there was a God who loved him as a person. Neither the prodigal, nor the older son, were loved by their father for their performance but because of their identity as sons.

We are also reminded by Seybert's witness that "passive piety" is hardly sufficient to enter into the kingdom of God's presence. When he recalled his penitential struggle, saying "I did not (at first) break through," we are reminded of our Lord's admonition to "seize the Kingdom with force" (Matthew 11:12).[1] To be sure, the prodigal son did not have to merit his father's love, but he certainly acted in a decisive way to be in the position to receive that love.

By contrast, the way to God that Seybert commends to us is by experiencing the sacred energy of the Father's love. When he speaks of being "thoroughly preached-through," he has in mind more than the sense of hearing. What he expresses is a veritable banquet of the Word, to be experienced by taste, sight, and feeling and smelling as well. This is nothing less than the banquet of the fatted calf prepared by the father for the lost son (Luke 15:22-24).

This breakthrough was commonly experienced in the milieu of the camp meeting, but in the case of Seybert it was described by the use of images drawn from the annals of Christian mysticism. Here is where his spirituality became distinct from that of our Anglo-American Methodist heritage. Seybert was firmly rooted in the themes of Wesleyan theology that had been taught by Albright, especially the themes he wedded to a group of images that he derived from his devoted reading of the great German mystical writers. His library, which was in his day the finest to be found in the denomination, included well-worn copies of Jacob Boehme, Tersteegen, Tauler, Thomas à Kempis, Gottfried Arnold, Rambach, and Schwenkfeld—indicating his strong affinity for Radical German Pietism.[2]

Mysticism, a term which is often vaguely used, has been defined as the direct intuition or experience of God, and a mystic is one whose life is centered on such a direct experience, and not merely on an accepted belief or practice.[3] The early church adopted this term from Greek religion.[4] The Christian mystic is one whose life is based on conscious, first-hand communion with God in Christ. It is always a communion of love, and in its perfection, it is so intimate and pervasive that the term "union" describes it best.[5]

Prominent Christian theologians have made careful, limited use of mystical terms. St. Augustine described this ideal when he said, "My life shall be real life, being wholly full of Thee."[6] The Protestant Reformers, as well as the mature Wesley, saw union with God's Word as the initial experience of every believer which identifies the beginning of the Christian life.[7] It was the birth of the believer, through justification by faith, into the body of Christ. For Boehme, a Protestant mystical writer— or radical Pietist— read by Seybert, the greater stress is not upon the basis of the faith-union, in God's pardon of the sinner, but on the possibility of a perfected experience of the faith-union. It is to have, in fullness, the God who has united himself with the believer. For Protestant mystics, including Seybert, this emphasis involved the use of medieval portrayals of ecstatic mystical transport to describe experiences of love for God possible for believers during intense seasons of devotional prayer. He may be cited as a forthright defender of the basic tenets of Wesleyan orthodoxy, but to this he blended his use of mystical insights as witnesses ("*Zeugen*") in the Christian life.[8]

What were some of the significant mystical undercurrents and images in Seybert's portrayal of the godly life? There is the language of Seybert's numerous recounted dreams and visions, which we shall examine in a later chapter. At a camp meeting near Orwigsburg, Pennsylvania, in 1835, at the preparation service of the Lord's Supper, some sank as though dead, into the deep sea of God's love".[9] "Breakthrough" (*Durchbruch*) was Seybert's term to describe our immersion into the depths of grace, and he prized deep rather than superficial conversions.[10] Familiar mystical language is evident in his description of the camp meetings of 1838: "All our camp meetings this year were blessed with awakenings, conversions, and reviving of the people of God." He concludes, "So the Lord did not forsake us," for our God is "He who walks among the seven golden candlesticks and who holds the seven stars in His right hand." He prayed, "O may He, always, with His sevenfold spiritual light and powers of His grace dwell among us to live, work, and to walk."[11] The golden candlesticks of Revelation 2:1 have intrigued mystics of all generations.[12]

It is also quite possible that Seybert's use of the parable of the lost son to describe his pilgrimage to the godly life was inspired by his mystical sources. In *The Way to Christ*, Boehme described true repentance by reference to the parable. The penitent discovers himself to be one who "lies captive in father's inheritance, God's love and mercy, in earthly pleasure with the devil's fatted pigs." He then enters God's presence "with the beautiful cloak of the innocence of Christ that he has soiled, as a dirty, tattered and ragged swineherd who has continually eaten the husks of vanity with the devil's pigs, and is not worthy to be called a son of the father and a member of Christ."[13] Johann Arndt, another favorite of the early Evangelicals and United Brethren, saw the prodigal son as the best example of the mystical union with Christ: "Beloved, what do the heartfelt embrace, kiss, and the beautiful new shoes signify, other than the fervent mercy, new gift-giving of lost goods and gifts, and the dear union.[14] Both Arndt and Boehme drew the distinction between true and false sonship.[15] Boehme wrote that it is hypocrisy and an "empty useless comfort" to say "Christ has paid and made satisfaction for our sins" if we do not "die to our sins in Him," for this would be "external hypocrisy, the externflly accepted sonship," which is false and useless.[16]

Unlike Wesley, Seybert apparently saw little need to rethink his mystical sources radically. This is evident in his emphasis on the theme of "resignation" or "yieldedness" (*Gelassenheit*) from Tauler, which worked easily into his order of salvation. Arndt had earlier appealed to this theme from Tauler when he described how we are to be the image in which God wishes to be seen. Being fully resigned to God is when "man does not act according to his self-will, but his will is God's will; man has no self-love, but God is his love; no self-honor, but God is to be his honor; no wealth, but God is his wealth and possession."[17] God is to completely possess us "from within and without " as is perfectly seen in our Lord Jesus Christ.[18] Once a person is resigned to God, said Tauler, "the Holy Spirit begins to enlighten him and to teach him properly since God keeps the true Sabbath and rest-day in his heart and frees it from all evil lusts, willings and work."[19] A resigned heart given to God is of greater value than a great knowledge of languages of formal learning.[20] Boehme wrote a treatise on "True Resignation" (1622), in which he described how one is to "sprout forth out of the death of the sinful man into a new mind and will in God."[21]

Who could experience this resignation to God and how did it find a place in the "bush meeting" religion of our Evangelical forebears? In counseling penitents, Seybert found that when their struggle to find pardon (*Busskampf*) reached a climax of breakthrough (*Durchbruch*), this moment normally would be attended by a twofold manifestation. One would inwardly experience inner peace (*Gelassenheit*) and outwardly there was the "shout" of victory, which expressed the convert's joy at "coming through." Here we examine the inward, more mystical side of that breakthrough experience.[22]

In a sense, quiet resignation seems antithetical to the active life-style of Seybert. He once wrote, "I must work while it is day. . . . When I get within the gates of the New Jerusalem, then I will rest. But so long as I sojourn in Mesech and dwell in he tents of Kedar, I have no rest, for it is written, work out your salvation with fear and trembling."[23] His longest "vacation" occurred when he paused, while ill, at the home of the aged John Dreisbach, a pioneer Evangelical leader who had been a colaborer with Albright. What memories, struggles, and victories these veterans could share! But how long did Seybert tarry and rest? One night and part of two days, for "the King's business required haste."[24] George Miller, another colaborer with Albright, had advised seekers of salvation, "you must not stand still" or "be still and quiet and let the Spirit of God work alone." However, once we have actively sought God, under the Spirit's leading, we can gain a "godly peace" that will enable us to walk—not retire—in God's power.[25]

At the same time, we need to recognize that the mystics' way of resignation did touch the lives of these Evangelical activists at several vital points. Foresaking all for the Gospel meant resigning one's bondage to temporal possessions and becoming "like a bird that escaped the snare of the fowler."[26] It meant guarding against the "spirit of (financial) speculation," which infected many professors of religion, who are "content to let the children of God have Heaven and God, if they only succeed in gaining large fortunes."[27] Being yielded to God involved self-denial in following Jesus, which included the avoidance of vain, world-attracting fashions.[28] In one sermon on the subject of serving God with humility "in heart and in appearance," Seybert bluntly recorded that the power of God became so manifest that "pride got sick." As many "useless ornaments of gaiety were thrown off," he gave the shout of "hallelujah!"[29]

Humility is closely linked to cross-bearing. In an episcopal letter shortly after his election as bishop, Seybert appealed to his preachers in words that remain prophetic today. "We lack the spirit of humility" which the master displayed in "the voluntary acceptance of the poverty and obscurity that marked the circumstances of His birth and early career." There is also "that voluntary submission to the shame of the cross; we are not willing to bear the derision of every fool and devil's imp." He also declared that we need "that willingness to suffer afflictions and tribulations without number, even unto death."[30] Seybert was already sensing, even in 1839, a debilitating loss of consecration within the Evangelical ministry, and the only antidote was to "behold the love of Him, who was constrained by His very agonies to pray for His merciless tormentors."[31] As he grew in years and in grace, Seybert visibly took on the appearance of consecration to his peers, even as my forebear Scheidler did for me.[32]

The early Evangelicals did not consider suffering per se to be a virtue of a mark of godliness. Resigning our selfish hold on our wills and submitting them to the will of our crucified Lord was the intent. George Miller was once privileged to spend several days traveling in the company of Albright and complained to him about his chronic illness and loss of eyesight. Albright replied, "Your sufferings are severe, but it is somewhat your own fault that they seem so burdensome and you seem so depressed, as you are unwilling to bow submissively to God." Resignation would be the key to ultimate healing, for "as long as you continue in this frame of mind, God will work no change in your condition." Miller could not begin to be yielded to God until he had "broken through" to find pardon for his sins; he then could not be wholly yielded until he was "entirely sanctified from all these weaknesses." Then, said Albright, "you would be satisfied and contented with the dealings of God with you, and praise Him even for all things." Only then could Miller, overwhelmed by a mighty stream of love, become "perfectly willing to kiss the rod and to walk before God in child-like confidence."[33] Even more important than whether bodily healing occurred, which often did in the bush-meeting experience, was the issue of whether full consecration had been achieved.

"Accepting one's lot," which is so difficult for present-day Christians, was another mark of the resigned believer. Unlike stoic fatalism, this means being at peace with passing circumstances after you have struggled to come to be in the center of God's will for ministering to others. Seybert never advised the unbelieving sufferer to accept his lot, but there are times when he so admonished believers, who needed to see that, despite their outward circumstances, they were blessed in Christ "with every spiritual blessing in the heavenly places" (Ephesians 1:3b). Thus, he commended the oppressed Evangelicals in New York when he found them "resigned to their lot and satisfied, whether the Lord let them live or die."[34] Once he was in dire pain from a severe buggy accident. Confined to a hotel amid "strangers and ungodly people," it was doubtful whether he would recover, but he remained "resigned and patient" until he found brothers to care for him.[35]

The spirit of the early Evangelicals might be called one of active resignation to their crucified Lord, as opposed to a more passive and contemplative resignation in the medieval mystics. It was never articulated apart from their burden for evangelization to the German-Americans. When Seybert became the first Evangelical to preach in Allentown, Pennsylvania, a "notoriously wicked city," he could secure only the cold and inconvenient market house while the authorities granted the use of the courthouse that day to an infidel who styled himself the World's Redeemer. Seybert reported that he and his colleague "submitted patiently" and they gained a hearing for God's Word, even among an unruly election-day crowd.[36]

Seybert was more than an individual mystic; he was a churchman, and had come to identify the will of his brethren in conference as an expression of God's will for his life. Thus, when he was first elected a deacon, he wrote that "I submitted as cheerfully as I could to the decision of my brethren, and will seek to do the best I can by the help of God."[37] The same sentiment was expressed when he was elected an elder, a presiding elder, and finally, a bishop. Perhaps the finest description of the life yielded to God is found in this testimony from Seybert's midlife, which weaves together the themes of mystical love for God through creation and redemption. "I am enjoying a most delightful and blessed experience after the inner man. I am fully translated into the marvelous light and liberty of the people of God." Winter is past, "The enemies of my soul seem overcome and driven from the field, and the everlasting arm of Jesus Christ is around me, as He presses me to His comforting bosom. I am therefore able to enjoy my travels," he concludes, "possessing as I do a healthy body, a contented mind and a quiet conscience, especially in this halcyon period of the year, when bright sunshine and gentle winds mingle the perfume of the flowers with the golden glory of the harvest fields. My heart is filled with peace."[38]

This old *Gelassenheit* teaching was one that was passed down through successive generations of Evangelicals, reaching me via the living witness of Monroe Scheidler. In one of his early letters to his Mina, he fondly referred to his home church near Cambridge as his "dear old Sabbath Home church," for this was the place where he had found eternal peace with his God. Characteristic of Evangelicals of the middle generations, he related the theme of resignation to the Sabbath, which he regularly greeted as a season of godly refreshment and as a foretaste of that Sabbath rest which is the inheritance of the children of God. "Your good wishes for a pleasant Sabbath to me were fully realized," he wrote her in March 1889. "It was indeed a happy day to me. I preached in the morning about 'Jesus and the Storm'—His cheering presence was very near."[39] The durable and resilient quality in the witness of our Evangelical forebears is bound up with Monroe's prayer to Mina, "May Christ be thy stay in the darkest night...in the weakest hour...in each moment's fall, may Christ be thy all."[40]

Notes

1. From the Preface of Seybert's *Journal*.

2. His collection, now in Naperville, Illinois, also includes the Puritan John Bunyan. Tauler and Kempis were medieval Catholic mystics, and a German translation of á Kempis *Imitation of Christ* was published by the Evangelicals on their press in 1838.

3. Evelyn Underhill, *The Mystics of the Church*, (New York, Doran, n.d.), 10.

4. The *mystae* were those initiates of the "mysteries" who were believed to have received the vision of the divine. Underhill, 10.

5. Underhill, 10.

6. Quoted by Underhill, 10.

7. Luther wrote that faith in the Word of God "unites the soul with Christ as a bride is united with her bridegroom" and, after Aldersgate, Wesley wrote, "I could taste the good word of God in the anthem." See "The Freedom of a Christian Man" (1520), in Hans Hillerbrand, ed., *The Protestant Reformation* (New York: Harper, 1968), 11; and "Journal of John Wesley" in Albert Outler, ed., *John Wesley* (New York: Oxford, 1965), 67. Despite the use of such mystical terms, Augustine, the Reformers, and Wesley (in contrast with Eastern Orthodoxy) understood salvation as being more relational than unitive in nature.

8. Johann Arndt (1555-1621), had earlier embellished Lutheran tradition with similar mystical impulses. See Peter Erb, tr., Johann Arndt's *True Christianity* in *The Classics of Western Spirituality*, (New York: Paulist Press, 1979), 16.

9. Seybert's *Journal*, entry for August 21, 1835.

10. See his self-description of being "converted deep into eternal life" (*tief ins ewige Leben hinein bekehrt*), discussed in Chapter 1.

11. *Journal*, entry for September 10, 1838.

12. Yoder, 59. He notes another Pennsylvania example, *The Vision of Isaac Child* (Philadelphia, 1826), a Quaker tract describing the "candlesticks" vision of Isaac Child (1734-69), in Seventh month, 1757. The use of the lampstand theme from Revelation was also a feature of German Philadelphian thought, derived from the work of Jane Leade in England. It would play a promient role in German radical Pietism. See Hans Schneider, *Radical German Pietism* (Lanham, New Jersey, 2007).

13. Peter Erb, tr., *Jacob Boehme's The Way to Christ* in *The Classics of Western Spirituality* (New York: Paulist Press, 1978), 28f.

14. Peter Erb, tr., *John Arndt's True Christianity* in *The Classics of Western Spirituality* (New York: Paulist Press, 1979), 28f.

15. Arndt, 37; Boehme, 133.
16. Boehme, 133.
17. Arndt, 30f.
18. Arndt, 30f.
19. Tauler, quoted in Arndt, *True Christianity*, 175.
20. Tauler, quoted in Arndt, *True Christianity*.
21. Boehme, *The Way to Christ*, 114.
22. The outward manifestation of the "shout" will be explored in Chapter 18.
23. Seybert's illness occurred in the fall of 1835; this remark is cited by Spreng, 156.
24. Seybert's *Journal*, entry for December 3, 1852.
25. George Miller, *Practical Christianity*, 24, 60.
26. "The Life and Labors of George Miller," in Yeakel, *Albright and His Co-Laborers*, 198.
27. Seybert's *Journal*, entry for July 28, 1854. Seybert evidently did not buy into the bourgeois spirit of the Protestant work ethic.
28. This was the theme of a message preached by Seybert at a "union camp meeting" held in 1828 with John Winebreener of the German Reformed Church (later founder of the Church of God), discussed in Spreng, 107.
29. From Seybert's farewell sermon on the Salem District in May, 1833, reported by Spreng, 128.
30. Bishop John Seybert, "An Appeal to the Ministry of the Evangelical Association," 1839, cited in Spreng, 203.
31. Spreng, 203.
32. See Seybert's *Journal*, entry for October 20, 1859.
33. "The Life and Labors of George Miller," in Yeakel, op, cit., p. 228.
34. Seybert's report from the Lake Circuit, New York, written in April, 1859; see Spreng, p. 295.
35. *Journal*, entry for September 11, 1856.
36. Spreng, p. 178.
37. *Journal*, entry for Thursday, June 6, 1822.
38. Seybert's *Journal*, entry for Monday, July 5, 1824.
39. Letter from M. L. Scheidler to Mina Hall, March 15, 1889.
40. Letter from M. L. Scheidler to Mina Hall, March 15, 1889.

Chapter 16

Dreams of the Spirit

"The Third night after leaving home, I had a remarkable dream....I felt greatly encouraged by this dream, but had a terrible conflict with the devil the next day." Seybert's Journal, *entry for September 14, 1820.*

References to dreams, as indicated above, form an important part of John Seybert's *Journal*. They reveal another aspect of mystical faith in his self-portrayal of the godly person. His dreams and visions were the fruit or ecstasy of the yielded life. His dreams help us to clarify his image of the prodigal son, by which he understood himself and his horizons. Just as the prodigal meditated upon life in his father's home "when he came to himself" (Luke 15:17) before his return, so also we may describe Seybert's recorded dream life as being visions on the homeward journey. They were divine signposts pointing the way toward the faithful completion of his earthly calling.

Dreamers are often regarded today with skepticism, especially those who see a relation between their dream or vision and their Christian faith. However, our early Evangelical forebears had a special place for them. Attending to dreams was more than a way of unraveling the torments of the inner life, as seen in the work of Freud and much of modern depth psychology. Persons like Albright, Miller, and Seybert found that their dreams opened them to another dimension of reality, through which God reached out to them.

Many religions have recognized the numinous quality of dreams, including Hinduism, Azrathustra, the Chinese and American Indian folk religions, and the ancient Greeks and Romans.[1] The biblical faith and the witness of the early Christian apostles shared this belief, though with a far different theological grounding from that of the non-Christian world.[2] Against this background, we can better grasp the reliance upon dreams and visions by our early Evangelicals. Because of their grounded belief in the reality of the spiritual world, which transcends space and time,[3] they were able to maintain vital contact with people's lives at a level deeper than the merely rational or conceptual. This will be evident in the examples of spiritual discernment through dreams that Seybert recorded.

With their grounding in the spiritual world, these forebears stood apart from most segments of the church after Copernicus, when the narrow religious world view of the Middle Ages reflected an obsession with "Dreams of the Spirit" in an untenable way. As Kelsey has asserted,[4] the church continued to teach the doctrines of Christ's Ascension and life after death without any grounded belief in the reality of the spiritual world. Modern Western theology, including prominent trends within the theology of mainline Methodism,[5] has been more concerned with the conceptual, time/space world than the numinous world of the Spirit, and has given little attention to the human psyche or to meditation. By refocusing the spiritual dimension in dreams, the early Evangelicals and United Brethren placed themselves in the normative tradition of the biblical faith and the early church, which together affirmed the reality of a spiritual world in which God contacts us through dreams and visions. We need think only of the formative dreams of the patriarchs, Abraham, Jacob, and Joseph;[6] Moses' vision of the burning bush;[7] the voice that called the sleeping Samuel;[8] the visions of the prophets;[9] and the dream references in the Psalms.[10] Jesus' birth was accompanied by dreams and visions,[11] and these manifestations fill the accounts in the Acts of the Apostles.[12] The church fathers who gave serious attention to dreams as vehicles of divine communication include Hernias, Justin, Origen, and Tertullian, as well as the Emperor Constantine, whose celebrated vision. resulted in his conversion to Christianity.[13] It has been asserted[14] that this tradition of dreams came to an end in the thirteenth century with Thomas Aquinas, who followed Aristotle in teaching that we can experience reality only through sense perception and reason. Thus, he concluded that no direct knowledge of God is available to us through dreams or visions. Seybert and the early Albright brethren stand as significant exceptions to the widespread trend in Christian thought since Aquinas that says human beings can experience reality only through sensory perception and reason. This tendency to think in conceptual terms only permeated "mainline," nineteenth-century Methodist theology. Chiles[15] has shown that Methodist theology became increasingly rational and moralistic, isolating Methodists in the pew more and more from any familiarity with the life of the Spirit.

In discovering Seybert's dreams, we find that his numinous experiences were expressly Christian, for they are unintelligible apart from his ardor to be a witness for Christ. His dreams thus formed a central vision, which governed the living of his life. Also, we find that their content was not concerned with moral do's and don'ts, but with defining his life's purpose under the calling of God. Here again, his reading of the German Pietists and mystics, expecially Arndt and Boehme, helped open him to the dynamics of the contemplative life. Arndt reminded him that the contemplative life was to be entered by humility, which "creates inner peace and brings about silence." He said, "In short, it is a little room, full of heavenly treasures. Man gains it, however, through meditative prayer and contemplation of the. crucified Christ." This path of contemplation reveals that man, himself, is as "a shadow or a dream."[16] Boehme spoke of the important role of imagination which is to be cultivated by the person who "desires to attain to divine contemplation within himself and speak with God in Christ."[17]

The dreams I have selected from Seybert and other early Albright brethren illustrate how they helped them to set priorities in using their resources, to provide encouragement amid adversity, to offer insight on the nature of the church and the task of evangelism, and to provide admonition to humility.

First, they discovered that their dreams could help them see how best to use their resources so as not to dissipate their energies, gifts, and opportunities. Their dreams helped set the main trend for their lives, so they could accomplish what they knew they had to finish, under God's calling. This objective is illustrated in an extraordinary dream recorded in the autobiography of George Miller (1774-1816). He was a member of the original circle of Albright's followers and had been commissioned by the conference of 1808 to complete the task of preparing the Articles of Faith and Rules of Discipline for the denomination after the untimely death of Albright. His dream prepared him for this important life task.

After preaching on Christmas eve,

> I went to bed contentedly, comforted of God, and, as far as I knew, was physically well, and had the following dream. I walked on a street, positively certain that it was the way to heaven. I walked a long distance with great courage, until my way led through a vast thicket, through which I hurried the more that I might not be overtaken by night in this dense forest. Soon I arrived at a place where the bushes were covered with snow and ice, on both sides of the road, and the branches of the trees

bent over the road on account of the weight upon them, so that with much effort I stepped over some, and others I shook off, and finally crept through under the rest on my hands and feet, until at last I was so exhausted, that I laid myself upon my knees and elbows, and rested and got breath again. [I] did not trust to lay my head down, on account of the extreme cold and fear of being overtaken by sleep.

After coming through obstacles with much exertion, Miller's dream shifted to a new plane.

It seemed to me as though someone had opened a door and let me out. I looked back, and was astonished when I saw the woods on both sides of the road, through which I had come, full of wild and savage beasts, who in their rage wanted to devour me. I thanked God, who had so graciously delivered me out of this danger, turned quickly and walked on where, after a short distance, I saw the city of God, the new Jerusalem lie before me.

His description of the heavenly city is reminiscent of the Revelation of John and of Dante's Divine Comedy.

I leaped for joy, and courageously hurried on until I noticed a stream of water which was between me and the city. I was perplexed and concerned how to cross it. Meanwhile an angel came toward me, seized me and led me in a quick flight toward the city, and it seemed to me as though I had wings myself and was flying by the side of the angel. The city was white as snow and clear as transparent glass. We flew through a brightly illuminated door, and with many thousands of thousands of saints we soared up and down through heaven. But I knew no one of those who were basking in joy, on account of the great glory that surrounded them. My body and clothes were as white as snow, and as clear as crystal, and in my hands I had a transparent clock, upon whose dial plate there moved a bright stone, similar to gold, more wonderful than be described. The angel showed me a great hall in the distance, by which, in looking at it, I was more quickened than by all the rest I had seen here.

At this climactic moment, the meaning of the dream for his life mission was disclosed to him.

As I was longingly looking thither, my guide said, "*Behold, this is the place of your rest and joy.*" I requested him to bring me to this place of the glory of the Lord. "As soon as you will have perfectly obeyed the Holy Scriptures and the Discipline, which you will compile from the same," said he, "but now you must first go back to the earth and complete this important work."

Miller was then left with a bodily imprint from his encounter with the angel in the dream.

> I gave him as an answer: if God would write upon my heart His Word and that which I was to compile out of it, I would be ready to go back again; but if not, then I would refuse to do it, for unless God would write it upon my heart, I could not complete it. Now the angel took the stone that was found in my clock, and with great power stamped it upon my breast, and I felt as though an arrow had pierced me through, and I had become mortally wounded.

As his vision of the city vanished, he saw himself standing upon earth beside a ladder whose top reached to heaven, an allusion to Jacob's dream in Genesis 28.

> The angel said, "You must get on this ladder and step from one round to another, until you have arrived at the place of your rest." Although I felt very sick on account of the pain in my breast, nevertheless, I hastened and got on the ladder, and with great effort reached the top of it, where, to my joy, I could again see the place of my rest. Here I had to press through a very narrow door, and having entered it, I arrived at the desired place, and sank into a sweet slumber. No doubt I should have continued longer in this slumber, if I had not been awakened by a severe pain.[18]

After awakening, he felt sick with a pain in his breast, and in the morning he related his dream to his colaborer, John Dreisbach. Miller believed he was mortally wounded, but despite his weakness he began to work on his Articles of Faith and Discipline, which was approved and ordered to be published at the conference of 1809. His conclusion, based on the dream, that he would die soon was wrong, for he lived eight years longer. The dream was a parable of his life, depicting the difficulties on the pilgrimage to Heaven. The ladder indicated to him that he would have to pass through numerous trials during the remainder of his life, after his vision of Heaven. Had Miller not been forced by his impairment to abandon his circuit riding, he would not have had the time to become the literary spokesman of the early Evangelicals. As one historian noted, he was, like Paul, kept quiet in order to write the epistles for the churches.[19] During these latter years, Miller was also granted extraordinary spiritual acumen and was sought out for counsel and prayer. It may be, as Howard Ervin has suggested to me, that by this wound he received, as did St. Francis of old, the stigmata, or the imprint of the wounds of our Lord upon his body.

Seybert's recorded dreams were more numerous, though no single dream had as much decisive impact on his entire life as Miller's. When he set out for his first appointment, the third night after leaving home he dreamed he was standing in his brother's meadow and saw streams of water flowing from the south and turning toward the east. "I then went under an overhanging rock that is in this meadow, and saw other springs of water, one of which was much stronger than the rest, and had exceedingly sparkling water—indeed it seemed to be literally *living* water."[20] This dream encouraged him to persevere in his mission, despite adversity, and it probably recalled to him his own regeneration that occurred while washing his face in a watering trough.

In a second dream built around the image of water, he was awakened to a confident expectation of conversions in his ministry. He dreamed of a deep, water-filled pit, into which several persons had fallen. His companions were afraid to approach the pit, since the earth around it was undermined, and only a frail, thin crust remained. Overwhelmed with compassion for the victims in the pit, Seybert hastily seized a stick of wood and began to break off the loose earth until he found solid footing. Taking a windlass, of the kind used in old-fashioned wells, he pulled two men and one woman from the pit with a rope. He was dismayed by their miserable condition. He then watched as the pit was utterly destroyed and, astonishingly, a bright stream of water gushed from it.[21]

Seybert eagerly anticipated the fulfillment of his dreams. One night he dreamed he caught fish with his bare hands, then a beautiful dove, and finally a cross young bear. Awakened with curiosity and expectation, he visited a family of new converts the next day. When both the man and the wife desired to unite with the church, Seybert thought, "Here I had now caught my fish or my dove in reality. I was now on the lookout for the bear." He had not long to wait. Soon he was preaching in a house when some malicious listener threw a brickbat through the window at him, cutting his face with glass. Seybert recorded, "This was the cross bear."[22]

The need to persevere in ministry was the theme of another dream, which had far more remarkable detail. He dreamed of arriving at a dark and forbidding locale, which he thought must be a place "where Satan's seat is." He noticed a dilapidated sawmill, whose broken wheel covered a darkened pit, which appeared to be the "nest" for evil spirits. He flailed the dark hole with a leather strap he happened to find, until at last the "old demon" came rushing out and left the sawmill. The place then grew brighter, and a stream of clear water flowed from the pit. Numerous fish were in the water, which he had begun to catch when he awoke.

While traveling the next day, Seybert saw an old mill exactly as he had dreamed of it. He had never seen this particular mill before the dream. He closed his account with the note that a work of grace might be expected in that vicinity, though not without conflict.[23] He then discovered the preachers in that vicinity were about to "quit the field" owing to intense resistance and persecution. Being at that time their Presiding Elder, he urged them to continue, and a revival presently erupted.

In another dream which possessed deeper theological insight, Seybert discovered an important insight in the work of evangelism. He found himself in a beautiful flower garden, whose buds were just ready to open. He noticed another person in the garden who was breaking off the buds. Reproving him, he said "Do let these buds alone until they open of themselves, and do not pluck them prematurely." He concluded, "We should never comfort seekers of religion too soon, but let them experience the grace of God for themselves....Let them open."[24]

Seybert was possibly inspired by Boehme in his appeal to nature to describe the dynamics of kingdom living. Boehme wrote, "You adorn the earth with fair plants and flowers through Your eternally shining light and make joyful all that lives and grows. You point out to us men Your majesty in it so that we might know Your kingdom that is hidden inwardly...where You dwell in a hidden way and fill Your creatures."[25]

The dream which Seybert told most frequently was one that was told to him by an anonymous friend. It is nothing less than a parable of the secret of the godly life, and he frequently related it to warn Christians against seeking the honors of the world and the applause of men. A minister fell asleep after a Sunday morning service. He imagined himself resting and meditating in a garden, when he heard the sound of footsteps. He was met by a ministerial friend who was widely known for his gifts and who was honored for his zeal in public service. However, he noticed an expression of distress on his friend's face. The newcomer asked the time of day. *Twenty-five past four*, was the reply. Said the other, "It is exactly one hour since I am in the spirit world, and I am damned!" "What! Damned? Why?" exclaimed the shocked dreamer. Solemnly, sadly, but deliberately the answer came. "Not," he said, "because I have not preached the Word of God, not that I have not been useful, for I have many seals to my ministry—there are many in glory today who can testify that I was the instrument of their salvation." Rather, it is *"because I sought the praise of men and the honor and fame of the world, rather than the glory of God. I have my just reward!."*

The minister awoke, deeply impressed by the dream, and proceeded to his evening worship service. On the way, he met a friend who asked him whether he had been told of the great loss that the church had sustained that day, for the celebrated and talented Reverend _____ was dead? "No," he replied, and with faltering voice he asked what time he had died. The reply was,,"At twenty five minutes past three o'clock this afternoon."[26] Seybert's greatest insight in the godly life, that we are to live for the praise of God and not ourselves, was the result of this dream "in the Spirit."

The power of dreams in the lives of our founders offers to us an important insight. The symbolic representation of events through dreams can be God's way of guiding and even healing us by directing us to issues that need to be disclosed to us at the redemptive or the "kairos" moment. The "dreams of the Spirit" remained to the end a vital part of the witness of the godly in the Evangelical heritage.[27]

Notes

1. These are described in Morton Kelsey, *Dreams: A Way to listen to God* (New York Paulist Press, 1978, Chapter 1).

2. The widely held pagan belief in spiritual reality helped prepare the way for the Christian mission, as seen in Acts 17:22-34.

3. See biblical bases for this belief in John 1:1-5, Col. 1:15-17, Hebrews 11:1-3.

4. Kelsey, 15.

5. See Robert Chiles, *Theological Transition in American Methodism* (Nashville. Abingdon, 19). This is especially applicable to the rational and ethical concerns in Watson and Miley.

6. See Genesis 15, 28, 32, 40, and 41.

7. See Exodus 3.

8. See I Samuel 3.

9. See Jeremiah 1.11, Amos 7:17 ff, Habakkuk 1, Zechariah 1.7 ff., Joel 21:28f.

10. See Psalm 126.

11. See Luke 1 and 2; Jesus dealt with the spiritual world of angels and demons throughout his ministry.

12. See Acts 7:56, 9:3-9, 10:9-16, 12:7, 18:9 f.; also, the Revelation of John.

13. These are discussed in Morton Kelsey, *God, Dreams and Revelation* (Minneapolis: Augsburg, 1968), Chapters 5-7.

14. The view described here is developed by Morton Kelsey in his *Dreams: A Way to Listen to God* (New York: Paulist Press, 1978), 76 ff; and 17-19, where he lists four modern schools of thought in Christian theology that have undermined the belief in the miraculous.

15. See Chiles, Chapter 1.

16. Arndt, 208.

17. Boehme, 65.

18. "The Life and Labors of George Miller," found in Yeakel, 240-242.

19. Miller's *Articles of Faith and Rules of Discipline* were not altogether visionary, as they were in large measure derived from that of the early Methodists, with some significant additions and adaptations (such as the article on the last judgment and an extensive discussion of entire sanctification, which are embodied in the E.U.B. Confession of Faith. See the 1980 U.M. *Book of Discipline* (Nashville: U.M. Publishing House, 1980), Part I, 63-68.

20. Seybert's *Journal*, entry for September 15, 1820.

21. Seybert's *Journal*, entry for December 5, 1821.

22. Seybert's correspondence for February 1821, as cited by Spreng, 59.

23. This dream occurred during his trip to Northampton County, Pa., which began on February 7, 1837; see Spreng, 169.

24. Seybert's *Journal*, for October, 1833.

25. Boehme, *The Way to Christ*, 95.

26. From the memoirs of John Seybert, cited by Spreng, 246f.

27. Through the years, the heirs of Albright and Seybert continued to give heed to dreams. When Monroe Scheidler was sleeping shortly before his death in 1953, he spoke so audibly in a dream that his daughter, seated nearby, could hear. She perceived he was trying to uproot weeds in his garden to make the ground fertile for growth and, clasping her arm, he repeated, "I must get these out!" At last his hands relaxed in peace, and with an expression of contentment he was released from his long earthly life of wayfaring for his God. From an interview with Mrs. Nellie Scheidler Biser, July, 1958.

Chapter 17

Songs of the Spirit

"I went to Erie County over a difficult road and deep marshy soil. But I got the blessing and felt the presence of God; as the fierce wind drove the heavy snow into my face, I sang 'Sei getreu bis in den Tod.'" Seybert's Journal, entry for Monday, November 25, 1833.[1]

The hymn to which Seybert refers above is from the old "bush-meeting spirituals" of the pioneer Evangelicals, that were an inner part of the praise-filled, homeward sojourn of the godly pilgrim. This is a tradition that few in our present generation have experienced. Its heyday was in the German-American communities stretching from Pennsylvania to the Midwest in the pre-Civil War years of Bishop Seybert's ministry.

As Yoder has documented in his massive study,[2] there are only a few isolated pockets, primarily in rural Pennsylvania, where these spirituals are still remembered and sung. Even great-grandfather Scheidler, whose ministry began in Indiana in 1887, had only faint recollection of those songs. We learn in his letters to his betrothed that he was a singing evangelist,[3] but his favorites were the gospel songs that made their first appearance in the American churches after the Civil War. Gospel songs, with which many older United Methodists are still familiar, are to the older spirituals as the "gingerbread-laden, scrollwork-happy Victorian mansion is to the frontier log cabin."[4] With his Pennsylvania-Dutch ancestry, great-grandfather preferred the more earthy and straightforward gospel songs. The more flowery gospel song grew out of the humble spiritual that preceded it, much as the urban revivals of the Civil War era were an outgrowths of the rural camp meetings of the frontier.[5]

As I review the cold German script in the old hymnals of Seybert's day, the once-flourishing German spirituals peer out at me, begging to be sung once more. How did these songs help promote godly living among our Evangelical and United Brethren forebears? Who were those gifted German-American poets who produced them? How did they come to be the unique literary contribution of the E.U.B. heritage in United Methodism? What were the main themes of these spirituals that were quietly lived out in the lives of our forefathers?

The songs were taught to generations of early E.U.B.s from the cradle to the death bed. They were sung in corporate and private worship, at camp meetings and in the lonely quiet of isolated frontier homes. They were sung while traveling or working in the field or shop. When they began to be recorded in later generations, they were usually written without musical scores. There were sometimes as many versions of a given spiritual as there were singers who had taken them to heart. They promoted godly living because they were the concrete expression of the hopes and aspirations of the people who sang them. They were the Psalter of the "bush-meeting Dutch."[6] Unlike the Negro spiritual of the South, there is missing an undercurrent of sadness and frustration. Instead, they struck a note of joy and confidence, calling to mind the harsh but hopeful daily work of the Pennsylvania farmer, who sang with assurance:

> Ich vill shoffen
> Ich vill shoffen
> Bis ich aivich sailich vat
> (I will labor
> I will labor
> Till I gain eternal joy.[7]

In addition to conferences, baptizings, and camp meetings, the bush-meeting Dutch sang going to and from meeting. "Mother could hear us a mile away," recalled one aged Evangelical.[8] One folk tale recalls a group of neighbors singing in the Spirit the hymn, "Veer reisen nuch dar Himmel tsu" ("We're Journeying Toward Heaven") as they passed the home of an old settler who ran out and shouted "Eer Leit sin oof em letza vaig—dar vaig gait nuch Veirich-shdeddel!" ("You people are on the wrong road—this road leads toward Weirickstown!").[9]

Singing the old choruses was a favorite form of relaxation for Bishop Seybert. Relaxing after an 1829 conference, he wrote: "Last night as we were at Meese's an ungodly man with his violin (came) and walked along the creek which was near the house playing violently, apparently to molest and tease us as we were singing on the porch." He later reported a sequel to the story: "This man named Manerer lived near New

Berlin, and in November 1829 was found lying on his bed with his feet upon the floor." It was learned he had committed suicide by taking poison and, concludes Seybert, "The violin music was heard no more."[10] Thus did the music of the godly prevail.

The spirituals prevailed in the stillness of sleepless nights, when the choruses "came rolling in." They also prevailed at the deathbed of the aged "mother Erb," an early United Brethren saint, who died shouting "Hallelulah, Glory," closing it all out with a last "Amen."[11] During Bishop Seybert's final illness, he attended church despite his weakness, and as he heard the shouting and praising of God begin, "he became as inspired as in the days of his youth, and sang with great joy his 'O seliges Leben' (O Blessed Life) or 'O droben ist Freude' (O Yonder is Joy)."[12]

Who produced these "Dutch" spirituals that were so influential in promoting godly living? These choruses were written and sung in an environment of spontaneous worship, thus their use declined as education and increased formalism in worship progressed in the later nineteenth century. They were a distinct folk product that arose before the advent of instrumental music and choir singing. A spiritual usually consists of a chorus, verses sung to the chorus, and a tune[13]. The largest number of the choruses were derived from English revival "songsters," imaginatively recreated by translation into the Pennsylvania Dutch dialect. The sources from which the verses were drawn include hymns from the German Pietist genre (particularly Tersteegen),[14] the English revival hymns of Wesley and Watts translated into Pennsylvania high German, Pennsylvania translations of American camp-meeting hymns, and original revival songs by "bush-meeting Dutch" folk poets.[15]

The Evangelicals were the most prominent in composing original spirituals, which became loved by all the German-speaking revival denominations.[16] There was a trio of Evangelical hymnists in the early 1800's, consisting of Walter, Bertolet, and Dreisbach, whose songs were spread throughout the Midwest through the missionary labors of Evangelical itinerants, notably John Seybert. John Walter (1781-1818), who was called Albright's "Beloved Disciple," wrote the two most popular German hymns ever composed in America—"Kommt, Bruder, kommt, wir eilen fort" ("Come, brethren, come, we're hastening on"), and "Wer will mit uns nach Zion gehn?" ("Who will go with us to Zion?")[17] The first was written in 1806 as a group of Evangelical missionaries was crossing the Allegheny mountains in a snowstorm.

The antislavery leader Daniel Bertolet (1781-8167) wrote hymns that encouraged Evangelicals to persevere in the "narrow way" unto salvation, such as "Bruder, wacht, im Glauben steht," ("Brethren awake, stand in the faith") and another that was inspired by a mystical vision of Christ.[18] John Dreisbach (1789-1871), a colleague of Seybert, composed more than thirty five German hymns and was the chief compiler of the leading Evangelical hymnal (*Der Evangelisches Gesangbuch*) and the revival songster (*Geistliche Viole*).[19] The tunes used by these poets came from secular sources, often by way of the English camp meetings, such as "Wer kempfa heer in da vilderness" (We're struggling here in the wilderness"), sung to the tune of "The Bear Went Over the Mountain."[20]

In addition to these early composers of spirituals, Evangelicals of later generations achieved prominence as gospel-song writers. Elisha Albright Hoffman (1839-1929) composed more than 2,000 hymns, including the famous "I Must Tell Jesus," "Are You Washed in the Blood?," "Leaning on the Everlasting Arms," and "Down at the Cross Where my Savior Died." His father was Francis Hoffman, an old Evangelical itinerant who was one of Seybert's early associates.[21]

The early spirituals of our bush-meeting Dutch ancestors were created to meet the specific religious needs of our Evangelical and United Brethren forebears. They were spirited and spoke in the earthy idiom of the immigrant frontiersman. For this reason they were resilient and lived longer in popular German usage than the literary music of the "Church Dutch"—the Lutherans, Reformed, and Moravians. Our three Evangelical poets wrote their hymns in high German, but as generations sang them they were transformed into the vernacular dialict known as Pennsylvania Dutch, especially with the decline of the German secondary schools in America during the 19th century. They originated in the decade after 1800 to fill the need for "spiritual songs," after the biblical injunction, "Let the word of Christ dwell in you richly in all wisdom, teaching and admonishing one another in psalms and hymns and spiritual songs, singing with grace in your hearts unto the Lord" (Colossians 3:16). They were folk dominated and "live," not clergy dominated and "literary."

John Wesley had discouraged his preachers from composing such "spiritual songs," viewing these homemade hymns as "doggerel double-distilled."[22] "Old-fashioned" Methodist hymns, composed before 1800, were literary hymns. The official Methodist hymnals were weighted with the hymns of Charles Wesley and other English Revivalists, and the folk spirituals of the campground were banned from these hymnals. Instead, they found other publishing outlets in the press of the Evangelical Association and the United Brethren in Christ, printed first in German. It is these groups that have helped keep the old spirituals alive in the annals of United Methodism.

What were the major themes of the spirituals of Seybert's day? They were built around a chorus and expressed such devotional themes as conversion, pilgrimage, and "happiness in the Lord."[23] Series of "rhyme pairs" or couplets were often added to the revival chorus by "bush-meeting" poets. Sometimes they were drawn from favorite hymns and were attached to various choruses. Such a "wandering rhyme-pair" was

> Ei ei! vee iss des duch so seess,
> Vos ich in Yaisoo shoon ganeess!
>
> (Oh, my, how sweet this is—
> what I already enjoy in Jesus!)[24]

This couplet gradually freed itself from Bertolet's hymn, "Der Heiland rufet mir and dir" ("The Savior calls me and you") and set out on its own.[25] With such variations, each spiritual became a new creation.

These spirituals were also rich in biblical themes. Some were allegories, such as Dreisbach's folk hymn, "Die Geistliche Schiftfahrt" ("The spiritual Sea Voyage"). Traveling through stormy waves, the little ship has the Bible as its compass and winds of prayer to fill its sails. Holding firm to the rudder,

> Bald kommt mein schiff in Hafen,
> dann werf' ich Anker aus.
> Kein Sturm mich kann wegraffen,
> Wann ich ins Vaters Haus
> Einmal bin eingekehret.
>
> (Soon my ship comes into the harbor,
> then I throw the anchor out.
> No storm can snatch me away
> once I have entered into my Father's house.)[26]

In another early-day favorite from the *Geistliche Viole*, the theme of conversion is portrayed by the image of the blacksmith, forging, clamping, filing, and polishing the heart of the sinner as a "Geistliche Schmiede-Kunst" ("a spiritual blacksmith").[27]

In preparing a person for the "new birth" experience, several hymns lauded the "narrow way" that leads to life.

> Sein' bahn ich seh' und ihm nachgeh
> Den engen weg, bis ich ihn seht.'

> (His track I see, and I'll pursue
> The narrow way, till Him I view.)[28]

Sometimes, other early Evangelical hymns warned against supposing that "mere" churchgoing and sacramental observance can of themselves bring salvation:

> Was ist Beten, Kirchengehen,
> Was hilft Beicht' and Abendmahl?
> Ists im alten Sinn geschehen,
> Höhrt es nur die höllen-quaal.
>
> (What is praying and church-going,
> How does confession and eucharist help:
> If it is done in the old (unconverted) sense,
> it is nothing more than the torment of hell.)[29]

Only the converted believer knows true inner joy and can sing his declaration that "religion is the best of all" ("Bakeiroong iss des beshda varrick").[30] He now lauds Jesus as Savior in the warm words of praise, "O how lovely' is Jesus" ("O vee leeblich...iss Yaisoos"),[31] and he finds the heavenly manna to be "sweeter than honey".[32] Onward the pilgrim travels, looking toward the day when he can sing his beloved "Hoolelooya tsoo dem Lommai" ("Alleluia to the Lamb") in the eternal presence of his crucified Lord, on the other shore. Even in heaven, the bush-meeting folk will be content to "sing to their Lord the simple and moving songs of the tented grove." As Yoder has so aptly said, "Who is there to say that these simple songs, the homemade tribute brought by simple lives and simple heart, with a Dutch accent, to be sure, do not rank with other tributes in song brought to the Father and the Son in all ages of Christian history?"[33]

How did the decline of the spirituals occur? They thrived among folk who represented low economic class and educational levels, and they began to decline in use as the "sects" became "churches" and Evangelicals and United Brethren rose in their sociological status. By Monroe Scheidler's day, articles such as the following were appearing in the denominational press, which decried the passing of the old spirituals: "It seems that some of these good old hymns and choruses have died and gone to heaven with the people who used to sing them....We have now in the multitude of song books a radically different type of sacred songs." The writer considered these to be "in better literary form" and have in them Bible truth "in various degrees," but they are "a very poor substitute, for our solid and unsurpassed Evangelical meetings was largely due to their soulful singing," when "the glowing hearts of the people swept heavenward in a fiery chariot of spiritual songs." With yearning he exclaimed, "Oh, that we might have some spirit and power today!"[34] Ill suited for the divided chancel churches of our day, they were made for the meeting house and the grove. In Seybert's singing, as much as in his preaching, "the spiritual arrows of God's grace were poised on the bow, ready to fly at the heart of the sinner."[35]

It is hoped that future revision of the United Methodist Hymnal may include selections from our spirituals. All the themes of the godly life are there. They are the "songs of the victors in the lifelong struggle against sin. They were those who could say, like Andrew to his brother Simon, "Come and see."[36]

Although we cannot restore the culture that produced these spirituals, it is possible for us to be drawn by their moving themes into a greater awareness of God's directing presence in our lives. The loss of these vibrant spirituals from the memories of God's people was a major factor in the "eclipse of godliness" in the church. Any recovery of our heritage of godliness that may occur shall surely involve a recovery of their singing "in the Spirit," as was portrayed by the beloved poet of the Evangelicals, John Walter:

1. kommt, Bruder, kommt, wir eilen fort
   Nach Neu-Jerusalem!
   Vermerkt ihr nicht die goldne Pfort',
   Die dorten vor euch glimmt?

10. Dort singen sie ja immerdar
    Die schönste melodie,
    Die neimals je gesungen war
    Im ganzen Leben hie.

1. (Come, brethren, come, we're hastening on to new Jerusalem!
   Don't you see the golden gate that lies there yonder before you?

10. There sing the brethren forevermore the most beautiful melodies,
    that no one has ever sung in their whole lives before.)[37]

Notes

1. Translation: "Be True unto Death."
2. Don Yoder's *Pennsylvania Spiritiuals* has provided much of the primary research for the data in this chapter, in addition to the author's collection of early Evangelical camp-meeting songsters.
3. Letter from Monroe Scheidler to Mina Hall, dated April 11, 1889. Scheidler published a volume of gospel choruses while serving as pastor in Elkhart, Indiana, in 1893. *Special Songs and Choruses for Revivals and Praise Meetings,* compiled by M. L. Scheidler (Elkhart, Ind.: Truth Print, 1893).
4. Yoder, 423.
5, Yoder, 423.
6. The reader should recall that the word "Dutch" used in these pages does not refer to Holland but to the Americanized, "low" Germans of Pennsylvania and their western descendants.
7. This chorus may be modeled on the German hymn *Schaffet, schaffet, Menschenkinder* by Ludwig Andreas Cotter (d. 1735), based on Philippians 2:12. Yoder., 460f.
8. Anna Foglesonger of Orrstown, Pennsylvania, interviewed by Yoder, 144.
9. From Jacob Shively of Lillmont, Pennsylvania, by letter, February 25, 1952, to Yoder, 145.
10. *Journal* of Bishop Seybert, entry for Saturday, June 6, 1829.
11. *Deutscher Telescop,* January 1, 1848, cited by Yoder, 146.
12. S. Neitz, *Das Leben u. Wirken des seligen Johannes Seybert, Ersten Bischofs der Evangelischen Gemeinschaft* (Cleveland, Ohio, 1862), 455, cited in Yoder, 146.
13. Yoder, 343.
14. Especially the hymns of the German Pietists, such as Tersteegen's *Kommt, Kinder, lasst uns gehen* and Sesse's volume of *Geistliche Lieder,* analyzed by Yoder, Chapter 7.
15. Yoder, 354.
16. Yoder, 357.
17. Yoder, 357.
18. Yoder, 356f.
19. Yoder, 343.
20. Yoder, 380.
21. Yoder, 425.
22. Yoder, 134.
23. Yoder, 12.
24. This is from v. 5 of hymn No. 141 in *Geistliche Viole,* 1835, cited by Yoder, 12.
25. Yoder describes four patterns followed by the spirituals, including the "chorus-verse" type, the type with a couplet interpolated with a chorus refrain, the family type that introduces to us godly heroes and heroines, and the spiritual without a chorus. Yoder, 12-16.

26. *Geistliche Viole*, 1855, No. 126, cited by Yoder, 371f, (translation mine).

27. *Die kleine Geistliche Viole* (New Berlin, Pennsylvania, 1825), 2nd ed., no. 46, cited by Yoder, 375.

28. This is a German translation of an English revival hymn by John Cennick (1718-1755), and in No. 187 in an early United Brethren hymnal entitled *Lobgesangen u Ehren dem Heiligen* and *Gerechtigen in Israel* (Hagerstown Md., 1808); cited by Yoder, 390.

29. This is from v. e of "Sichre Welt, wie kannst du leben," which is No. 39 in Johann Walter's *Eine kleine Sammlung alter and neuer Geistreicher Lieder, zur Erbauung and Gebrauch aller Gott-liebenden Seelen* (Reading, 1810), the earliest Evangelical hymnal, cited by Yoder, 391, (translation mine).

30. Recorded by Yoder, song-text No. 4, 192-194. Note the translation of "religion" from "work" ("Varrick", from the high German "Werk").

31. This hymn calls to mind the hymn of the medieval German mystic, Bernard's "Jesus the very thought of Thee with sweetness fills the breast." Yoder, 451.

32. "Der fühlet solche Süssigkeit, (He feels such sweetness,) Die ubertrifft den Hoing weit, (that even surpasses honey.)" This is from Bertolet's *Der Heiland rufet mir and dir*, in *Geistliche Viole*, 1835, No. 141, cited by Yoder, 456.

33. Yoder, 458.

34. *Evangelical messenger*, March 13, 1895, article on "Our Evangelical Hymn-Book," by J. B. Kanaga, A. II., quoted by Yoder, 154.

35. Yoder, 449.

36. Yoder, 458.

37. *Geistliche Viole*, 1855, No. 160, (translation mine).

Chapter 18

Surprised by Grace

"Genuine conversions have taken place (among our people) in a manner that is often witnessed. The newly converted...have found the priceless pearl of a changed heart." Letter from John Seybert to Der Christliche Botschafter, *Winter 1852.*

The climax to the prodigal's homeward journey was the "welcome home" by his father, when his worst fears were transformed by the astonishing breakthrough of pardoning grace. In this chapter we shall explore the hopeful, God-expectant, "come and see" attitude of our godly forebears that counterbalanced the cross-bearing and self-denial prominently displayed in their pilgrimage of faith. While shunning "worldly" amusements, they found "holy joy" in their life of faith that left them radiant and victorious even when beset by apathy and adversity. John Seybert moved in the pulse of this joy. It was nurtured by the expectant outlook that he expressed in the close of his letter quoted above. Citing Psalm 103, he exhorted his brethren to "wrestle with tears and prayers, with all the heart, until you are purified from all sin, delivered from all evil, fully healed, and transformed by divine truth."[1]

In the preceding chapter we noted how the breakthrough into godly living was celebrated in song. Here we shall observe the extraordinary ways in which God's Spirit was manifested among our forefathers to bring release from oppression, physical and spiritual healings, and ecstatic expressions of worship and prophetic utterance.[2] Once again, Seybert's *Journal* offers a treasury of witnesses to God's miraculous dealings with these humble Christians who were sensitized to the Presence of the divine flooding their lives. As we explore these testimonies, let us recall that they are not the reports of wild-eyed zealots laden with a self-declared Messiah complex. They are the records of a churchman with a heart of compassion for God and the wounded, broken lives of God's people everywhere. These extraordinary works are nothing less than the signs of the normal Christian life, in the early days of our E.U.B. pioneers.

The first outward sign of the supernatural breakthrough of grace in their lives was the "shout." This was the outward manifestation of their inward experience of peaceful yielding to the Spirit, which we have described by the term *Gelassenheit*.[3] It also signifies an important assumption held by Seybert and his audiences that is not often shared by present-day worshipers.

This is their belief in the mysterious presence of the spiritual world with which communication is mandatory for vital Christian experience. By spiritual reality we are not alluding to the occult or the bizarre. Morton Kelsey has reminded us that this phrase asserts that man knows the reality of God not only through sense experience and reason, but also through "direct experience of the nonphysical world."[4] The world view of Jesus gave ample room for this dimension of experience.[5] By contrast, the effort to formalize religious experience in "textbook theology" has often relied on the Aristotelian idea that we can know God only indirectly, through sense experience of the physical world and by inferences that reason draws from the physical realm.[6] Seybert not only knew the reality of the divine Presence. He also rejoiced with his audiences in celebrating that Presence.

Paging through Seybert's *Journal*, we can almost hear the bush echoing the shouts of converts. Here we learn anew what it means to experience the empowering Presence of God in worship and praise. Reminiscent of Israel's shout that triggered the wall-tumbling victory of Yahweh over Jericho, the shouting originated in the warmth of the bush meeting to express the convert's joy at coming through," "crossing the river," or "finding peace."[7] At one big meeting early in his ministry, he reported that "we had a glorious time; some struggled for liberty, while others leaped for joy and shouted victory."[8] Another meeting was so blessed that it ended with a shout.[9] After preaching on the text, "To him who conquers I will grant to eat of the tree of life, which is in the paradise of God" (Rev. 2:7 RSV), he reported that there was a general "breaking through into eternal life." This caused such a rejoicing among God's children that their shouts and songs were heard afar as the hills caught the echoes and "Lebanon shook with praise."[10] Or again, "This evening ...we were blessed with a marvelous manifestation of the eternal life of God. The friends from town are still shouting on their way home—I hear their voices now praising God on the highway, while I am writing this journal entry."[11] He surmised, "The air is so clear and still this evening....

I guess the Lord has bidden the wind be still, so that His praise may be heard afar!"[12]

Seybert intuited that folk who had been oppressed by guilt or hostile adversaries needed the release that the shout provided. In one meeting he ceased preaching amid the shouting, his heart being "too full for utterance," and he wrote, "Let the children of God, who suffer so much persecution for righteousness' sake, rejoice; then let those who have been led to Gethsemane and Calvary march down Olive with shouts and songs and hosannas to their King."[13] The preacher considered the shouts of the redeemed as a foretaste of our Lord's return in judgment, "when He shall come with a shout, and a great noise as of a trumpet."[14]

In addition to the shout, Seybert used other expressions to portray the surprising manifestations of God's grace. He described an elderly and feeble brother who became powerfully blessed while relating his Christian testimony that he sank from his chair under the "weight of glory" that filled his soul.[15] While praying with another aged and enfeebled saint, he discovered that "When the Lord blessed her, she expressed herself with holy laughter," reminiscent of Psalm 126.[16] In one meeting, persecutors set fire to the meeting house while Seybert was preaching. The fire was discovered and extinguished by two of the brethren while the service continued uninterrupted. Seybert later remarked that "the devil's fire under the building was put out by the brethren, but the fire of the Lord burned mightily inside. Hallelujah![17] Reading like the book of Acts, his *Journal* described a camp meeting that climaxed with a "sound as of a mighty rushing wind," and a great commotion among the "dry bones." Filled with life from God, many began shouting "Life! Life! Eternal life! Hallelujah!"[18]

Seybert elsewhere reports that the friends became so powerfully blessed during preaching that some became "spiritually drunken."[19] In one remarkable midcareer camp meeting, Seybert noted "the convicting energy of the Spirit" and the "Word" was so extraordinarily manifested that "many sensible persons who were cool enough to observe, declared that the earth trembled, especially on Friday night."[20] Seybert's followers surmised that it is not harder for God to shake the earth than to cause human spirits to tremble under divine grace.

The greatest revival in Seybert's ministry began at Orwigsburg, Pa., in July 1823 and continued uninterrupted for three years. It was a turning point in the history of the fledgling Evangelical Association as numerous future leaders of the church were then brought into the ranks of the ministry. In the words of one pioneer, "the devil is very angry with us and roars terribly, and his emissaries...attempt to close up the gap (in his citadel) with hypocritical work, but the Lord sends heavy showers and causes the gaps to become wider than before!"[21] Seybert traced the beginning of this revival to an odd experience. While preaching in a grove near the town, he felt strangely tempted to stand during his opening prayer. Nevertheless, "breaking through" as he called it, he fell upon his knees to pray, and instantly a wonderful "baptism of power" came upon him. The multitude began to "melt down," the Word had free course and God was being glorified. Seybert proceeded to erect a stone on the spot, calling it Ebenezer[22] and engraving the date upon it as a spiritual memorial. He elsewhere described the effect that singing produced during this remarkable meetings during that summer of 1823. Using mystical language, he portrayed the outpouring of the Holy Spirit upon the worshipers until "many of the friends seemed quite overwhelmed in the sea of eternal love."[23] This seemed to Seybert to be a fulfillment of Joel's prophecy that sons and daughters, old men and maidens, and indeed all flesh would be filled (Joel 2:28-29).

So great was his enjoyment of this midharvest meeting that he harbored the desire that "during the remainder of my earthly life, I could have a vivid realization of this wonderful prayer-meeting at least three times daily! I know it would nerve me for the battle, and would be an incentive to faithfulness in the midst of tribulation." He concluded his entry by praying, "Blessed art Thou, eternal King and Saviour of the world, that through Thy holy blood Thou hast triumphed over the night of hell, and hast delivered us from Satan's power, and has pardoned our transgressions, and hast overcome principalities and powers', and divided unto us the spoil! We praise Thee both now and forever! Hallelujah!"[24]

How did Seybert believe that one ought to prepare to receive these surprises of divine grace? A basic prerequisite is the need for "holy unction" that comes from viewing others with the compassion of Jesus. This might be described as the capacity to see with the eyes of faith.[25] He once heard what he considered an orthodox sermon on the cleansing power of the Cross, though he noted, significantly, "He may have been a messenger of God, but he lacked one thing, an unction from the Holy One."[26]

Seybert sometimes recognized that the unction he sought came only when he admitted his weakness. Once when he was troubled with a sense of "spiritual poverty," he withdrew into a forest, where he wrestled all day until the sun set. That night when he preached, he began in weakness and fear. Soon, however, "the Lord lent the light from the glory world into his soul."[27] The result was such a demonstration of "the Spirit and of power" that a 90-year-old sinner broke down and pleaded unto God for mercy. Another prerequisite was the right sense of God's timing. Toward the end of his life, Seybert passed among friends at Bethlehem, Pennsylvania. They noticed that he kept scanning the landscape and fixing his gaze toward the setting sun. "Why, brother Seybert! Is it possible that you are here? Whom are you looking for, anyway?" "I am not looking for anyone here, sister," was his reply. "I am going down here to Texas—the Lord's saving sinners there!"[28] He desired to be where and when God's saving presence was operating on behalf of the lost. That was the absorbing thought of this man. He wanted nothing better.

The record of John Seybert stands as a vibrant witness to those who doubt that the supernatural operations of the Holy Spirit are still available for the ministry of the church. He knew from firsthand experience that God meets our needs miraculously, in his timing, so long as we are involved in meeting the needs of others with compassion. As he began one camp meeting in Illinois, a minor storm approached. His enemies were already exulting that the meeting would soon be disrupted. At the last moment, the storm parted and swept by either side of the encampment, with furious destruction, leaving the spot chosen for divine worship completely untouched.[29] Even unbelievers saw the finger of God in this demonstration. In his later years, Seybert ministered intensively in communities where fatal epidemics of cholera were raging and he remained unharmed as he spent himself in the service of others.[30]

In addition to such supernatural acts of deliverance, Seybert's *Journal* contains the record of extraordinary manifestations of the Spirit that fall into the categories of healings, prophecies, miracles, and the phenomenon that is currently called "resting in the Spirit."[31] Seybert reported these phenomena with no evidence of boasting. They were not the basis of his spirituality. They were gifts and manifestations that surfaced in the context of his ministry to others. Further, they were integral to his ministry as a churchman, and not as one who had abandoned the church and her ordinary means of grace. Instead, his witness infused new life into these ordinary channels, such as the sacraments.

Gifts of Healing (1 Cor. 12:9)

During an attack of malarial fever during October, 1823, Seybert dismounted his horse in a forest to pray, but then collapsed in exhaustion.

There lay the zealous apostle, far from human help, and burning with fever. Like Elijah, faint and ready for death under the juniper tree (I Kings 19:4), Seybert received a healing touch from God. After lying still for some time, his fever subsided and he began to breathe deeply, feeling new life filling his frame as if a ministering angel had visited him with divine strength. Thanking God, he immediately rose, saddled his horse, and went his way.[32]

His theology of healing is made more explicit during a visit to the home of brother "J. Drometer," one of his Illinois preachers who had become dangerously ill with a fever. Seybert also noticed that the man's family was depressed. While visiting him one day, Seybert felt a mighty inward constraint to pray. He fell on his knees by the bedside, and in earnest simplicity sought the Lord to restore the sick brother in accordance with his will. After prayer, Seybert departed, leaving his benediction upon the family. Soon Drometer was out of his bed and had resumed his preaching journey with Seybert, riding thirty miles that same day and giving thanks to God for his instantaneous healing.[33]

Seybert found that God's healing mercy was sufficient for beast as well as man. As he reached South Bend, Indiana, in 1841, his horse became sick. Leading it into a grove near the city, he tried in vain to relieve its misery. As he saw his faithful beast lie on the ground at the point of death, Seybert turned from the creature to the creature's God in prayer. On his knees, with tearful eyes and upturned face, he told God he needed that horse to fill his appointments. He said, "Thou hast often helped me in marvelous ways, and Thou can help me also in time of need."[34] Arising, he looked toward his horse, and was thrilled to see it standing demurely, quietly grazing as if nothing had happened. Returning to the city, he fed the animal and soon was ready to travel.

Healing was also manifested in relation to baptism. Once after being asked to baptize the infant child of unconverted parents, Seybert discovered the child was sick unto death. After leading the parents to begin seeking their salvation, he baptized the child, noting briefly in his *Journal* that immediately upon its baptism the child became well.[35] In another instance, the grace manifested in baptism prepared a sick child to experience physical death with peace, with sure trust in God's mercy, even admonishing her parents to prepare for eternity.[36] Seybert believed the vital factor in baptism was neither the water nor the mode of applying it. Instead, it was the inexpressible gift that he called the baptism of the Holy Ghost.[37]

Prophecy (I Cor. 12:10)

In one account, Seybert testified about a time when he manifested both prophecy and the gift of healing in the course of ministering to those in need. He was in a season of spiritual poverty, needing to learn anew that "God alone is mighty, that all depends on His blessing, and that He must be all in all, if the work is to increase." Once, he reported, "I had a series of appointments a thousand miles in length, and when I began I was taken with a fever." He recalled how he had to rest each morning before traveling by horse to his evening preaching appointments. Finally, he became so feeble that as he arrived at the home where he was to preach, he went directly upstairs to bed, "sick almost unto death."

As evening came and he heard the house "filling up with many people," he thought it was a pity that so many should come to hear God's Word and be disappointed. Staggering downstairs, he saw many strangers present and thought, "Why, you ought to try to pray with these people anyhow." While making the attempt in great weakness, a text came to mind that he determined he would announce. He said, "As soon as I began, the eternal power of God came down from heaven, and I felt suddenly perfectly well, and in the congregation there occurred a tremendous commotion." Sinners cried out and found mercy, blessing God with a loud voice, "while God's children wept and shouted at the same time, because of the rushing among the dry bones that were coming to life."

The next day he "went on his way, perfectly restored." Seybert continued his message with this prophecy: "We must not give up so soon. Only keep on prophesying. The mighty breath of the Spirit causes a rushing in the valley of dry bones, and the spiritually dead will be made alive." He continued, "The life of God will enter into them, and they will stand upon their feet, when the servant of God prophesies."[38]

Some of Seybert's most notable prophecies concerned the prospects for the work of the Evangelical Association in the mountain valleys of central Pennsylvania. He gave this prophecy in 1827 concerning those valleys, saying, "There is at present much excitement about salvation, and many inquiries after the way of life. The people are uneasy in their sins," and this uneasiness "is destined to become general, for the morning twilight of the day of grace is breaking upon the midnight of these valleys and mountains." Then reaching a glorious crescendo, he prophesied, "It will soon be daylight, for the day-star has arisen, and the Son of

Righteousness will speedily burst upon the scene with His glory, and darkness will flee away. All the efforts of Satan to prevent it will be in vain." He went on to say: "These valleys will be redeemed. This desert will yet rejoice and blossom as the rose; it will blossom abundantly, and rejoice with joy and singing. All flesh shall see the salvation of our God."39

After entering Ohio, and facing westward, Seybert prophesied, "Notwithstanding all efforts to the contrary, these beautiful groves with their wealth of flowers, and their grassy slopes, shall no longer belong to the father of lies, but to the Lord Jesus, to whom belong the riches of the Gentiles. Let these groves and prairies be consecrated to Him, for the truth has already triumphed."40

Miracles (1 Cor. 12:10)

In addition to miracles of deliverance that we have previously noted, Seybert recorded as miracles other instances, both great and small, in which grace was operating in deeds that appeared supernatural in character. Exemplifying a large-scale miracle, he once reported that a woman had been translated to heaven without experiencing physical death. Her name was Barbara Eckert, and she was among the most devoted and pious laywomen among the early Evangelicals. She was bitterly hated and persecuted by her ungodly father and relatives for her earnest Christian testimony. After being driven from her home for erecting a family altar of prayer, she became an itinerating Christian mystic, enjoying "in a remarkable degree the life and power of God."41 She fasted for an entire week before a "big meeting" Seybert held in 1825. The persecuted saint left the meeting to go to a neighbor's house, and she was never again seen. Many conjectured that she had been murdered, but Seybert concluded, along with those who knew her most intimately, that "God can do today what He did in Enoch's day" (Genesis 5:24).42

On a smaller scale, a stranger once unexpectedly delivered a book to Seybert that he had previously ordered but no longer expected to receive. He was preparing to preach, and lacked the dollar needed for payment. After the sermon, another stranger who had been moved by the message crowded his way through the throng and grasped Seybert's hand warmly. After withdrawing his hand, he found a silver dollar had been left in his palm, which he promptly used to pay for his book.43

Wherever Seybert identified the miraculous in his experience, it was without any trace of magic or superstition. He was careful to give credit to the saving power of God. Once he felt compelled to cross the rain-swollen Schuylkill River to join a revival in progress. Although he was warned not to attempt the ford, he said, "I have an appointment across the river, and in the name of the Lord I am going to ride in! The Lord can help me through!"[44] The horse swam the mad torrent, astonishing spectators on the shore, and Seybert filled his appointment that evening. Immersed in ministry, he relied on the miraculous deliverance of God to make a way where there was none.

Resting in the Spirit

(See Paul's celebrated experience of a man in Christ who was caught up into paradise; II Cor. 12:2-4). This manifestation of the Spirit, which is also sometimes described as being "slain in the Spirit," has been traced by MacNutt through Catholic and Protestant traditions alike. Tauler, the medieval Catholic mystic with whom Seybert was conversant, once preached to his Dominican brothers with such effect that "fully forty men staid behind in the churchyard lying as it were in a swoon."[45]

In like manner, Seybert reported participating in an unusually powerful "experience meeting" in December 1820, where he prayed with a class leader who was seeking a deeper awareness of God's grace. After fasting and prayer, grace "poured like a river" into his soul until, as Seybert recalled, he became "unconscious, or rather entranced" for a period of time. As a result, the congregation was immersed in God's love. One sister, under the "powerful effusion of God's Spirit," lay entranced for thirty two hours and awoke feeling "unspeakably happy."[46] Such experiences set apart the worship of our Evangelical forebears from the formalism that often prevailed in the old-line churches. They became even more convincing as signs of grace when they were accompanied by godly living.

There were times when Seybert experienced moments of virtual transfiguration, and these always occurred in relation to his compassionate ministry to others. They were never private experiences of spirituality isolated from that mission. One morning in July, 1850, he "felt a most blessed influence from the world of light" and received a word of knowledge concerning Romans 13:12, "The night is far spent, the day is at hand! Let us therefore cast off the works of darkness, and let us put on the armor of light."[47] He felt God's gracious presence that day, despite the heat and the fact that he had to travel on foot, staff in hand. His experience of transfiguration enabled him to envision God's moving upon His people. He later remarked that "the Spirit of the Lord brooded with His Light-creating influences over the moral darkness" as the brethren "labored on in faith" and the people became "convinced of the necessity of conversion."[48]

Being "surprised by grace" was a continuing trait of those Evangelicals who followed in the example of Bishop Seybert, although the supernatural operations of the Spirit became less evident as the years passed. Those extraordinary accounts of the miraculous we met in Seybert are missing in Scheidler's shoebox of letters from the 1880's that I inherited. However, enough of the shape of godly living appeared in them to keep alive the fire of the Spirit until the present generation.[49]

Notes

1. Letter for John Seybert to *Der Christliche Botschafter*, winter, 1852, cited in Spreng, 306.

2. In our day, these manifestations might well be called "charismatic," meaning the life that is empowered by the extraordinary manifestations or gifts of the Spirit (as listed in I Cor. 11:1-11) in addition to the normal means of grace in the life of the church (as listed in Acts 2:42).

3. See Chapter 15.

4. Morton Kelsey, *Tongue Speaking; An Experiment in Spiritual Experience* (Garden City: Doubleday, 1964), 170.

5. Kelsey, 175. There are 196 references to angels and demons in the gospels.

6. Kelsey, 184.

7. Yoder notes that this practice was borrowed from the early English-speaking camp meetings of the Methodists. Yoder, 87.

8. Seybert's *Journal*, entry for October 6, 1820.

9. Seybert's *Journal*, entry for February 10, 1821.

10. Report of Seybert from 1836, cited in Spreng, p. 164.

11. Spreng, 164; entry for July 7, 1834.

12. Sprang, 164.

13. Seybert's *Journal*, entry for August 10, 1835.

14. The text for the sermon was the Song of Solomon 6:9, with emphasis on the words, "terrible as an army with banners." Spreng., entry for January 18, 1823.

15. Spreng., entry for July 7, 1829.

16. Report of Seybert from April of 1831, cited by Spreng, 126.

17. Spreng, 126; entry for February 20, 1835.

18. Seybert's *Journal*, entry for June 5, 1837.

19. Spreng, 126, entry for October 13, 1848.

20. Report of Seybert for 1834, cited by Spreng, 148.

21. Letter from Brother Peter Erb to John Walter, dated January 14, 1812; printed in Yeakel, *Albright and his Co-Laborers,* 162. His account is typical of the opposition that Evangelical missionaries regularly encountered, including Seybert at Orwigsburg.

22. The term "Ebenezer" recalls the "stone of help" Samuel erected after the defeat of the Philistines in I Sam. 7:12. He declared "hitherto the Lord has helped us." From Seybert's *Journal,* entry for July 15, 1823.

23. Seybert's *Journal,* entry for July 13, 1823.

24. Seybert's *Journal,* entry for July 13, 1823

25. John Wesley also described faith in terms of such a "spiritual perception" in his "An Earnest Appeal to men of Reason and Religion," found in Outler, 386f.

26. Report of Seybert for June, 1824, cited by Spreng, 85.

27. Seybert's testimony following the conference session of 1830, cited by Spreng, 119.

28. Seybert's *Journal,* entry for October 26, 1857.

29. Seybert's *Journal,* entry for July 15, 1841.

30. Seybert's *Journal* entries for the last week of July, 1848, in Indiana.

31. This is the term used by Francis MacNutt, *The Power to Heal* (Notre Dame: Ave Maria Press, 1978), 189ff.

32. Seybert's *Journal,* entry for October 10, 1823.

33. Seybert's *Journal,* entry for June 30, 1846.

34. Seybert's *Journal,* entry for August 13, 1841.

35. Report of Seybert for spring, 1826, cited by Spreng, 79.

36. Seybert's *Journal.,* entry for March 16, 1825.

37. Seybert's *Journal,* entry for September 18, 1835.

38. Sermon preached on Rev. 20:6, entitled "The Blessed and Holy Lot," reprinted in Spreng, 414-420; see especially 417f.

39. Seybert's report to his brethren in conference, spring, 1827; cited in Spreng, 101.

40. Report of Seybert from Spring, 1844, cited in Spreng, 258.

41. Report of Seybert for the Winter of 1825, cited by Spreng, 88.

42. Report of Seybert for the Winter of 1825, cited by Spreng, 88.

43. Seybert's *Journal,* entry, for February 14, 1824.

44. Spreng, 78.

45. *The Sermons and Conferences of John Tauler,* 39f.; cited by MacNutt, 195.

46. Seybert's *Journal,* entry for December 6, 1820.

47. Seybert's *Journal,* entry for July 4, 1850.

48. Seybert's *Journal.,* entry for July 30, 1852.

49. Monroe Scheidler, who put me in touch with the heritage of Seybert, experienced anew the surprising work of grace in his travels as an itinerant evangelist during the 1880's and 1890's. Like Seybert before him, he took delight in discerning God's presence in those he met, in the succession of the seasons, and in learning to walk with humility before others.

Part Three

Home at Last

Chapter 19

Mingling with God's People

"I told the constable it is too hard that a man with a family should lose the instrument by which he earned their support, and I concluded I would pay the debt, and give you back your loom." John Seybert's words to an impoverished weaver whom he met in the winter of 1846.[1]

Seybert knew that God's children include the younger brothers as well as the dutiful, elder brothers. He had been a prodigal himself and so, once he discovered the Father's mercy, his heart went out to God's prodigals wherever he found them. He was never more "at home" with the Father than when he was ministering to God's prodigals. He found them scattered, helplessly assailed by the world, and separated without hope from their Father's estate. Still, he knew they were among those for whom Christ died and so should have an opportunity to receive their inheritance among the people of God. After all, no one earns a share in that estate by nature, save Christ alone, who is the only-begotten Son of the Father. One becomes an heir of his kingdom by adoption, and yet for Christ's sake each of us is treated as though he or she alone is the lost son of the parable, beloved of the Father.

Our task in this chapter is to discover the social consciousness of our Evangelical forebears, through the witness of Seybert. His encounter with a weaver gives us a vivid picture of godliness activated in serving our neighbor. It was on a cold winter day in 1846, during one of his many horseback trips through Ohio, that Seybert encountered someone hauling a weaver's loom on a sled. Starting a conversation, he soon discovered that the man was a constable who was preparing to sell the loom in payment for a debt. Its unfortunate owner was a poor weaver with a large family, and he had no other means of support. After learning the amount of the debt, Seybert exclaimed, "This is hard!" The constable replied, "I must do it, hard as it is." After a pause, the bishop asked,

"Would you mind taking the loom back to its owner again, if I pay you the amount of the debt?" The constable gladly consented. As they approached the house, the man and his family met them with astonishment. As Seybert announced what he had done, he dismounted his house, reached into his pocket, and counted out the exact amount owed to the officer of the law. The embarrassed family wanted to know who their benefactor was and from where he had come. "My name is John Seybert," he said. "My family place is Manheim, Pennsylvania, but I am a traveling preacher, who hardly knows that he has a home except the heavenly one, where all the saints shall rest forever."[2] After spending the evening with the family, they invited him to set an appointment to preach in their home. Many came and were deeply moved by the preacher's message. The weaver and his family were converted and a class, and later a church, were organized there, of which the weaver became the class leader. Seybert's selfless investment in the need of another became a well-planted seed of faith. When the weaver was able to repay Seybert, the bishop accepted the principal, without interest.

As Seybert spent himself for those in need, he was manifesting a vital dimension of the godly life. He was interested in more than the surprising manifestations of the Spirit's gifts. He knew that the Spirit's fruits (Gal. 5:22 f.) are what we are by virtue of the new birth. The fruits are the attributes of the new nature that we share in Christ. Seybert regarded the Holy Spirit as a self-effacing and a serving Spirit. He seeks to live within our lives until we become God's saving presence for others.

A similar social consciousness, rooted in godly faith, was present in John Wesley and the early Methodists. However, there is a difference between the moral theology of leading Methodist theologians of the second-half of 19th-century America and the witness of Seybert and the early Evangelicals.[3] Seybert was not interested in inculcating moral principles of living apart from the vital "unction" of the Spirit. He saw the Christian as the vital extension of Christ's life into a torn and brutalized world. Together, the social witness of the godly represented the living church dispersed for service in the world. Seybert's keen social consciousness was rooted in his mystical experience of an ever-present faith union with God, that permeated his living with a sensitive reverence for life, reminiscent of St. Francis of Assisi. We have discovered that Seybert, unlike Wesley, saw little need to rethink his mystical sources radically. Tauler's emphasis on yielding oneself to God *(Gelassenheit)* worked easily into his teaching on salvation.[4] It has also been observed that Seybert was likely influenced by Boehme, the great German Protestant mystic, in relating the parable of the father's love for his prodigal son to our compassion for those in need. As Boehme's two favorite images convey, the prodigal returns (Luke 15:11 ff.), but work still remains to be done in the vineyard (Matthew 20:1-16). For Boehme, with a will resigned to God "the journey back is undertaken and with a resigned will until the work in the vineyard is completed."[5]

Rising as they did from this unique blend of Protestant and Catholic mystical piety, the Evangelicals had a vision of kingdom living that was to transform the German-American communities in which they ministered. After these communities were subjected to the refining fire of "bush-meeting evangelism," their converts were to walk on the Narrow Way as examples to their neighbors. When the Indiana ministry of the Evangelicals began on the land of Monroe Scheidler's forebears in 1839, the missionary on the field reported to Bishop Seybert that "the work of conversion made but slow progress on this field of labor, til several families from Pennsylvania settled here." Through their "deep interest and exemplary lives," they "confirmed the truth of the word preached, and thus gave the cause a new impulse."[6] The next year, the first German services ever held in Chicago were conducted by Evangelical missionaries under appointment of Bishop John Seybert. This was a small but growing town,[7] a center of migrants that was rampant with immorality. One missionary reported, "In spite of our having been pelted by stones by (the devil's) servants, and denounced by the priests of Babel, the Sun of Righteousness begins to shine into many a heart. Some have already been translated into the liberty of God's children, while others are almost persuaded to become Christians."[8]

Owing to the outreach of Seybert and his German-American itinerants, the prevailing folk culture of such communities was often upset and an alternative one, more godly in tenor, was brought into being. One of its features was the breakdown of former class and racial prejudices with the formation of new loyalties in Christ. Seybert reported on one occasion when a native American attended his service in Ohio. He candidly remarked, "A great many, who have all their religion in their mouth, could learn from this native American how to behave in the house of God, in a manner becoming a civilized and enlightened race."[9] The great Orwigsburg revival of 1823-1826 began when Seybert started preaching in the courthouse and schools of the town until the public facilities were closed to him. He then accepted the invitation of an African American named Wilson and preached in his humble home and soon a class of 25 members was organized.[10] Likewise, when

Evangelicals moved into the "godless" city of Allentown in 1835 with the gospel, no one opened a home for preaching except a black man.[11] Seybert frequently mentions his contacts with Negroes in Dutch-speaking areas, and on one occasion he ordained a black evangelist.[12]

Other features of the new redeemed communities that were spawned in the wake of Seybert and his itinerants included the decline in alcoholic consumption and gambling and the renewal of family life. After a "pentecostal" meeting in New Holland, Pennsylvania, in 1837, Seybert exclaimed that "there are good prospects of better days. One infallible proof of this is that the whiskey distilleries (poison machines) and beer breweries are growing fewer, and liquor drinking is on the decline."[13] Evangelicals and United Brethren incorporated into their Books of Discipline strong statements against liquor, profanity, slaveholding, and other identified social evils. Their smaller size enabled them to maintain a more consistent stand against slavery than did their Methodist cousins, who became divided on a national scale over this issue.[14]

We need to remember that those were days when the disciplinary rules were read on a regular, devotional basis by church members and were taken seriously as the guide to growth in the godly life. These rules were never any better preached than when they were lived out in the lives of Evangelicals. It was said of Seybert that his life spoke even louder than his words. His compassion for others in the Spirit of Christ was never better expressed than one day in 1831 when he walked into a pathetic situation. He heard that a sheriff was preparing to sell the home of an impoverished widow to pay a debt her husband had left. After investigating her case, he appeared in the crowd on the day of the sale and bid for the house, until he was declared the buyer. He then announced to the officer, "Please deed the property back to the widow." The officer was astonished as Seybert paid the full debt in cash. The woman uas speechless. She wanted to know who her benefactor was and how she could repay him. Seybert merely replied, "I want you to lead a pious, godly life now, avoid luxury, extravagance, and every evil forbidden in the Word of God, and if you think you can pay this back in annual small installments, all right."[15]

He believed this money had been invested in kingdom work, as much as if he had given it for the erection of a church building. His heart was more burdened to meet the needs of God's children, wherever he found them, than to enhance the stature of his denomination. And the paradox is that the cause of the Evangelical Association mightily flourished under his selfless leadership.

As this incident with the widow indicates, the message of these forebears was a gospel for the disinherited. The "Dutch country" of Pennsylvania and Maryland, where they originated, was already well "churched" by 1800. For this reason, the lay preachers of the Evangelicals and the United Brethren found a hearing among the poor hillfolk, whom even Methodism itself had missed.[16] Some headway was also made amid the rich farms of the "Plain Dutch" country, including Mennonite regions in central Pennsylvania (by United Brethren) and Dunker regions of Ohio and Indiana (by Evangelicals).[17] However, it was when they ministered to the disinherited poor that they fulfilled their calling to bring the message of the godly life to the hopeless backwoods of God's prodigals.

At the other extreme, Seybert also found himself mingling among recent German immigrants in the upper Midwest. These folk had been aligned with the "Church Dutch" traditions of the Lutherans and Reformed, but many had surrendered themselves to "Rationalism" and "Infidelity." Seybert called this a "powerful host of darkness" with two wings, one of "popularity Christians" and the other of "superstitious bigots."[18] This referred to persons who conformed their lives to standards of this world rather than to God and to those who took undue pride in religious acts devoid of godly piety. Bishop Seybert used a number of untranslatable words in opposing extravagant dress and opulent lifestyles, such as "modesucht" and "Luxus."[19] We must recognize that the real reason for his attitude was not quaint eccentricity. It was because "worldliness makes us poor in benevolence."[20]

In opposing the styles of the old folk culture, Seybert brought into focus the key to godly social witness. It is recognizing the sphere of influence that God has given to each of us and imparting the light of the gospel to those whom we encounter within our sphere.

George Miller, the compiler of the first Evangelical *Book of Discipline*, reflected deeply on this subject. His book, *Practical Christianity*, was written from Scripture and experience to show "how each one in his sphere should serve and honor God."[21] He discovered that obeying God's call to ministry led to unexpected temporal as well as spiritual blessings. Although he received only $200 during eight years of itinerant preaching, his family remained well provided on his farmstead. After giving top priority to God's ministry, he found, to his surprise, that "I was apparently prospering, even in worldly matters, much more than other members of the family, although they were doing all in their power to become rich."[22] He discovered the truth of Jesus' words, "But seek ye first the kingdom of God and His righteousness, and all these things shall be added unto you" (Matthew 6:33). In his popular book, which Seybert frequently recommended, Miller stated that "ceasing from...works of love is as unjust as avarice...itself, both will palsy heart and hand, and drive men into many foolish and hurtful temptations and snares, that will at last bring them to destruction."[23]

Seybert's social witness also led him to envision the possibility of a new ecumenical brotherhood of all godly believers. This vision had earlier been evoked by Philip William Otterbein, the chief founder of the United Brethren Church. The German scholar Heinz Kloss has suggested that the revival Otterbein guided can be considered the successor to the work of Zinzendorf (1700-1760), the great Moravian leader.[24] Zinzendorf had envisioned a "Congregation of God in the Spirit" as a fellowship that would unify the German-language groups across denominational and variant backgrounds. Otterbein believed that Christians of different backgrounds might participate in a "higher unity" in Christ without renouncing their "original ecclesiastical relations."[25]

John Walter, Albright's early preaching assistant, demonstrated in a conversation with a Lutheran pastor how the enmity that the revival preachers fostered could be transformed into a higher unity that transcends folk divisions. While traveling toward an evening preaching appointment, Walter met this unnamed minister who lived in the same neighborhood where he had the appointment.

> Minister: "Whither are you traveling, and what is your profession?"
> Walter: "I am a preacher, and am on my way to my appointment."
> Minister: "A preacher? And where did you study for the ministry?"
> Walter: "At the feet of Jesus, in the school of the Lord."
> Minister: "And what is your name?"
> Walter: "My name is Walter."
> Minister: "Walter, Walter! But not the Walter who so fearfully condemns the people?"
> Walter: "Oh, no, I condemn no one who does not condemn himself."
> Minister: "But there is one, by the name of Walter, as I have been informed, who passes through the country and condemns the Lutherans, the Reformed, and, in fact, all who do not belong to his sect."
> Walter: "Why, he must be a rude, ill-mannered man! I preach, that the Lutherans, the Reformed, Catholics, and all others, if they are pious Christians, and die as such, will be saved."
> Minister: "And where do you preach, if I may ask?"
> Walter: "Up in Penn's Valley, in the house of a man by the name of

Weis."

Minister: "Why, he is my neighbor! There can be but few hearers there."

Walter: "There may be a cause for that. There are neighborhoods where the people do not like to hear the truth, and many even are kept away by their pastors. But you certainly will attend?"

Minister: "Why yes, that might be possible. And would there be liberty for me to say a word, too, if something should be said that would not be in accordance with God's Word?"

Walter: "Oh yes, perfect liberty! I should be very much pleased to be corrected, if I should teach erroneous doctrines."

Meanwhile, they arrived at the home where preaching was to be held. The neighbors were astonished to see their pastor, who had often warned them against these meetings. Young Walter took the pastor by the arm to the table where Walter was to speak, After preaching with great fervor and spiritual power, he turned to the pastor, saying, "Now there is liberty." The pastor shrugged his shoulders in confusion, but seeing the congregation waiting for him to respond, he finally arose and said: "Well, neighbors, I must acknowledge, this young man has proclaimed unto us the word of God, the truth, and nothing but the truth."[26] Upon this unplanned ecumenical encounter, conversions followed, a strong class was organized, and a new era of kingdom living began in one community.

Seybert, ministering in the wake of the mighty Walter, acknowledged worth wherever he found it, nor did he forbid anyone to cast out devils because he was not of his company. In addition to having an eye for "false religious keepers," he was alert to find pastors in the "mainline" denominations (e.g., Lutheran, Reformed, and Mennonite in particular) who gave a living and godly testimony to Christ. He once reported, "I visited a Reformed minister named Felix" and "I have never found another...possessing withal such a Christ-like Spirit as this man.[27]

What lessons do we as *United* Methodists learn the social witness of Seybert and ur forebears? First, we see that God's love becomes real to us as we become willing to let God open our eyes to see in the Spirit the needs of others. Second, in responding to those needs in love, class and creedal barriers are superseded and a greater dimension of Christian community can be realized. With this discovery of community we recover our real connectional roots as one people under God. Third, however much John Seybert and his colleagues became servants to others, the reader of his *Journal* senses that he did not live for the glo-

154   Bishop John Seybert and the Evangelical Heritage

rification of the poor as a class, nor for the glorification of his denominational program, but Christ.

The social witness of our godly forebears lived on to touch my spirit in quiet wonder, so that I sense in my bones, as did Seybert of old, that how we live is exceedingly more important than what we say about our lives.28 To the end, I want to be found mingling with God's people, as had Bishop John Seybert.

Notes

1. Cited in Spreng, 274f.
2. Spreng, 274f.
3. These heirs of Wesley in mainline Methodism, such as John Miley of Drew University, shifted toward an ethical emphasis based on "Christian moral principles," owned by men as free moral agents. Wesley's sense of the dynamic operation of the Spirit had receded from view. See Chiles, 88 & 96; Karl Barth referred to this tendency as the "moralization" of theology; see his *Protestant Thought from Rousseau to Ritschl*, tr. by Brian Cozens, (New York, 1959), Chapter 1.
4. In chapter 15 we noted that there seems to be a theological tension in Seybert to uphold Wesleyan theological orthodoxy and also to draw upon mystical insights as witnesses (*Zeugen*) in the Christian life. A similar comparison can be made between the Lutheran Pietist Johann Arndt and Martin Luther. See Peter Erb, *Johann Arndt*, 16.
5. Erb, 21. The influence of Boehme on Seybert was discussed in Chapter 15.
6. Report of Brother Absalom Schaefer, 1839, 217 cited in Orwig, Vol. I, 279f.
7. In 1840, there were 4,853 citizens in Chicago. Orwig, Vol. I, 312.
8. Report of Brothers A. Stroh and J. Holl, missionaries in Cleveland, Ohio; cited in Orwig, Vol. I, 310.
9. Seybert's *Journal*, entry for May 12, 1822.
10. Albright, *History of the Evangelical Church*, 155.
11. Yoder, 24.
12. Ibid.
13. Seybert's *Journal*, entry for May 7, 1837.
14. See *The Doctrines and Discipline of the Evangelical Association* (Cleveland, 1893), Part II, Rules for Members; also, the *Origin, Doctrine, Constitution and Discipline of the United Brethren in Christ* (Dayton, 1885), Chapter 4. The United Brethren, being a smaller group than the Methodists, also adopted certain progressive, even radical practices in the 19th century, such as lay representation and women in the pulpit. Yoder, 459.
15. Seybert recorded this conversation in September 1831; cited in Spreng, 121f.

16. Yoder, 100f.

17. The Dill and Scheidler farms, where Seybert's missionaries visited in 1840, were part of a Dunker community north of Cambridge City, Indiana. These plain Dutch sects had made a virtue of the ascetic life, with the denial of worldly amusements and ambitions, but they had also become spiritually stagnated in the years when Seybert traversed their lands. He sensed that their religion had become petrified into a legalism devoid of grace.

18. Seybert's report of his trip to Wisconsin in the spring of 1855, Spreng, 322.

19. Spreng, 328.

20. Seybert's response to a poor woman's generous financial gift; Spreng, 327.

21. George Miller, *Practical Christianity,* cited in Yeakel, *Albright and His Co-Laborers,* 250.

22. George Miller, *Practical Christitanity,* cited in Yeakel, 251.

23. Miller, *Practical Christianity,* 151.

24. Heinz Kloss, *Um die Einigung des Deutschamerikanertums* (Berlin, 1937), 117f; cited in Yoder, 109.

25. Arthur Core, *Philip William Otterbein, Pastor, Ecumenist* (Dayton, 1968), 32. The United Brethren trace their origin to the meeting of Martin Boehm, a Mennonite, and Otterbein, who was German Reformed, at the Isaac Long barn, Lancaster County, Pennsylvania on Pentecost 1767.

26. Yeakel, *Albriqht and His Co-Laborers,* 139-142.

27. Seybert's *Journal,* entry for January 26, 1821. This spiritual outreach also crossed racial lines. At a U. B. camp meeting reportedly attended by 7,000 persons near Hagerstown, Maryland, in 1838, the African-Americans drowned out the whites with their singing and shouting. Yoder, 24.

28. I personally encountered this dimension of social witness through Monroe Scheidler, who was my living link with the heritage of Seybert. In his shoebox of letters he wrote warmly of his ministry to children and youth in the pioneer communities where he served. He placed kingdom interests above his own. I recall seeing him in his later years taking produce from his garden to an indigent family who lived in a tarpaper shack by the railroad tracks in Cambridge. There are postcards he sent home from Florida, where he was visiting his brother's family as a widower in his eighties. Instead of biding his time, he mentioned witnessing to travelers in train stations and holding temporary jobs peeling potatoes in restaurant kitchens, where he could "be useful" and have occasion to share his love for his Lord.

Chapter 20

Whither the People of God?

"It seemed as though Satan (was) bound in chains...and the ungodly were quiet . . . and the 'little flock,' to whom is promised the inheritance of the kingdom, had a most precious waiting before the Lord." Seybert's Journal, *entry for July 27, 1835. (Spreng translation).*

We need now to demonstrate that the godly life is not a solitary pilgrimage, but rather inherent within it is the germ of a new order of community. As we probe the dimensions of this new order, we deal with the important issues of the meaning and purpose of the church. Seybert did not leave us a detailed or systematic treatment of this issue, but we may profitably explore the numerous images of the church that appear in the pages of his *Journal.*

One prominent image is the one that saw the church as an "association" (*Gemeinschaft*), which is a body of persons "in connection" with one another. Each member had his or her own sphere of influence to impact with the gospel, and gathered together each one found a common bond of purpose that was expressed in different ways. Sometimes this was referred to as "the missionary spirit which filled the whole Association in those days." This described the mood of the General Conference of 1839, when John Seybert was elected bishop.[1]

Seybert expressed their common purpose in terms of meeting the neglected spiritual needs of the German people, for if the Evangelicals do not help them, "nobody else will."[2] The early Evangelicals were convinced that the means of achieving this end was by teaching and living the doctrine of entire sanctification. As one church father put it, "if there ever shall be a time when the Evangelical Association rejects this doctrine, and discards it, then should 'Ichabod' be written in place thereof, for then 'the glory is departed from Israel.'"[3]

Each of these expressed purposes was an effort to define the meaning of their common life "in connection" with one another. If faith is only private, the believer is not accountable to others. Further, we cannot be rightly connected with God if we are not rightly related to others.[4] As in early Methodism, Seybert used the "love feast," the weekly "class meeting" and the "quarterly meting" as structures for accountability under God.[5] In October 1831 he held a "remarkably powerful" quarterly meeting on the Mohawk River in New York in which seventeen members of the Niagara Falls class participated, coming from as far as ninety two miles for the occasion.[6] He believed this meeting was empowered by God in part because of the great sacrifice the people had made to meet together "in the Spirit."

Among the major attributes of Seybert's ministry, according to his contemporaries,[7] was his care for the church. He loved the church for the sake of Christ and for its sacred mission in the world. Another prominent image that he used to describe this mission was the "marvelous light and liberty of the people of God."[8] This calls to mind Paul's admonition "that we may prove ourselves to be blameless and innocent, children of God above reproach in the midst of a crooked and perverse generation, among whom you appear as lights in the world" (Philippians 2:15 NAS). He also highly favored the image of the church as the "bride of Christ." Describing a time when he was preaching from a favorite text, Revelation 22:17, he said, "I was explaining that the bride, spoken of in the text, meant God's true church, and was showing how the Church says 'come,' when a woman in the congregation suddenly began to cry out Lost!"[9] For Seybert, the church is alive when it is going forth to call people, and not when it is sluggishly awaiting some stirring of life from the people.

These images of the church are brought more clearly into our focus when we view them against the background of other influential concepts of the church that have emerged in Christianity. These concepts are closely related to the way grace has been understood. For Roman Catholics, the church has often been seen as a divine/human community embracing the entire world and headed by a priestly hierarchy that confers grace sacramentally, especially through the sacrifice of the Mass. For the Protestant Reformers, grace is seen as God's unmerited good will or benefit for mankind that is discovered in a community of faith. This community is outwardly recognizable where the Word of God is visibly preached and sacramentally received by believers.[10] Being a community of faith, it assumes different institutional forms that are usually allied with the state.[11] For the Anabaptists,[12] the church became a voluntary, gathered fellowship of believers who experienced grace to the extent that they submitted to a life of cross-bearing discipleship following after Jesus Christ (*nachfolge Christi*).

In the movement of Christian renewal called evangelical Pietism,[13] the true church became recognized more by the lives of its reborn members. They are the living body of Christ. The theme was Christ living in and through a regenerated laity, and credal and liturgical structures were secondary to their personal witness. Their small groups, called conventicles, were considered "little churches within the church" (*ecclesiolae in ecclesia*). John Wesley's English Methodists reflected this pattern when he referred to his class members as those "having the form and seeking the power of godliness."[14] These early Methodists gave their witness within the context of the Church of England, where their official church identity was found. Similarly, Seybert's Evangelicals gave their witness chiefly within the context of the "church Dutch" (Lutheran and Reformed) and "plain Dutch" (primarily Mennonite and Dunker) traditions, to which they were unofficially and often uncomfortably related, as we have seen.

However, Seybert's view of the church was not merely a German photocopy of the Methodist pattern of class structure. To this pattern he added themes derived from the German radical Pietist tradition.[15] Prominent among the titles in his library were the works of Arnold and Boehme. From Gofftried Arnold he acquired the conviction that the church is to be "unsectarian" (*unparteiisch*), in the sense that there should be no striving about "things to no profit, such as water baptism and other forms and figures. Formalists and hypocrites should consider that the essential thing about religion is the kernel and not the shell."[16]

When Seybert spoke of this "kernel," which is vital, godly Christian faith, he reflects insights that we find in Boehme. In Boehme's *The Way to Christ*, which Seybert admired, it is written that the church is ensnared in formalism because she has been seized by a "false Babel" where men "order and direct by rational conclusions."[17] He likened a church guided by this kind of cerebral faith, devoid of the Spirit, to a man who "hang(s) onto the husks." Mindful of the parable of the prodigal son, Boehme continued, "What does it help...that the bestial man keeps the patterns of Christ's service, but...cannot reach the treasure of the service?"[18] The godless man, wrote Boehme, hears externally, and "If there is stubble or straw in the sermon, then he sucks vanity out of it...and brings forth wicked fruit.[19] All of this agrees with Seybert, with one exception. When it comes to the order that the godly life takes, Boehme taught that "the saint has his church in himself where he hears and teaches internally."[20] Seybert, however, taught that the Spirit leads the godly into a new order of a community life, which he called an "Evangelical Association" (*Evangelische Gemeinschaft*). Nevertheless, Seybert would undoubtedly agree with Boehme that much which passes as Christian worship is vain and hypocritical. "Babel has the stone-heap," alleged Boehme, "into which it goes with hypocrisy and flattery, permitting itself to be seen with beautiful clothes, pretending to be devout and pious. The stone church is its god in which it puts its trust."[21] This disdain for "cultural Christianity" is one major reason why Evangelicals and United Brethren resisted calling themselves a church (*Kirche*) for more than a century and preferred the warmer, more intimate title of "Association" (*Gemeinschaft*) and "Brotherhood" (*Bruderschaft*).[22]

This picture of the church that we see emerging in Seybert's *Journal* takes on vital, living dimensions when we view the Association's becoming energized in worship. It has been observed that the early Evangelicals and United Brethren—apart from what some might think of their theological outlook—were the most deeply folk-based of all the German-American churches and sects in their worship.[23] Although Seybert read high German and did so voluminously, he frequently used dialect and folk expressions in preaching and song leading, whether in meetings among thousands or only with three.[24] The mood of joyful love and freedom in the Spirit was dominant wherever he engaged people in worship. He would have agreed with the words of his elder colleague in the gospel, George Miller, who wrote, "I heartily loved my brethren, but still more frequently did I love my God."[25] Seybert walked in the admonition of Albright, who had charged his colaborers to "prosecute the work of the Lord with still greater earnestness."[26] This "work" was best expressed by picturing a house "visited with a powerful outpouring of the Spirit of God, and sinners...calling upon God in every room,"[27] until "in all parts of the house there (would be) also heard the voice of thanksgiving and praise (with) great joy among the brethren."[28]

Spirit-led worship is also sacramental. Seybert was less concerned with the inspiration of the elements in the sacraments than with the way they inspired the godly.[29] We previously noted instances where baptism effected miraculous healings, even in the case of young children.[30] At one large camp meeting Seybert baptized several persons in a creek, and "the blessing of God came in showers upon the various candidates, but most especially upon the witnessing multitude who lined the banks of the stream."[31] Seybert believed that baptism in the Holy Spirit should normally accompany baptism with water. He once found that "the Lord made no difference" between the immersed and the sprinkled, as "the baptism of the Holy Ghost came down upon all the subjects of baptism on this occasion.[32] This witness of the Spirit is what distinguished these people of God from the "German baptized heathen."[33]

The Lord's Supper was not a service of memorial to Christ in a cognitive sense alone. The Supper was open to all the reborn in Christ, regardless of their church affiliation, and it was the concrete embodiment of their living witness to the "suffering Christ." Quarterly meetings normally closed with a "sacramental service." Seybert reported after one such service that "my heart was moved in such a measure that I could scarcely preach...as I was presenting the suffering Christ as man's only Savior."[34]

The Supper visibly signified an inward, continuous communion with Christ. As such, it should not be only an evening meal" (*Abendsmahl*). On his deathbed, John Walter had prophesied "in the Spirit" that "Whoever permits the Savior to come in, in early life, or at noon, with such he will keep the morning (*Morgen*) and also the mid-day meal (*Mittagsmahl*)." [35] It was the Lord's supper that made this "Association" a "Church," at least in the eyes of the German civil authorities, who forbade Evangelical missionaries to administer communion in the 1860's as a violation of the laws regulating the German state church.[36]

The association (*Gemeinschaft*) of the godly, the true church that Seybert loved, was also actively reproducing itself. We might wish that there had been a more positive emphasis upon discipleship in Seybert's preaching, so that church growth could have been achieved as much by the ministry of the laity as the clergy. Still, it is evident that his burden for the lost was often contagious. He believed that the church is to measure its gain by conversions and not mere accessions to church buildings. At one meeting-house dedication, he observed, "We had a right glorious dedicatory feast in our plain house of worship there." This was in part because it was "an edifice without a tower, without a bell, and without debts, erected by poor people" to God's glory. It was also because the dedication service itself was marked by the awakening and conversion of sinners.[37]

Furthermore, our Evangelical forebears were able to distinguish between false religious affection, based upon pretense, and true, godly affection that yields the fruit of love in daily living. George Miller once reported attending a "big meeting" where people became so boisterous that no one could be edified. After a prolonged period of intercession,

Miller arose when it was his turn to preach. "At the conclusion the manifestation of the power of God became quite general, but instead of disorder and confusion, there was solemnity and power, followed by shouts and praises unto God."38

It was in the "parting" ritual that the shift took place from being the church gathered for worship to the church dispersed for service. The farewell songs were filled with admonitions to brotherly love, and hopes of meeting at the next camp meeting as well as in heaven.39 Seybert, describing a "big meeting" held in Penns Valley in May 1833, tells us that the circuit preacher preached his farewell sermon on Sunday evening and the farewells lasted late into the night: "After the sermon there was great commotion of weeping, shouting and praising the Lord. The people threw their arms about each other's necks, loving one and another. This exercise continued far into the night."40 Seybert apparently originated several terms describe closing services at camp meetings, including the "Farewell Ring," "Ring Service," and "Parting Hand."41 At a German and English camp meeting held in 1822 with the Methodists, Seybert described the closing service. "Then friends gathered in circles and groups variously and bade each farewell which caused streams of tears of love to flow, and we gathered for song and to pray with young sinners for mercy."42

A basic reason for church discipline was to equip Evangelicals to be effective witnesses when dispersed into a hostile world. Seybert's watchword, "Give me children, or I die!" was often adopted by his hearers, who found themselves challenged to be living witnesses to the faith by word and deed. One negative consequence of this emphasis was the frequent signs of struggle to avoid the excesses of discipline on the one hand, and the neglect of it on the other. At times he erred on the side of excess concerning negligent members. One early historian, commenting upon the 1830 session of the Eastern Conference, complained that offenders of the *Discipline* "were often too rigidly dealt with" under the apostle's command, "put away from you every wicked person."43

Perhaps referring to Seybert, who was then a presiding elder, this critic continued, "Had more patience and forbearance been exercised, no doubt many members and preachers could have been saved" who were expelled.44 On the other hand, the price of neglecting church discipline was considered too great to be courted. The church periodical admonished in 1841, "Let every Church preach the pure gospel with power and unction, keeping up lively services in the sanctuary, and enforcing the *Discipline*, and there will scarcely any room be left for complaints of deserting members." Here was the way, it was thought, to maintain "the missionary spirit that has animated the Society at large...for so many years" and to prevent backsliding (*Ruckfall*) into the ever-present temptations of the world.[45]

Although an advocate of church discipline, Seybert was alert to avoid the trap of the occult, in which discipline meant conformity to the arbitrary authority of a charismatic leader. His mother was attracted to the Harmony colony at Economy, Pa., a utopian cult founded by a German mystic named George Rapp. He visited her regularly at the colony but was opposed to the colonists' views that they alone were the elect of God and that the millennial reign of Christ was to become synonymous with the village of Harmony. By contrast, Seybert recognized that there is a place for spontaneity in godly living that should not be stifled in the name of discipline. The purpose of discipline is to enable each member to become engaged in every person's world as a living witness to the "crucified Redeemer."[46] By voluntarily submitting one to another in a discipline we learn "the spirit of humility, which (Christ) displayed in the voluntary acceptance of poverty and obscurity" in this world." We also learn that "voluntary submission to the shame of the cross" is what empowers us to suffer tribulations and ultimately to "surmount all difficulties, in order to execute the command of Christ, to bring to the world the glad message of her crucified Redeemer."[47]

It is within this context of a church immersed in witness within the world that Albright's insistence upon "entire sanctification" becomes meaningful to us. He had testified to his brethren at the outset of the Evangelical Association that "I entered into a state in which my heart was almost constantly lifted up to (God)...for God in Christ quickened my soul, so that I did not live unto myself, but to the glory of God and the salvation of my fellow men."[48] Those who lived and breathed this doctrine were regarded as the pillars of the church. As one brother testified a decade after Seybert's death, "Many (who taught this doctrine) have gone home to their eternal rest, others still live and are pillars in the house of God. The work which they have built upon this ground is still standing."[49]

A final aspect of the church that appears in the testimony of these forefathers is the important role of the home. In the heritage of evangelical Pietism, as in Judaism, the home had a special place in inculcating religious practice. It was a "little church within the church" (*ecclesiola in ecclesia*), especially when the churches were under attack during the Age of Rationalism in late 18th-century Europe and amid the hardships of the American frontier. One must see the early "Albright people" at home and in daily life to perceive how pervasive was their commitment to godliness. The grace of conversion was lived out each day in disciplined lives, in everyday work, in family love, and in neighborly kindness. We can envision the discipline, the resignation, and the joy etched on their faces and hands. Although Seybert was not himself a married man, he visited many homes in the course of his travels. On one occasion, while staying at "Brother Alspaugh's," the family was so blessed while engaged in morning prayer "that they were constrained to praise the Lord aloud before they could eat breakfast...or even prepare the meal."[50] At another time, a family was so filled with joy during prayer that they did not care to eat their meal at all. In that community he says, "The Devil and wicked people try in every way to hinder the Lord's work, but it is useless, as long as the fire of God's Spirit burns like that on the family altars."[51]

At the peak of revivals, extraordinary manifestations of the Spirit were sometimes manifested within families. Seybert related an unusual incident of this type that he said occurred during a revival at Warren, Pa., in 1834. One evening while the Arnet and Gross families were away at a prayer meeting, their six children engaged in a childish prayer meeting at home. After a lengthy exercise in prayer, the youngest somehow became offended. Mocking the others, this seven-year-old child slunk under the table in a sulking manner. When the others looked under the table, they were astonished to see an immense black dog with glaring eyes, sitting by the sulking child. Realizing there had been no dog in the house, one of the children said, "This is the devil!" The beast now circled the group, tugging at their clothes and leaping on the table. The children remained calm. One of them was unable to see the apparition. They continued their prayers as the father, Conrad Gross, returned home. Refusing to believe the report of the children, he said, "Nonsense! What would the devil want in our house? Now does he look?"

"It is a dog with great yellow eyes," exclaimed the children, pointing to where they saw him."

Unable to quiet them, Gross finally said, "Let us pray." As he fell on his knees, he noticed a thick, dark mist appearing before his eyes. He opened the door and ordered, "Satan, I adjure thee in the name of Jesus Christ to depart from my house!"

At that point, the childun said they saw the beast slowly leave the house.[52] This drama shows how the petition of Charles Wesley's hymn was made a vital, living practice in the homes of these Evangelical pioneers:

> I want a principle within of watchful, godly fear,
> A:sensibility of sin, A pain to feel it near.[53]

Among the thousands of books that Seybert personally distributed during his numerous crossings of the Allegheny Mountains by buckboard was Miller's *Practical Christianity*. This pioneer Evangelical manifesto on the godly life was especially directed to families. Above all, the father is to "be a pattern of godliness unto his family."[54] He should not "rule over them, according to his own temper," but "lead them according to the Spirit and mind of Christ."[55] Any good that he "would imprint in his household must first be imprinted on himself by Christ."[56] Although he advocated biblical instruction for children, including use of the Evangelical Catechism in the home, he knew that "children always notice more attentively how we speak than what we speak."[57] For persons contemplating marriage, he gave advice that surely deserves to be heeded today. One should approach this decision in "watching and prayer," for "whoever does not crucify the lusts and desires of the flesh, will be led into many temptations and snares,...or must during his lifetime be unequally yoked, which will cause him many necessary sorrows and trials, and which he will not be able to endure."[58] The human struggle between love of spouse and love of ministry is played out in the beautiful correspondence by John Walter, the pioneer Evangelical poet/preacher, to his wife. Writing to her in 1809, he prayed, "may God be your husband and comforter! I have entrusted you to him in my absence....My soul pours itself out daily for you in prayer. At the throne of grace you can daily meet me, at least in the morning, at noon, and in the evening, even though we must be separated in body."[59]

Our focus upon the home reminds us that godliness is not so much taught as caught, as it is modeled in one's formative years. It is in the family that the truest expression of "connectedness" (*in Gemeinschaft*) could be expressed. I am writing this book because an Indiana pioneer named John Dill opened his farmstead to Seybert's Evangelical missionaries in 1840. From his heirs have come a succession of ministers in the tradition of Albright and Seybert, including Monroe Scheidler. Bushnell was right on this: the founders were "great in their unconsciousness."

Notes

1. Orwig, Volume I, 266.

2. From Seybert's address before the General Conference, assembled May 25, 1835, at Orwigsburg, Pa.; cited in Spreng, 151. Seybert sometimes attempted to preach in English, when the occasion required, and sometimes he did so with effect, as on March 23, 1821, or March B, 1831. Evangelicals resisted the transition into English in part because their first venture into this area resulted in a schism; see the "John Hamilton Affair" in Albright, *History*, 221f.

3. This is a reference to I Samuel. 4:21 in an address by John Dreisbach, the first presiding elder of the Evangelical Association; Yeakel, *Albright and His Co-Laborers*, 307.

4. See Mark 7:9-13.

5. See Seybert's *Journal*, entries for October 1831 and for February 5, 1841.

6. See Seybert's *Journal*, entries for October 1831 and for February 5, 1841.

7. Spreng, 386.

8. Seybert's *Journal*, entry for July 4, 1838: the reversal of this theme came when Seybert called godless communities the "land of moral midnight," as on February 21, 1821.

9. Seybert's *Journal*, entry for January 12, 1821.

10. By the Word of God, Luther's primary meaning was God's living, redemptive encounter with mankind, to which Scripture gives written witness. See Paul Althaus, *The Theology of Martin Luther* (Philadelphia: Fortress Press, 1966), 73.

11. Lutheran Germany, there developed the principle of the territorial state church; in Calvin's Geneva, the pattern was theocratic; in England, a comprehensive church state plan emerged that has been called "Erastian."

12. The Anabaptists, which means the "rebaptized," were also called "Radical Reformers" because they sought to restore the apostolic church. Among their present-day descendants are the Mennonites.

13. It was rooted in the late 16th century, with Arndt among the Lutherans and Taffin among the Reformed; See F. E. Stoeffler, *The Rise of Evangelical Pietism* (Leiden: Brill, 1965), 121, 202.

14. John Wesley, "The Rules of the United Societies," (1739), cited in Outler, 178.

15. For a list of the major titles in Seybert's library see Albright, *History*, 262. Rejecting the old church structures of the day, radical Pietists included those seeking a new age of the Spirit that would supersede those structures. See Hans Schneider, *German Radical Pietisim*.

16. Seybert's *Journal*, entry for May 13, 1037; Arnold, in his *Unparteiische Kirche- and Ketzer Geschichte* (1699) defended the concept of the "free unsectarian church" and said that "those who make heretics are the real heretics;" See discussion of Arnold in Norwood, *The Story of American Methodism* (Nashville: Abingdon, 1974), 107.

17. Erb, 118.

18. Erb, 160.

19. Erb, 162.
20. Erb, 162. .
21. Erb, 162. Similarly, Seybert once described the ordeal of a "converted Lutheran" who tried to remain within his church but "soon he was driven out from his Babel...and he united with our church." *Journal*, entry for December 18, 1836.
22. The title "Evangelical Association" was adopted in 1816 and was changed to "Evangelical Church" in 1921; the title "United Brotherhood in Christ Jesus" was adopted in 1800 and was changed to "Church of the United Brethren in Christ" in 1889.
23. Yoder, 116.
24. Seybert preached at a camp meeting numbering several thousand at Lebanon, Pa., in 1836; on March 4, 1821, he had preached to three persons.
25. Yeakel, *Albright and His Co-Laborers*, 234.
26. Yeakel, 227.
27. Yeakel, 226.
28. These are George Miller's words as recorded in Yeakel, *Albright and His Co-Laborers*, 182.
29. He used different modes of baptism as well; on October 8, 1833, he reported baptizing four *in* water, and one at the water beside a stream, one brother three times forward *under* water and one sister with *pouring*.
30. 5ee Chapter 18.
31. This was during an 1836 camp meeting at Lebanon, Pa., cited by Spreng.
32. Seybert's *Journal*, entry for September 18, 1836.
33. Seybert's *Journal*, entry for June 12, 1833. Lutherans in Europe had long charged Anabaptists as "Rebaptizers." The tables are turned in 1850 when Seybert catches an "unconverted" Lutheran pastor rebaptizing a child who had been baptized by an Evangelical missionary. He wrote, "Does not the (Lutheran) Augsburg Confession...say, in the article on Baptism, that 'all rebaptizers are accursed'?" Spreng, 297.
34. Seybert's *Journal*, entry for October 13, 1833.
35. The testimony of John Walter in 1818, in *Albright and His Co-Laborers*, 166.
36. This ruling was made at Esslingen, Germany, in 1863, as reported in Yeakel, *History*, II, 271.
37. Seybert's *Journal*, entry for July 11, 1853.
38. Yeakel, *Albright and His Co-Laboreres*, 238.
39. Yoder, 463; he refers to several "Songs of Farewell" (*Abschiedslieder*), including "*Jetzt scheiden wir dem Leibe nach*" (no. 168 in *Geistliche Viole*).
40. Seybert's *Journal*, entry for May 19, 1833.
41. Yoder, 58.
42. Seybert's *Journal*, entry for June 2, 1822.
43. Orwig, Vol. I, 147.
44. Owig, Vol. I, 147.

45. Orwig, Vol. I, 323.
46. From an episcopal letter issued by Bishp John Seybert in June 1839, cited in Spreng, 204.
47. Spreng, 204.
48. Yeakel, *History*, II, 147. Yeakel, a staunch defender of entire sanctification, links this testimony from Albright to that doctrine, but it is also descriptive of what the new birth signifies.
49. Yeakel, *History*, II, 152.
50. Seybert's *Journal*, entry for January 27, 1825, (Spreng translation).
51. Spreng, 87.
52. Spreng records this report of Seybert from April 1834.
53. *The Methodist Hymnal*, (Nashville: The Methodist Publishing House, 1966), No. 279.
54. Miller, *Practical Christianity* (English edition), 84.
55. Miller, 86.
56. Miller, 87.
57. Miller, 113.
58. Miller, 144.
59. Yeakel, *Albright and His Co-laborers*, 157.
60. It would be hard to overestimate the impact of one godly person in fostering *Gemeinschaft* and in building a sense of community that spans generations. Little did Scheidler know the full impact that would come from his stories, his singing about the piano, and sharing with others in need. Here is where I felt the deepest impulse of the "communion of the saints."
61. Horace Bushnell, "The Founders Great in Their Unconsciousness," in *Work and Play* (New York: Scribner, 1864), 124.

Chapter 21

This Your Brother Was Dead, And Is Alive

"And ye, who have been blessed of the Lord with worldly goods, will ye not open your hands with benevolent deeds and gifts to support the Gospel..., when ye see how much good the Lord does through this means!" From Seybert's report of the work of the Evangelical Association in Tioga County, Pennsylvania, during the summer of 1838.[1]

Seybert knew that the amazing deliverance of the prodigal was his own story, and so he dedicated his ministry to the rescue of God's prodigals, wherever he found them. This dedication is what distinguished John Seybert the churchman. In the last chapter we considered the images of the church that he held. Here we shall see the way he functioned as a churchman who applied the themes of personal godliness to the obligations of his office. As the quotation above indicates, he tried to awaken all "elder brother" types in the Association to the task of becoming a compassionate church.

What happens when our memory is lost or distorted? One of the hardest things about visiting my elderly aunt, who knew great grandfather intimately, is that her memory, once keen with inspiring memories, had become dim and incoherent. Like many in the church-at-large, the elder brother in the parable could not claim senility, but he failed to perceive what happened to the lost son because he was focusing exclusively upon his own need for self-worth in the Father's eyes. The father then recalled to this son's memory the miracle of his brother's return, saying, "This your brother was dead and is alive; he was lost and is found" (Luke 15:32).

Considering Seybert as our model, what does it mean to be a "godly churchman"? First, it means having a missionary spirit. In 1833, after serving two terms as a presiding elder, Seybert offered himself to the church as the first regularly appointed missionary of the Evangelical Association.[2] After being elected as the first president of the denominational missionary society in 1839, he commented, "If anyone wishes to see me, *let him look for me pretty well in the front, where they are still breaking ice.*"[3] Because of his missionary priority, his churchmanship was never stuffy or rigid. With him, souls were all important and reputation in itself meant nothing.

He would attempt anything to reach a lost person for the Gospel. In 1848, when the first steps were taken to send a missionary to Germany, Seybert was appointed to procure the funds for that vital mission.

It also means establishing a vital balance between the head and heart, the discipline of the intellect and the "unction of the Spirit." Although Seybert had little opportunity for formal education, from the beginning of his ministry he pursued an arduous reading program that supplemented his diligent and prayerful study of the Bible. He excelled among his peers in his ability to explain and defend the great doctrines of the faith. However, he desired more to speak in "the demonstration of the Spirit and of power" than in human wisdom.[4] The observation of Albright by one nineteenth-century scholar would also apply to Seybert. "God raised up a man from among the people who could feel and think with them . . . so that the glory will be given to Him and not to the feeble instrument."[5] That Seybert supported higher education solidly Christian in basis is attested to by his episcopal declaration of 1843, urging all ministers "to endeavor to become learned and literary men, who have also the unction of the Holy Spirit."[6] He wisely knew that the heat of revival can be rendered ineffective for the Kingdom if it is not informed by the light of the redeemed mind.

Another trait of the godly churchman that Seybert exhibited was the way he deferred his own needs to those of others. Saving a widow's house at the auction block demonstrated his generosity.[7] In his later years he maintained a home at Freeport, Ill., that he dedicated as "none other than the house of God, the gate of heaven" (an allusion to Genesis 28:17).[8] It contained a prophet's chamber," where every preacher of the Gospel would be at home, and the tenant was under contract to give hospitality to God's servants at Seybert's expense. However, the Bishop balanced this generosity with frugality toward himself, as when he boarded his horse twenty-eight miles outside Philadelphia to save stable expense while ministering in that city.[9] He walked the round trip! Likewise, clothing was for protection and not for display, so he thought nothing of a patch on the knee or elbow, since his greater concern was to be adorned with the beauty of godliness. After preaching in Cleveland in 1845, he was invited to dinner at the home of a German whose wife was considered "unconverted." She had dutifully exploited her culinary art to prepare a meal she thought would be "fit for a bishop." She finally saw her husband approaching the house—but no bishop. Instead, a poorly clad little man, with a broad-brimmed hat, leather shoes, and a badly worn coat was accompanying him. Disappointed and angered, she complained, "Now I've gone to all this work and trouble for nothing," for, "instead of the bishop, he's got nobody but some common old man."

The wife greeted him at the door with, "I thought you were going to bring Bishop Seybert; what did you bring this fellow for?"

"Why it is the bishop, my dear," was the reply.

"This a bishop? This is no bishop!"

She finally was convinced that her guest was the renowned and powerful preacher of whom she had heard, and dinner was served. As Spreng observed, if she had known his character, she would have prepared a plain, common meal, without so much ado.[10]

Only rarely in his effort to find the proper balance between deference and boldness in witnessing to others did Seybert err on the side of hesitation. He once felt "heartily ashamed" for his "lack of moral courage" in failing to offer prayer for guests who were sharing lodging with him in a hotel.[11] Every such failure was to Seybert a reversion to the insensitive state of the elder brother, who did not remember what had been the condition of the lost son.

Deferring to the spiritual and physical needs of others above one's own is an outgrowth of the early Evangelicals' preference for the mystic doctrine of yielding to God (*Gelassenheit*).

Seybert also applied this terminology of submission to his attitude toward the authority of the church. Yielding to the consecrated will of his brethren in conference was, he believed, tantamount to yielding to the will of God. It enhanced his compassion for the lost, since the collective will of the Association was in those days consecrated to the mission of personal evangelism. For example, when as a youthful preacher he received the report that he had been elected to the office of a deacon, he was at first agonized in spirit. He wrote in his *Journal*, "Could I have chosen, I would have greatly preferred to be retained a while longer as a probationer, for I felt that I was not fit for anything else." However, his sense of churchmanship prevailed, and he concluded, "I submitted as cheerfully as I could to the decision of my brethren, and will seek to do the best I can by the help of God."[12] Not only was he inwardly directed by the Holy Spirit, he was also able to accept the verdict of the church as an expression of God's will for his ministry.

Being a churchman, he was not a "lone ranger" missionary who lacked accountability to the body of Christ. Describing the episcopal office that was entrusted to him, Seybert said, "The higher the office which the church, entrusts to a brother, the more humility is required,...and a greater treasure of grace and unction in the heart" until "the world is crucified unto me." Only then can a church leader be delivered from undue pride of office, "lord(ing) it over God's heritage."[13]

Seybert once contrasted his office as a churchman with that of a politician. He was visiting with John Dreisbach, the first Evangelical presiding elder who was at that time a member of the Pennsylvania Legislature. After touring the imposing capitol buildings at Harrisburg, he commented to Dreisbach that he was glad to see his ministerial brother serving there to the glory of God. "But," he exclaimed, "how much greater is the dignity and honor of a minister of the Gospel which I am permitted to hold!...Though I were a thousand times better than I am, I would by no means be worthy of this dignity...of such an office as the Gospel ministry!"[14]

He was filled with gratitude that God had counted him worthy, through Christ, to minister to the lost among God's children He regarded his election to five quadrennial terms as bishop[15] only as adding certain administrative responsibilities to his primary work of living and preaching the gospel.

The seals of Seybert's ministry were not temporal success nor security. They were his "spiritual children,"[16] and he took a parental delight in visiting them wherever possible. As the friars of old, he shied away from accepting a regular salary, preferring to pay his own expenses from funds that were freely contributed to him. All the salary that he did accept he contributed to the missionary enterprises of the church, practicing in deed the liberality that he preached.[17] He sometimes contrasted his preachers with those among the "professional clergy" of his day who "gather no sheaves into the Lord's garner" but "only money into their own pockets."

Evangelical preachers are those "who have no desire as yet to serve the god of this world and the god of luxurious fashions" since they give their substance "for the service of the God of Heaven."[18]

A final emphasis in Seybert's ministry as a churchman was the need for godliness in the conduct of church conferences. The sessions where he presided were like "antechambers of heaven."[19] Victory over the powers of darkness "by the conquest of many hearts and sections of the country for the Lord Jesus Christ" was the grand purpose that brought the brethren together "united as one man."[20] How did these itinerants feel who were being sent out to go great distances to new mission fields? One observer wrote, "Intense brotherly love constrained them to give each other the holy kiss of love amidst the flowing of tears."[21] Conferences in Seybert's day were never to deteriorate into mere business meetings.[22] Rather, they were to contribute to the preacher's growth in grace in the "fullness of God" until the men would be clothed with power to go forth in mission. A conference that was bearing true fruit for God would also be "blessed from day to day with conversions," the way Seybert described the General Conference of 1843.[23] A conference was never a comfortable retreat from the world; it was a preparation for a more effective penetration of the world. "I am bound to die on the walls of Zion!" he told the brethren.[24]

Perhaps the finest tribute to Seybert's practice of godly churchmanship was a comment he made to a young man who later became an influential Evangelical leader. The youth was helping Seybert set up an encampment for a camp meeting in Wisconsin in 1859, during Seybert's last summer of mortal life. He asked the boy to help him bring up some poles from the woods. The bishop remonstrated with the boy as the latter eagerly grabbed a heavy pole. "No, no," he said, "you take this end; I will take the heavy end!"[25] How faithfully he consistently "took the heavy end" has become readily apparent in our sampling of his life.

Here is the kind of serving spirit that was the finest hour of our Evangelical heritage. It became known to me in the latter-day churchmanship of one of Seybert's spiritual descendants, Monroe Scheidler.[26]

Can anyone deny that we today have need of "churchmanship" with that beautiful quality of joyful submission of self to the needs of others? Seybert and all whose ministry he has inspired could surely say with the Apostle Paul that "I have learned to be content in whatever circumstances I am. I know how to get along with humble means, and I also know how to live in prosperity; it any and every circumstance I have learned the secret of being filled and going hungry and suffering reed" (Philippians 4:11b-12 NAS.) The end is that Christ may be all in all, to the glory and praise of God.

Notes

1. Quoted in Spreng, 188.
2. At the session of the Eastern Conference (the original conference of the Association) on June 3-7, 1833.
3. Comment by Seybert made during his visit to Northhampton County, Pa., in 183?, recorded ii Spreng, 168.
4. Spreng, 33.
5. From a letter by Dr. M. J. Cramer, Ph.D., of East Orange, N. J., to Reuben Yeakel, cited in Yeakel, *History*, II, 215.
6. Episcopal Resolution by John Seybert and Joseph long, Bishops, and Absalom B. Schaefer, Secretary, at the General Conference of 1843, in Greensburg, Ohio; cited in Yeakel, *History*, I, 216f. One college was established by the Evangelicals during Seybet's lifetime, Union Seminary in new Berlin, Pa.that later became Albright College in Reading, Pa.
7. See discussion in Chapter 19.
8. Spreng cites this service of dedication; according to the *Journal*, this visit to Freeport occurred on September 22, 1854. Spring, 314.
9. Entry for November 28, 1835.
10. Reminiscence recorded in Spreng, 266f.
11. Seybert's *Journal*, entry for October 10, 1825.
12. Entry for June, 1822. The Evangelicals, like the Methodists, had two levels of ordination, deacon and elder. The probationer was a preacher "on trial" who was not yet elected to the order of deacon. The higher offices above elder, including :hose of a presiding elder and a bishop, had only functional superiority.
13. An extract from Seybert's sermon on "The Episcopal Office" (n.d.), cited in Spreng, 412.
14. Seybert's *Journal*, entry for January 30, 1828.
15. Seybert recorded that his fifth and final election took place on September 24, 1855; see also Spreng, 326.
16. It will be remembered that Seybert was devoted to celibacy by choice.
17. Spreng, 291. Spreng also records that during the 1850's the *Discipline* of the Evangelicals fixed the amount of salary for preachers, both married and single, and this was to be the maximum allowed, not the minimum tolerated.

Every preacher reported all money he had received, and this was collected and equably divided. They often received less than the disciplinary allowance, but if the average was above the allowance, the remainder stayed in the treasury to cover future deficits. This was real "*Gemeinschaft*," economically as well as spiritually. The plan was abandoned by the time of the Civil War. Spreng, 323.

18. Seybert reported in his *Journal* that he visited Iowa between July 15 and 27, 1854. This quotation, recorded during this visit, is cited in Sprang, 318.
19. This was George Millers description of the Evangelical Conference of 1810, recorded in Yeakel, *History*, II, 17.

20. Yeakel, *History*, II, 17
21. Yeakel, *History*, II, 17
22. Yeakel, *History*, II, 26.
23. Seybert's *Journal*, entry for October 20, 1843.
24. Seybert's address before the East Pennsylvania Conference in the spring of 1856, as cited by Spreng, 330.
25. Reminiscence of Seybert from 1850 recorded by Spreng, 353.
26. It became evident in the way he ordered his life with discipline and frugality so that he would be ready on the spur of the moment to expend himself without fanfare in meeting the needs of others. There was the time during the Second World War when he met an army wife traveling across country by train with three unruly youngsters. Sensing her desperation, he changed his plans so he could take care of her children for her until she arrived at her destination. He was not at all deterred by the fact that he was then almost 80 years old. In "retirement" after the war, he read a report in the church paper, *The Evangelical messenger*, that indicated a church in faraway Minnesota was unable to find volunteers to peel vegetables for a large gathering of Evangelicals that was planned for that area. He soon found himself on a bus for Minnesota, where he spent a week working and sharing Christ's Spirit with new friends. He had a way of finding his place at the heavy end of the log, without complaint or a desire for recognition.

Chapter 22

I'll See You On Tuesday

"If nothing comes up to hinder I will come over... next Tuesday and spend a few hours with you....Your Great Grandpa. M.L.S." Letter to the author from the Reverend Monroe L. Scheidler of Cambridge City, Indiana, June 5, 1952.

In this chapter we shall consider the final goal in the pilgrimage of the godly life that theologians denote by the imposing title of eschatology, or the doctrine of the "last things." The letter quoted above was sent to me by Monroe Scheidler during his last year of earthly life but I do not recall receiving it until the spring of 1981, when my mother sent it to me among some of my personal items that she had found. Receiving it then, three decades after its writer's death, the letter has come as a "word from beyond." I am reminded that our present lives are energized when we discover that significant others are in our lives who have a stake in how we complete the course set before us. The "cloud of witnesses" (Hebrews 12:1) that surrounds and supports us is not a faceless crowd. It consists of persons who have much invested in how we keep the faith. I am also reminded that a meeting has been appointed—a time of accountability before the One we serve.

The Evangelicals included a statement in their Articles of Faith on "The Judgment and the Future State" that may have been derived from the Lutheran Augsburg Confession. It has been preserved in our present United Methodist Book of Discipline in the words, "We believe all men stand under the righteous judgment of Jesus Christ, both now and in the last day. We believe in the resurrection of the dead; the righteous to life eternal and the wicked to endless condemnation."[1]

Realizing that we now see the harvest of godly living "in a mirror dimly, but then face to face," the early Evangelicals lived as people of hope because they were furnished with a sense of destiny under the

Providence of God. As the prodigal of old, they had made their pilgrimage to their Father's house in the wonder of the new birth. However, they knew that the fullness of the Father's presence was a joy reserved for those who had faithfully completed their earthly course.

How common it is to find among the elderly those who have become embittered by the ravages of time, especially when the gifts of health and spouse are removed. Then it is truly seen whether one's happiness had been dependent upon these gifts alone or on the Giver himself. It appears that age only intensifies within us what we were earlier. If one's early life is truly motivated by the Great Commandment, that quality of life is what is refined and intensified with the passing of time. Our Evangelical forebears designed the songs to achieve that end. While they labored in the world, knowing that faithful work is prayer, heaven was their Fatherland.

> Mein Leben ist ein Pilgerstand;
> Der Himmel ist mein Vaterland.
>
> My life is a pilgrim's stand;
> Heaven is my Fatherland.[2]

After leaving the inordinate love of this world behind in the experience of the new birth, they set out resolutely Zionwards and sang while grasping their pilgrims' staffs:

> I'll never turn back, into the world
> Oh no, not I, not I!
> I'll never turn back, into the world
> Oh no, not I![3]

Theirs was a religion of discovery, confidence, and a "come and see" expectancy. It was a life that had gained wisdom through incessant struggles with the Tempter here below.[4]

Eschatological hope had prompted the Puritans of Old and New England to embark upon social revolutions that would inaugurate the heavenly kingdom among God's covenant people on earth. The great Pietists, too, were touched by these eschatological impulses, though in a cautious and reverential way. Seybert once stated that he had studied "the writings of pious and learned authors" on the millenium and had concluded, "I will see to it that I am a child of the King, so that I may have part in the first resurrection, and then in course of time I shall find out what the millenium is and shall myself reign with Christ in the millenial kingdom."5 Philip William Otterbein, the chief father of the United Brethren in Christ, has left us a letter on the "millenium"6 in which he laid the foundational hope "that there is in prophecy a more glorious state of the church than ever has been; and this we call the millenium."7 Such a hope, free from disputatious, apocalyptic date setting for the end time, would energize generations of United Brethren and Evangelicals to work for the renewal of the German Americans in the power of kingdom living. Immortal life was for them not merely a reward for the individual; it meant sharing victoriously in the life of Christ's Redeemed Body together with all saints.

The emphasis on "entire sanctification," that was especially strong among Seybert and the Evangelicals, is to be closely linked with their anticipation of sharing in this immortal life. A Lutheran Pietist whose writings Seybert prized was Johann Jakob Rambach (1693-1735), whose study of the life of Jacob concluded that the ladder of heaven (*Himmelsleiter*) in Jacob's dream was "a vision of Jesus Christ as the only way to life." Following the scheme of this typology, our entry into Christ's kingdom is pictured as a step-by-step progression until we shall become fully reconciled to God, "who stands over this ladder." Being our Regal Guide, "our Saviour... had to humble Himself before He could be exalted." Likewise, we will do best not to "change His order" and demand an "easier way to heaven." Instead, "whoever humbles himself and climbs down with Christ will be raised with Him."8

The final hours of Seybert's life, as described by witnesses, capture in images the demeanor of one who was about to climb that final rung of the ladder (*Himmelsleiter*) that ascends into God's full presence. Seen in this context, we can understand why it has been said that the life of a truly godly person is more striking than his teachings. First, we catch a glimpse of him attending his last General Conference session in 1859. Seen through the eyes of one of the participating delegates, Seybert was observed kneeling at a table to receive the Lord's Supper. "I had quite forgot myself, so intensely did I observe Bishop Seybert's manner and appearance." He thought, "you are undoubtedly nearing the end of your earthly career, and are approaching the boundaries of the spirit world, for out of your countenance there shimmers already the countenance of a glorified one." Here was the final public testimony to the power of his life of godliness: "I shall never forget that face until I see him in the transcendent lustre of the resurrection morning. His great spirit of self-denial, the marks of his sufferings, his sacrificing love...together with his great zeal against all wrong—all this seemed to me to be shining in his almost transfigured face." His final perception of Seybert, that reminds me of my last meeting with great grandfather, probes the mystery of that narrow boundary that separates time and eternity: "He seemed so near heaven that the possibility dawned upon me that, should his spirit at that moment depart and step over, his body might remain kneeling at the chancel just as he was, with folded hands, until someone should carry him away."[9]

A second glimpse into Seybert's final moments of devotional insight occurred on his last day upon earth. His spiritual faculties and his capacity to savor the fellowship of the godly grew only more intense. On a cold December 29, 1859, Seybert arrived at the home of Brother Isaac Parker, near Bellevue, Ohio, after a final preaching tour. The previous day he made his last journal entry, that consisted of the terse phrase, "One soul saved."[10] Exhausted but intending to rest here only a few days, he spent a little time conversing in low tones of God's work and much time reading his pocket Bible that lay by his side on a chair after his death. On his last day he joined the family at breakfast and then sat in the family circle, a devotional custom in German Pietist homes, relating a remarkable dream he had during the night. He spoke of being at a large gathering of preachers, who appeared delighted at his arrival. He wanted to shake hands with them all, but there were so many that he could not, Then, in a moment of silence, he said, "How terrible death must be to a wicked man!" Motioning toward his feet, he remarked, "Death begins at the extremities, then it come further up, and then it gets here," touching his heart, "then it is over. So too will I fall asleep."[11] His last words had been uttered. His spirit departed. His friends were quietly aware that his final dream of joining that transcending community of the godly had been achieved. No eloquent testimony in words had been made, but his numerous sons and daughters in the faith, who wept at their loss, sensed he was on "mount Zion, and in the city of the living God," and had come "to the funeral assembly of the first born," and "to the spirits of just men made perfect" (Hebrews 12:22f).

His witness still comes alive with force within us by manifesting qualities too little noticed among "church folk." One was his boundless compasion for all of God's prodigals. Another was his unclouded vision to live for the unseen world of God's kingdom. Seybert's trusted colleague, Bishop Joseph Long, preached a funeral sermon in the presence of Evangelical and Lutheran ministers, and his appropriate text was "And they that be wise shall shine as the brightness of the firmament; and they that turn many to righteousness, as the stars forever and ever" (Daniel 12:3). Memorial services were held in thousands of Evangelical churches and homes across the country. A man of valor had fallen in Israel, and the church somehow felt orphaned.

Evangelicals usually referred to the state of the dead as the "sleep of the godly" who are awaiting the general resurrection (I Cor. 15; Phil. 3:20 f). This contrasts with the eschatology of Lutheran orthodoxy, that revived the medieval tradition that souls live in a blessed condition with Christ apart from their bodies.[12] This teaching, notes Althaus, weakens both the significance of death and the biblical hope in the resurrection. By contrast, Luther had said there is no problem of an intermediate state between physical death and the resurrection, since "There is no time" in God's presence. "Just as soon as your eyes are closed, you will be awakened," and so "Each of us has his own Last Day when he dies."[13] In the incandescent light of Christ, the limitations of time and finite bodily existence are finally transcended and subsumed. How can we be sure of this? The living witness of our godly forebears proclaims it more powerfully than has the best-versed doctor of theology.

As United Methodists, we are reminded that a meeting has been appointed for us with the One for whom we claim to be living. God's greatest truths come to us as insights and hopes borne by messages that are fragile and easily overlooked. Coming to me across the years is a letter from one whose life was in touch with the durable heritage of Seybert and the early Evangelicals. I remain more intrigued than ever with the line in great grandfather's letter that announced, "I'll see you on Tuesday."

Notes

1. From Article XII of the Confession of Faith of the Evangelical United Brethren Church, in The Book of Discipline of the United Methodist Church, 1980, paragraph 68. The Methodist Articles of Religion (see also paragraph 68) contains no article devoted to this theme, although it was surely emphasized in early Methodist preaching as well as among Evangelicals and United Brethren. It will be recalled that Albright and George Miller, who in 1809 compiled the Evangelical Articles of Faith and Discipline, were both Lutheran in background.

2. From *Eine Sammlung von Geistlichen, Lieblichen Liedern* (Baltimore, 1840), Anhanq, 30; quoted in Yoder, 452.

3. This chorus was sung by a twentieth-century Pennsylvania Dutchman, Peter M. Kershner, and it was recorded by Yoder, 453.

4. Yoder comments on their pilgrimage songs: "And who is there to say that

these simple songs, the homemade tribute brought by simple lives and simple hearts, with a Dutch accent, to be sure, do not rank with other tributes in song brought to the Father and the Son in all ages of Christian history?" Yoder 458.

5. Seybert's sermon on Rev. 20:6, entitled "The Blessed and Holy Lot," printed in Spreng, 414ff.

6. "Millenium" refers to the 1,000-year reign of Christ mentioned in Revelation 20:6.

7. Philip William Otterbein, "Letter Concerning the Millenium," in Core, 102f. Early-day United Brethren and Evangelicals took no definitive stand on the current controversy over pre- post- or amillenialism. If anything, Otterbein's emphasis upon a coming "better age" for the church, to be followed by Christ's return, could be considered post-millenial. His major emphasis was for believers to live prepared, "to make our call and election sure."

8. Here we detect the interweaving of German Pietism and Wesleyan holiness themes. George Miller defined for the early Evangelicals the condition of entire sanctification that characterizes the believer who ascends this *Himmelsleiter* with Christ: "whosoever will surrender himself, soul and body, unto God, and by faith lay hold upon the sanctifying life of Christ, will soon attain to the happy state of grace," submitting to the providence of God with resignation *(Gelassenheit)* but also with gratitude. This leads to Christ's "complete victory in us, so that we can momentarily resist and overcome all temptations to sin, so that evil or sin can neither inwardly nor outwardly reign over us. But the sanctified person dare not think for a moment that he is not exposed to the danger of being tempted and lured into sin; he has much rather reason to be watchful and prayerful, and to work out his salvation with fear and trembling; but he can also be assured that the grace of God, through Christ, is stronger than the devil, the world and the flesh." From George Miller's *Practical Christianity*, 44f, and his autobiographical testimony in Yeakel, *History*, II, 150.

9. Testimony from the 1859 General Conference cited in Spreng, p. 358.

10. Seybert's *Journal*, entry for December 28, 1859.

11. Account reported by Isaack Pakrer to Bishop Samuel Spreng, as found in Spreng, *Life and Labors of John Seybert* (Cleveland: Lauer and Mattill, 1888), 365.

12. Paul Althaus, *The Theology of Martin Luther* (Philadelphia: Fortress, 1966), 412.

13. Martin Luther, *Weimar Ausgabe*, 14:71, cited in Althaus, 416.

Chapter 23

A Summons to Evangelicals

"Now, beloved friends, who hear this, how is it among you?... Are you still rooted and grounded in that love that is as strong as death?...Ye messengers of the Lord, have ye this love burning yet, or has she gone down?" From Seybert's sermon on Song of Solomon 8:6: "For love is as strong a death."

"The devil hates no one so much as those Christians who are so entirely swallowed up in God....Oh my brethren and sisters! Whatever you do, press deeply into God. Watch and pray, submit yourselves wholly unto the Lord, and trust him in the greatest adversities." From Se(bert's Sermon on Job.[1]

John Seytert preached out of the experience of his life, knowing that God's provisions of grace are ample to equip us for the vocation of ministry that summons us all. His counterpart among the United Brethren, Philip William Otterbein, had once preached on the theme of the prodigal son, "for Jesus is waiting for you. The garment of salvation is already prepared. All is ready. Come."[2] The invitation beckons. Among those who call themselves "United Methodists", too few have a grasp of the vital spiritual dimensions of that heritage, beyond a nominal acquaintance with its principal founder, John Wesley. Perhaps our encounter with Seybert will kindle a renewed appetite for those pioneers of faith whose lives are meant to enrich and make vital the witness of our lives to our Lord Jesus Christ. "The higher a degree of godly life a person reaches in this time," wrote Otterbein, "the firmer will be his hope for the future."[3]

As we come to the bicentennial of the death of the founder of the Evangelical Association, Jacob Albright (1759-1808),[4] the time seems very right for a renewal of our historical consciousness. As a church and as a nation, we are a people in search of a heritage. Many are decrying our youths' woeful ignorance of their nation's past.[5] They see little of it around them and often learn less of it in school, where it has tended to become a subject dictated by special-interest groups. The heritage of the church is even less visible. Few are being surrounded by history, as I was in my youthful visits to the old Scheidler home in Cambridge, where it was like a seemingly endless blanket. What most know of their civil and religious heritage they find in glass cases, where it is impossible to touch. And yet, knowledge of the past does breed belief in the future. The popularity that long surrounded the television show, "Star Trek," suggest psychologists,[6] was fed by the need of youth to believe that earth will continue to exist so far into the future. Furthermore, what a student meets in a core curriculum at age eighteen is too unfamiliar and too late to be called tradition in the strong and vital sense of the term. Unless they have been lived out before one in a robust, incarnate fashion, the traditions we value may look like faded hand-me-owns compared to the glamour of popular culture.[7]

What has been presented here is not another historical chronicle of a good man's life or of a denomination's flowering. It is more. This appraisal is set forth as a basis for evoking a renewed spirituality in United Methodism. The witness of Seybert and the early Evangelicals joins that of the Wesleys and Francis Asbury to provide us with resources for reinvigorating our common life and mission. The form in which Seybert expressed himself was more akin to poetry than prose, and poetry suggests that "to try to understand human things without being moved by them is to misunderstand them."[8] What seems unique in his witness is the way he joined the streams of Wesleyan theology and German mysticism, as channeled through Radical Pietism. The former emphasized free grace and the assurance of pardon and sanctification. The latter added to those themes an emphasis on resignation to God, reverence for life and meditation guided by dreams, visions, and the images of nature. As a result of this fusion, he gave new meaning to our present-day discussion of what it means to seek Christian renewal that is "Spirit-filled."

We have traced the distinctive features of Seybert's faith as they unfolded in his own self-analysis, as found in his long-unpublished *Journal*. We found that the parable of the prodigal son was a controlling metaphor that he examined to describe the progress of his vocation as a minister. The term "godliness" best expresses the character and goal of that pilgrimage. It evokes a quality of life that is to be commended to

United Methodists today as a vital but little appreciated aspect of our heritage.

We have emphasized "godliness" rather than the more familiar term "holiness," that is often associated with the so-called "holiness controversy" that disrupted Methodism in the late 19th century.[9]

However, there is no report of a "godliness" controversy! Godliness did not become a program to be championed or opposed, as did the more polemical term holiness. Godliness was either vitally present, in praxis, or else it was absent from the life of the church. Perhaps its apparent demise as a functioning concept in the generations after Seybert formed a felt void that helped give rise to the holiness debates. Many had by then sensed a change in the quality of church life. They were seeking a way to restore the spiritual power, vision, and confidence of the founders. A lesson we learn from this controversy is that the renewal of truly godly living can hardly be assured by developing strategies of doctrine and church program, however needed and helpful they may be. By contrast, the vision of the founders, that now summons us anew, was their redemptive love for all of God's prodigals, wherever they might be found, and also a commitment to live for the unseen world of God's Kingdom, heedless of discomfort or dishonor in this present world. These are qualities of faith that can neither be taught nor legislated without hearts that are willing to be resigned to God in gratitude and consecration.

They are qualities that we observed in the intimate conversation of Monroe Scheidler and his fiancee in the old shoe box of letters that I uncovered. They are also found in the mystical language of the Evangelical hymns of Seybert's day, that invite us to recover the rich "Urgrund" of our faith.

> O, der Alles hat verloren,
> O wer doch gar war' ertrunken
> In der Gottheit Urgrund See!
> Damit war' er ganz entsunken
> Allem Kummer, Angst and Weh.
>
> O, whoever has lost everything,
> O, whoever would drink fully
> In the Godhead's enveloping sea!
> He would wholly submerge therein
> All worry, care and grief.[10]

If we find ourselves being summoned by the pattern of godly living that we have gleaned from the life of Seybert, several features of that pattern may help guide the way we order our talents and resources for ministry. Heeding these features might even assist in recovering the direction toward becoming a vibrant people "on fire" for God. What are they? One feature is (1) the awakened capability to recall those forgotten places of sacred memory where we experienced the touch of God's transforming presence. Godliness is not born overnight, since its roots in our lives go back for generations. By getting in touch with our own "sacred histories," like my finding Bishop Seybert's writings in great grandfather's bookcase, our lives in Christ may begin to be rooted with new depth. Those qualities of faith in Seybert and his contemporaries that we have called "godly" were, it appears, largely communicated to the younger generation by the power of lived example and with a sense of sacred aura. This reminds us of the undervalued force of vivid narrative in transmitting the faith, like Israel's memory of her dealings with the God of "Abraham, Isaac, and Jacob." A healthy appeal to memory should not be construed as sentimentality. It is in part to know something against ourselves, like the prodigal's memory of his "godless appetites." Otherwise, memories are self-serving instead of God-serving.

Other features issue from this awakened sense of sacred memory. (2) Another is recognizing that genuine godly living does not draw attention to itself or count the cost. (3) Still another is the capacity to identify those bonds that tend, like the "lure of the keepers," to restrict our full, free response to God, and render us content with a diet of "husks," that is counterfeit Christianity. (4) It is willingness to reclaim a sensibility to the offense and pain of sin that is personal as well as corporate, an awareness that has sometimes been blunted among liberals and conservatives alike. (5) It is finding, like Seybert did on his road "dampened by tears," that it is hard to commit sin when we become vividly aware of God's presence. (6) It is recognizing that godly living involves courage and perseverance to live and act in the conscious presence of God. This is what Seybert meant by being "preached through." It is being so saturated with divine energy that this incandescent quality is reflected on our very countenances.

The features of the godly life that summon us also concern the way we witness to others. (7) It is focusing upon the "sense of the heart," yielding a character that is both gentle and sensitive toward the needs of others, yet tough-minded and realistic in its grasp of evil. (8) It is to be motivated to lose oneself in unreserved service to God and neighbor in the now, "mingling with God's people," until this becomes more important than to have our own needs gratified, or to be blessed, or even to be liberated from forms of oppression. (9) It is to rekindle our roots as a connectional people, whose fellowship is enlivened by manifestations of grace. These gifts surface in the context of our ministry to others, and not because we selfishly want to "possess" gifts. They also emerge as we begin to pay closer attention to the way God seeks to guide us through dreams and the imagery of music, that were such fruitful avenues of edification for Seybert.

(10) The godly life discloses its final meaning to us in the light of our ultimate destiny. The godly among the Evangelicals were more concerned with the kind of living that prepared them for the end time than they were with speculating about when it would arrive. Do we sense that our final destiny as those who aspire to the godly life is mysteriously interwoven with the destiny of the others for whom Christ died? The Great Commission requires that this be so.

As I set out to read the letters of Monroe and Mina, I soon realized that in their courtship they were unconsciously enacting a parable. He was an Evangelical, standing in the tradition of Seybert, and she was a Methodist. Our glimpses at their letters have disclosed their loving intention of introducing each other to their respective ways of living the gospel, with the expressed hope that their coming marriage might be consummated in Christ. As United Methodists, our wedding is past, but much remains to be done if we are to make a marriage after God's heart. Much remains if the latest chapter in his story of faith is to stand alongside those others.

Even in Seybert's day, spiritual decline was already threatening the Association. Warnings had begun to be sounded that the supernatural, redemptive quality of Evangelical worship had "degenerated into mere human effort."[11] Editorials had already appeared in the church paper reminding Evangelicals that no redemptive ministry is possible apart from "the power of the Holy Spirit which overwhelms the sinner's heart."[12] Said one leader, "Only a Gospel preached by a converted and divinely anointed preacher and a Church filled by the Holy Spirit—not a dead mass of members—is the true saving salt of the earth which is to penetrate and save fallen humanity."[13] Seybert was the embodiment of that ideal. It may be true that he belonged to the age of spiritual giants and, "take him for all in all, we shall not look upon his like again."[14] Be that as it may, our turn has come. Drawing from our godly roots, the world is ready for each of us to begin living out of our accumulated power within our God-given spheres of influence, where our witness can make an eternal difference for someone else.

Notes

1. From the extracts of Seybert's sermons printed in Spreng, 396ff. and 408-409.

2. Philip William Otterbein, "Die Heilbrigende Menschwerdung," printed in Core, 90.

3. Core, 90..

4. The Methodist Episcopal Church was formally organized at the Baltimore "Christmas Conference" of 1784; the official launching of the United Brethren in Christ occurred in 1800 and of the Evangelical Association in 1803, near the end of Albright's brief ministry (although this name was not adopted until the General Conference of 1816).

5. See, for example, the article by Linda Stevens, "Nation in Search of a Heritage," in the *Tulsa Tribune* (circa Monday, August 3, 1981).

6. Linda Stevens, "Nation in Search of a Heritage," in the *Tulsa Tribune* (circa Monday, August 3, 1981).

7. Michael Platt has written an illuminating article on this theme entitled, "On Tradition and the Soul," in *The Intercollegiate Review* Vol. 17, No. 1, (Fall/Winter 1981), 47-51. The stories we have shared from Seybert's life are to be seen as enactments of theological insights that can serve to illuminate our present-day pilgrimage of faith.

8. Michael Platt, 49.

9. Major holiness denominations that issued from the ferment within the Methodist Episcopal Church included the Free Methodist Church (1860) and the Church of the Nazarene (1895). The National Holiness Association, formed after the Civil War, sought to perpetuate the camp meeting tradition and included Methodist, Evangelical, and United Brethren participation, among others. There was considerable agitation over the holiness doctrine within the Evangelical Association prior to its unfortunate division in 1891.

10. From *Geistlich Viole*, 1855, No. 41, verse 3; (translation mine). These insights of Christian devotion, rooted in German mysticism and Pietism, emphasize a sensitive, discerning spirituality unimpeded by the defensiveness that characterized later Protestant fundamentalism in its struggles with liberalism. Also, in his use of mystical sources, Seybert balanced those others, like Boehme, whose power of supernatural transcendence led to a new appreciation for the natural world (i.e., Boehme wrote, "As you leave the world you will come into that out of which the world was made." Boehme, *The Way to Christ*, 172).

11. This complaint was made about camp meetings held in 1865; Yeakel, *History*, II, 134.

12. From *Der Christliche Botschafter*, (August 27, 1873); cited in Yeakel, 202.

13. From Yeakel's comments on the occasion of the founding of the Evangelical mission in Europe. Yeakel, 240. At the General Conference of 1859, the last he attended, Seybert opposed a resolution that favored receiving children into full church membership only on the basis of their baptism. This would have introduced the issue of the "Half-Way Covenant," that the New England Puritans had agonizingly debated two centuries earlier. Seybert's stance, that prevailed on that date, rested on the premise that "Such a step would be to lay the foundation for a heap of dead bones among us." Spreng, 354.

14. Spreng, 72.

Appendix 1

"The Doctrine of Christian Perfection"
An Excerpt from Chapter 3
(pars. 25-31) in *The Doctrines and Discipline of the Evangelical Association. Cleveland, Ohio: Thomas and Mattill, 1897 (first ed: 1809)*

§ 25. The Lord Jesus expressly says, Matt. v. 48, *Be ye therefore perfect, even as your Father who is in heaven is perfect.* And the Apostle Paul exhorts, 1 Thess. v. 16-18, *Rejoice evermore; pray without ceasing; in everything give thanks, for this is the will of God in Christ Jesus concerning you.*

He that would fully comply with these exhortations at all times, must be wholly resigned to the will of God; consequently all self will and selfishness must be perfectly subdued; he must bear everything that may befall him, as from the hand of the Lord, or he cannot meet every adversity with acquiescence and resignation, much less with gratitude. He must stand upon his guard so firmly and immovably that he can parry, and gain the victory over any temptation the moment that it may present itself, without yielding more or less, either voluntarily or negligently, as it does sometimes happen with weak Christians. If his rest, peace, and joy in God, as no more interrupted by any such vicissitudes or occurrences, he must indeed be firmly rooted and grounded in God; and of a truth, he must love God with all his heart, with all his mind, and with all his strength; sin has, as it were, lost all its power against such a one, he being surrounded by the love of God as with a wall of fire. The flesh, the world, and Satan, are under his feet, and he rules over his enemies, yet in watchfulness.

This is the state which the Evangelical Association understands by

CHRISTIAN PERFECTION.

§ 26. That such a state is attainable even in this life, is very evident, for Christ and all His apostles exhort thereto; yea, from this we learn that it is every Christian's bounded duty to strive thereafter. And how can he be a Christian, who does not desire to submit wholly to God, and to love Him in truth, with all his heart, with all his soul, and with all his strength?

By experience we are fully persuaded that such a state is attainable, and has been attained by many, who have happily persevered therein for many years, even to the end of their days. Many others had attained it, but for want of watchfulness lost it again. This we also have learned by sad experience. But experience has likewise taught that this blessed state, after it has been lost through negligence, may again be attained by the grace of god, and that a person may finally, after having been as a reed shaken by the wind, become as a firm and immovable pillar in the temple of God.

§ 27. With many others this work has never come to a perfect clearness; a great degree of grace was indeed visible, yet there were also infirmities discernible at the same time, which could not be properly distinguished by those who look upon externals only, whether they were but involuntary, natural infirmities, or slighter voluntary deviations and overcomings of sin.

Experience has moreover taught that, ordinarily, this state of Christian perfection is attained gradually, by an upright course of life in following the Lamb; however, during this gradation, this work is perfected in the soul, sooner or later, by a sudden and powerful influence of grace and outpouring of the Divine Spirit. Those who have actually experienced it describe this effusion of the Divine life as being similar to the grace of justification, yet, far exceeding the same. This grace is called SANCTIFICATION.

Notwithstanding, as all created beings will ever remain finite and circumscribed, and, according to the nature thereof, are forever less than God Himself; the most perfect man (or angel) will ever be inferior to God, though he become a partaker of the Divine nature by justification, and through sanctification be much more assimilated to the Divine Being; there he may, after having attained to this degree of sanctification, grow and increase yet more and more in grace, and proceed from one degree of glory to another.

And where this progression should cease cannot be conceived; rather may we suppose a continual advancement and progression to all eternity. Nevertheless, the happiest spirit will ever remain greatly inferior to God Himself.

§ 29. It is further to be considered here, that sanctifying grace does not take away the natural infirmities of man, yea, it does not even cover them; but, on the other hand, it sometimes rather manifests and exposes them. Such are, a weakly and morbid body, weakness of understanding, of memory, of judgment, and of the mind. Therefore such an individual may be imposed upon by false appearances, and through a misdirected judgment think more highly or derogatively of other persons than they really deserve. He may be indistinct, yea, confused in expression; give unfit advice; and through various kinds of such weaknesses, which God never imputes as sins, he may render himself ridiculous before a witty world. Such a one should, therefore, never refuse to receive instruction and good counsel from others who do not possess the same degree of grace with him, as far as he sees that God designs to instruct him in this way.

This much has been deemed necessary to be stated here, to prevent all misunderstanding of the matter, and to enable the reader to see this doctrine in a clear light, and to form just *conceptions* thereof.

Whereupon the Evangelical Association further declares:

§ 30. Let us then, seriously and explicitly admonish all believers, ardently to strive for Christian perfection. And in order that we may teach uniformly on this point, let us decide, once for all, whether we shall continue or give up this doctrine. We are unanimous to defend and maintain it; understanding by it nothing else than a total deliverance from all sin in the proper sense of the word, by means of the love of God being shed abroad in the heart, influencing and actuating the same.

Some indeed say: "This cannot be attained, till we have passed through purgatory." Others say: "No, this is accomplished at the moment when body and soul are separated." Again, others say: "We can attain this before we die, one minute after is too late." But we are unanimous that we may be redeemed from all sin, long before we die; that is, from all evil affections and desires. So this point remains settled.

§ 31. The next inquiry is: Is this happy change wrought gradually or instantaneously? Both take place. Shall we, then, insist upon one as well as the other, in our preaching? We must certainly insist upon a gradual change, and this zealously and continually. And have we not equally as good reasons to insist upon an instantaneous change, wrought by the effusion of grace in an instant? If we can expect such a blessed change, should we not earnestly exhort all believers to seek it? And the more so, because the more earnestly this instantaneous work of grace is sought, the more it is longed for, the more rapidly and steadfastly the gradual work of grace in the soul will progress. The more they are concerned about such a change, the more punctual will they be in observing the divine ordinances: whereas, on the other hand, the contrary may be observed in all those who are not expecting this work of grace. They are blessed in the hope and expectation of a total change, while gradually growing in grace. But where this hope falls away, the work of grace begins to stagnate, if it does not apparently decrease. Therefore, whosoever is concerned to promote the gradual progress of this work, should encourage believers in the hope of such an immediate influence of grace.

Appendix 2

Case Study from The Life of John Seybert[1]

Prepared by J. Steven O'Malley under the title "Whither the People of God?" at the Case Method Institute held at Wake Forest, N. C., June 1981; used by permission of the Institute. Case No. 9-482-657 (copyrighted). (Note: This case is intended for use in pastors' and lay study groups. The issues presented here are intentionally left unresolved to evoke discussion. The "teaching aid" at the end is designed to suggest ways to present the case.).

Sitting in his pew, John Seybert (1791-1860), the first constitutional bishop of the Evangelical Association, put his head in his hands. He prayed and he thought about the upcoming vote. This vote would be a simple "yes" or "no," but the issue was fraught with grave consequences for the church he had long served. It was a petition for enlarging the bishop's power. A positive vote would mean that the office of bishop would be patterned more closely after that of the Methodist Episcopal Church. Its adherence to an episcopacy with life tenure was a policy favored by some Evangelical leaders. The body preparing to vote on the issue was the 1859 session of the General Conference meeting in Naperville, Illinois. Joseph Long, one of two junior bishops attending with Seybert, was presiding.

Seybert had been ordained in 1821 and elected bishop at the General Conference of 1839. Raised a nominal Lutheran, he had undergone a life-changing conversion as a young man in 1810. His "penitential struggle" had been climaxed when he stooped to wash his tear-stained face in a watering trough. He instantly became aware that he had received the washing of regeneration and was now "a new creature in Christ Jesus." In later years he gratefully related to many a seeker of religion how "there by that well the Lord converted me deep into eternal life...and I will not forget it to all eternity." He had seen his church grow from a few thousand souls to become the largest indigenous American denominations devoted to the evangelization of the Germans in this country. When he was elected bishop, he felt overwhelmed by the responsibility of the office and requested the brethren to "pray for me and have patience with me." The bishop, who had by some estimates traveled 175,000 miles on horseback to reach his people with the gospel, was acclaimed by many as a nineteenth-century St. Francis.

The Evangelical Association was part of the German-American religious family. There were the "church Dutch," the Lutheran and the Reformed; there were the "plain Dutch," including the Mennonites, Dunkers, and Amish; and there were also the "bush meeting Dutch," including numerous revivalist sects, the largest being the Evangelical Association and the United Brethren in Christ. The Evangelicals combined vital personal piety with Methodist methods of discipline. Their preachers traveled throughout the German communities of Pennsylvania and the Midwest, offering a gospel of personal regeneration in Christ and relying heavily upon camp (or "bush") meetings in their strategy. They shunned the formal traditions of faith and order of the "church Dutch," and they insisted that the "plain Dutch," with their strict habits of dress and behavior, were lacking in the assurance of salvation apart from the new birth.

The venerable Seybert modeled this style of ministry for the Evangelicals of his day. He believed they were to be a Spirit-led movement of lay persons who had first banded together to bear witness to their faith among the Pennsylvania Germans. A purely functional order of ministry had evolved, without formal apostolic succession or clerical privilege. He had repeatedly admonished his preachers that the minister's office was not to be an exalted temporal position. Instead, the minister was to be yielded to God (called *Gelassenheit*) and was to bear his cross humbly for Christ in this world. Only men who evidenced such consecration were considered fit for the itinerant ministry of the Evangelical Association.

Jacob Albright (1759-1808), the founder, had been a farmer of Lutheran parentage who had first modeled this style of ministry for the Evangelicals. After a series of personal tragedies, including the deaths of several of his children from dysentery and his own narrow escape from death, Albright experienced conversion and had in 1796 embarked upon a brief but effective ministry to his German neighbors in eastern

Pennsylvania. Although they were laymen, his assistants had ordained him in 1803 with the simple conviction that he was "a genuine (*wahrhaftigen*) Evangelical preacher in word and deed, and a believer in the Universal Christian Church and the communion of saints." The act was done with no ecclesiastical recognition by any existing church body.

In the last year of his life he had been unanimously acclaimed a bishop—a position he had exercised de facto from the beginning. His colaborers had been left leaderless by his premature death, in 1808, and many Lutherans and other "church Dutch" who had opposed his ministry rejoiced that they were rid of this feared preacher of repentance and were confident that the "Albright people" would soon collapse. Although the movement did not collapse, it did suffer without his leadership, and a full thirty-one years passed before a successor to Albright was elected to occupy the episcopal office. That person was John Seybert.

During Seybert's years as bishop, the ministry of the Evangelical Association had been extended from its place of origin in eastern Pennsylvania in three directions. There were secondary extensions north into western New York and Ontario and south into Maryland and the Shenandoah Valley of Virginia, and a primary thrust west into the Great Lakes states and the upper Mississippi Valley. Among the Evangelicals in the West, the older Pennsylvania German families met the newly arrived German immigrants, Evangelical converts who spoke "high" German and had not yet been assimilated to American democratic values. Despite this diversity, these two groups found unity during the two decades of Seybert's leading in the Evangelical Association owing to a common commitment to genuine personal piety and Methodist discipline. Above all, it was Seybert who provided the vital link between the Eastern and Western segments of the church with his continuous preaching and visitation tours. He was the figure who above all kept potentially divisive forces from erupting.

As the Conference of 1859 opened, these parties of division were beginning to assert themselves. The leader of this drive was a young minister named John J. Esher, who believed it was time for the Evangelicals to "come of age" and deal with the realities of a new day. It was time for them to take their place as a denomination with a right to its "place in the sun." An emigrant from Alsace, Esher had been converted in an Evangelical camp meeting of the 1840's and had been elected as a "Western" delegate from Illinois. He was also chafing under the older, informal Pennsylvania Germans—the so-called "bush-meeting Dutch"—

who controlled the Association from its inception. He had been embarrassed and angered by the attack upon the Evangelicals by John Williamson Nevin of the German Reformed church, who influenced his denomination in 1849 to reject the validity of the ordination of the Evangelical minister seeking to transfer to his fellowship, and who proceeded to deny that they were a lawful church.

Further, Esher had been irritated by the earthly spirituals, such as "Kommt Bruder, kommt," that so many rural evangelicals were fond of singing in the crude Pennsylvania German dialect of their camp meetings. As an editor of the new church hymnal, he was laying plans to have those "bush meeting" favorites either rewritten or excluded because, as he said, they involved a "too familiar conversation with God and Christ." In their place, he would substitute more stately German hymns, such as "Ein Feste Burg." Some of these new hymns were composed by one of his allies, William Horn. In addition, Esher was preparing to write an improved catechism for the denomination that would be influenced by the work of Philip Schaff, the great German Reformed Church historian.

Esher believed that the office of bishop was the key vehicle for effecting those changes in the Association that would enhance its denominational standing. Esher and those delegates who sided with him believed that the office of the bishop had remained unfilled for 31 years because of a deep-seated fear of the responsibility of the office, since no one felt qualified to walk in the shoes of Albright until 1839, when Seybert was compelled by his peers in General Conference to accept the office. For his part, however, Esher was not timid in seeking this office for himself, for he held that bishops should not be humble servants of the people so much as "generals leading the army of God against the infidels." They were to strictly enforce the laws of faith and order, and especially the Evangelicals' prized doctrine of Christian perfection, until no minister would deviate "a hair's breadth from the Discipline." Soon after the Conference opened, a pro-Esher delegate named W. W. Orwig secured the condemnation of an Eastern delegate, a popular presiding elder named Solomon Neitz, for issuing a pamphlet that questioned the doctrine of Christian perfection heralded by Orwig and his allies. In accordance with his advocacy of a more formal, intrinsic episcopacy, Esher's petition urged that bishops be allowed to serve more than two 4-year terms and that they be permitted to move preachers at will, even across conference lines. At the same time, Esher and his allies were careful to pay courteous respect to the venerable Seybert, the patriarch of the church.

Seybert and those delegates who sided with him spoke for the older, Eastern segment of the church. They wanted the Pennsylvania Germans and the newer, Western German-Americans to remain united and harmonious. As for the office of bishop, Seybert believed that a bishop, like any elder, should mold policy by exemplifying personal godliness, rather than mandating policy by precept, as in the polemics over holiness fomented by the Esher delegates. The Eastern delegates were becoming fearful of the prospects of a one-man episcopal tyranny. They recalled that the early conferences, while the episcopal office was still vacant, had placed limits on the active power of the bishop, even deleting a form for the separate ordination of bishops from the Discipline of 1830. Although Seybert had long held the office of bishop, he believed that "the less power in the hands of the bishop, the safer for the society in the future."

As the time for the vote on the petition approached, several delegates noticed Seybert's attitude of deep thought and meditation. One delegate noted, "I had quite forgotten myself, so intensely did I observe Bishop Seybert's manner and appearance. . . . I shall never forget the face...his great spirit of self-denial, the marks of his sufferings, his sacrificing love..., his great zeal against all wrong—all this seemed to me to be shining in his almost transfigured face."

Meanwhile, the Esher forces were rising to argue their case for a newly defined episcopal office that would be more fitting for a church "come of age." Bishop Joseph Long, a close friend of Seybert, rose to warn the delegates that "you must remember, first of all, that when you vote power to men, they will use it. This may do, as long as you have Bishop Seybert and myself in office, but you will get men who will use all the powers you give them, and not always for the best interests of the church."

With that warning, the delegates were asked if they were ready to vote. Seybert heard Long call for the division of the house.

Teaching Note - Whither the People of God?

(The following outline suggests ways in which this case may be used with church and school classes.)

I. Teaching Goals

This case is a historical reconstruction. Based on data supplied by the unpublished *Journal* of Bishop John Seybert and informed by other materials, it intends to serve as a suitable occasion for pursuing the following goals:

1. Exploring the tensions involved in the development of a revivalist movement into a denomination with a strong institutional focus.
2. Analyzing the role of language and ethnic factors in the formation of nineteenth-century American religious life.
3. Engaging the reality of the perennial struggle between freedom and order in the life of the church at the general and congregational levels.
4. Probing alternative views of authority in the ministry of the church.

II. Design (assuming 90 minutes)
A. Part 1 (35 minutes)

After providing time to read the case itself (10-12 minutes), the following might occur:

1. Identify the central figures, constituencies, and conflicting parties.
2. Identify issues raised by the case.
3. Relate 1 and 2 together.

(This might be illustrated on a chalkboard or powerpoint with the use of connecting lines.)

B. Part 2 (45 minutes)

1. Arrange a role play, the scene being the General Conference, meeting in session to vote on the power of the office of bishop.

2. It should be assumed that the issues of the case are clearly focused in the minds of the participants.

3. Someone must be Bishop Joseph Long, who moderates the discussion.

4. The group should be divided arbitrarily into a group of "Westerners," who support Esher, a group of "Easterners," who are loyal to Bishop Seybert, and the uncommitted. Charge each group with presenting arguments that disclose issues from its point of view; the "uncommitted" might identify the "imponderable issues." (This step could take 20 miniutes.)

5. Debate the issues.

6. Bring the General Conference to a decision by vote.

7. Consult Resources. Reading from the following sources will assist the student in making use of the cases: (1) Albright, Raymond, *History of*

the Evangelical Church (Harrisburg: Evangelical Press, 1956); (2) Behney, Bruce, and Paul Eller, *A History of the Evangelical United Brethren Church* (Nashville: Abingdon, 1979); (3) Heisey, Terrel, "Immigration as a Factor in the Division of the Evangelical Association," *Methodist History* (Winter, 1980): 43-47.

8. Uses of the case: The design suggested in this teaching note is aimed at theological students or United Methodist church groups.

9. Supplemental information for use by the case teacher

10. After the vote is taken, the teacher might indicate that the consequences of this case were as follows:

The vote was defeated, but the issue was raised again in 1863. The two antagonistic parties continued their debate after the death of Seybert with increasing intensity, resulting in the division of the denomination in 1891-1894 into two churches, the original Evangelical Association (led by Esher, who became a bishop in 1863) and the "Eastern" oriented United Evangelical Church (led by Bishop Rudolph Dubs, a successor to Neitz). These groups were reunited in 1922, with the rise of a new generation of leaders, to form the Evangelical Church. In 1946, this church merged with the United Brethren in Christ to form the Evangelical United Brethren Church, in 1968, the latter church merged with the Methodist Church to form the United Methodist Church. In the 1880's and the 1890's during the heat of controversy, songs were devised in Pennsylvania Dutch by the supporters of each party. One example is as follows:

>Ta-ra-ra-ra boom-de-ay
>De Debsa hen ken karrich may!
>Ta-ra-ra-ra Boom-de-ay,
>De Esher hen ken leit may!
>(Ta-ra-ra-ra boom-de-ay
>The Dubsites don't have a church anymore!
>1a-:a-ra-ra boom-de-ay
>The Esherites don't have any people anymore!)

—See Don Yoder, *Pennsylvania Spirituals* (Lancaster, Pa.; Pennsylvania Folklife Society, 1961), 440-441.

Index

A
à Kempis 39–40, 104, 110
Albright 5, 8–11, 15, 23–24, 28, 31–32, 34, 37, 39–40, 43, 46, 50, 53, 55, 59–64, 71, 74–93, 97–104, 107–115, 121, 125–26, 143, 152, 154–5, 160, 163–70, 174, 181, 183, 188, 196–200
Althaus, Paul 166, 181–2
Aquinas, Thomas 98, 114
Aristotle 114
Arndt, Johann 38–40, 63, 98, 106, 110–11, 115, 121, 154, 166
Arnold, Gottfried 39, 104, 159, 166
Allentown 75, 109, 150
Asbury, Bishop Francis 76, 78, 184
Augsburg Confession 78, 167, 177
Augustine, St. 17–18, 49, 51, 58, 105, 110

B
Bainton, Roland 68
baptism 24–25, 33, 40, 81–82, 136, 138, 159–61, 167, 189
Benedict, St. 38
Bertolet, John 125, 127, 131
Bethlehem, Pennsylvania 137
Bible 15, 34, 59, 78, 127, 129, 170, 180
big meetings 28–29, 47, 134, 140, 161–2
Boehm, Martin 9, 29, 155
Boehme, Jacob 104–106, 110–11, 115, 119, 121, 148–9, 154, 159–60, 188
Bonhoeffer, Dietrich 74
breakthrough 25–26, 47, 103, 105
Buber, Martin 51
Bunyan, John 40, 110
Bushnell, Horace 17–18, 165, 168

C
Cambridge City, Indiana 17, 21, 24, 64, 155, 177
camp meetings (or "bush meetings") 3, 23, 25–28, 52, 105, 123–24, 126, 142, 162, 188, 198
Cell, George 39–40
charismatic 6, 33–34, 142, 163
Chicago, Illinois 52, 149, 154
Chiles, Robert 120, 154

church Dutch, the 71-72, 76, 81, 83, 93, 97-98, 103, 126, 151, 159, 196-97
churchmanship 6, 170-1, 173
Cleveland, Ohio 154, 171
conferences 9, 16, 31, 57, 62, 64, 86, 91, 109, 115, 117, 124, 143, 157, 162, 166, 171, 173-5, 179, 182, 189, 195, 197-8, 200
conversion 32-33, 58, 74-75, 81-82, 94, 96-97, 100, 102, 114, 127, 142, 149, 161, 164, 195, 196
Copernicus, Nicholas 114
Core, Arthur 100, 155, 182, 188
cross bearing 75, 83

D

death 9, 15, 20, 39, 59, 60, 62-63, 73, 75, 77, 96, 97, 98, 102, 106-107, 114-5, 121, 124, 130, 138-40, 163, 177, 180-81, 183, 196-7, 201
Der Christliche Botschafter 10, 28, 82, 86, 133, 142, 188
Dill, John 24-28, 62, 155, 165
discipleship 10, 159, 161
discipline 8, 11, 25, 31, 60-61, 63-64, 72, 85, 89, 115-7, 121, 150-1, 154, 162-4, 170, 174-5, 177, 181, 196-9
Doctrines and Discipline of the Evangelical Association 63-64, 85, 154
Downing, Jim 54-55
dreams 105, 113-15, 117-8, 120-1, 184, 187
Dreisbach, John 78-79, 107, 117, 125-7, 166, 172
Dunkers 24-25, 27, 71, 196

E

ecumenism 152-3
Edwards, Jonathan 34, 63, 91, 100
Episcopacy 31, 195, 198
Erb, Peter 40, 63, 102, 110, 125, 143, 154, 167
eschatology 177, 181
Esher, Bishop John J. 29, 101, 197-201
Evangelical Association 7-8, 10, 16, 23-25, 28-31, 39-40, 60-61, 63-64, 77, 79, 81, 84-86, 91, 101, 111, 126, 135, 139, 150, 154, 157, 160, 163, 166-7, 169-70, 183, 188, 191, 193, 195-97, 201
evangelism 115, 119, 149, 171

F

faith 5-6, 8, 11, 15-21, 28, 32-34, 38-40, 43, 50-51, 55, 58, 66-68, 73-75, 78, 83, 88-90, 95-96, 98, 100, 102, 105, 110, 113-15, 117, 121, 126, 133, 136, 142-3, 148, 158-59, 162, 170, 177, 180-88, 196, 198
forgiveness 81
Francis of Assisi 69, 148

G

Geistliche Viole 101, 126-27, 130-31
German Reformed, the 9, 73, 75-76, 81, 101, 111, 155, 198
Germans 7, 71, 88, 130, 196, 197, 199

Germany 40, 82, 84, 166–67, 170
godliness 7–8, 31, 33–34, 37–40, 43–44, 46, 60, 75–76, 81, 83–84, 87–91, 108, 129, 147, 159, 164–5, 169, 171–2, 179, 184–6, 199
grace 3, 9, 15, 17, 23–25, 27, 31, 33, 37–39, 44–47, 50–51, 54, 59, 60, 62, 66, 67, 74, 82–83, 88, 90, 94–96, 98, 101, 103, 105, 108, 119, 126, 129, 133–43, 155, 158–9, 164–5, 172–3, 182–4, 187, 192–4
Great Awakening 5, 7, 63, 71, 90
Gross 164

H

Hamilton 166
Harmony Society, the 163
healing 62–63, 95, 108, 120, 137, 138–9
heaven 68, 83, 107, 115–7, 124, 128, 139–40, 162, 170, 172, 178–80, 191
Henhoefer, Aloys 85–86
heroes 50–51, 53–55, 130
Hicksville, Ohio 50
Hoffman, Elisha Albright 126
Holy Spirit 5–6, 24–26, 33, 40, 46–47, 50, 58, 63, 72, 83, 94, 106, 136–37, 148, 161, 170, 172, 187
home 3, 8, 17, 19–20, 31, 39, 43, 45–46, 61, 71–72, 93, 100, 103, 107, 109, 113, 118, 124, 133–4, 138–40, 145, 147–50, 153, 155, 163–5, 170–1, 180, 184
humility 62, 107, 115, 143, 163, 172
humor 89
hymns 47, 125–8, 130, 185, 198

I

Illinois 10, 11, 52, 110, 137–8, 195, 197
illness 108, 111, 125
immorality 50, 87, 149
Indiana 10, 16–17, 21, 23–24, 28–29, 31, 50, 62, 64, 72, 91, 102, 123, 130, 138, 143, 149, 151, 155, 165, 177
Indians 67
intellectualism 89
intemperance 88
Iowa 67, 174

J

Jesus Christ 21, 27, 32, 46, 50–51, 57, 66–67, 72–73, 78, 87, 94, 96, 99, 100, 106, 109, 110, 120, 128, 131, 134, 159, 164, 173, 177, 179, 183, 191
justification 33–34, 38, 82, 85, 102, 105, 192

K

Kelsey, Morton 114, 120, 134, 142
Kierkegaard 73, 78

L

Long, Bishop Joseph 174, 180, 195, 199, 200

Lord's Supper 81, 83, 105, 161, 179
love 7, 17–18, 20, 23–25, 38, 49, 51, 54, 69, 72, 74, 82, 85, 95–96, 98–100, 102, 104, 105–106, 108–109, 136, 141, 149, 152–53, 155, 158, 160–62, 164–65, 173, 178–79, 183, 185, 191–3, 199
Luther, Martin 15, 38–40, 59, 65, 75–76, 110, 154, 166, 181–82
Lutherans 24, 45, 75–76, 81, 126, 151–2, 166–7, 197

M

MacNutt, Francis 141, 143
Manheim, Pennsylvania 96, 148
millenium 178–9, 182
Miller, John 10–11, 28, 37, 39, 59–60, 63, 74, 77–78, 89–91, 94, 97, 101, 107–108, 111, 113, 115–18, 121, 151, 152, 155, 160–2, 165, 167–8, 181–2
ministry 5, 7–8, 19, 23, 26, 32, 33, 37, 39, 44, 54, 60, 62–63, 67, 71–72, 77–78, 87, 89–90, 98, 104, 108, 111, 118–20, 123, 134, 135, 137, 141, 149, 151–2, 155, 158, 161, 165, 169, 170, 172–3, 183, 186–8, 196, 197, 200
miracles 137, 140
Moravians 82, 126
mysticism 81, 104, 184, 188

N

narrow way 81, 95, 125, 127–8, 149
National Road 21, 23, 64
Negroes 150
Neitz, Solomon 81–82, 86, 130, 198, 201
Nevin, John Williamson 101, 198
new birth 25, 27, 39, 40, 47, 71, 76, 91, 94, 102, 127, 148, 178, 196
New York 18, 40, 51, 55, 63, 68, 108, 110–11, 120, 154, 158, 168, 197
New York City 75
Noblesville, Indiana 16, 37, 50

O

Ohio 21, 37, 66, 69, 72, 87, 90–91, 130, 140, 147, 149, 151, 154, 174, 180
Orwig, Bishop W. W. 10, 40, 79, 101, 154, 166, 198
Orwigsburg, Pennsylvania 105, 135, 143, 149, 166
Otterbein, Bishop Philip William 9, 11, 29, 39, 40, 63, 71, 73, 75–78, 100, 101, 152, 155, 179, 182–3, 188
Outler, Albert 50, 52, 101, 110, 143, 166

P

Parker, Isaac 180
parting, the 162
penitential struggle 46, 47, 94, 95, 97, 99–100, 103–104, 195
Pennsylvania 8, 20, 23, 25, 44, 47, 59, 62, 67–69, 71, 74–75, 77–78, 81, 86, 88, 91, 94–96, 98, 101, 105, 109–10, 123–6, 130–1, 137, 139, 148–51, 155, 169, 172, 175, 181, 196–9, 201
Pennsylvania Dutch 69, 101, 125–6, 201
Pentecostalism 32, 34

Philadelphia 78, 89, 110, 166, 170, 182
Pietists 39, 40, 47, 58, 73, 98, 115, 130, 166, 178
plain Dutch 71–72, 76, 93, 103, 151, 155, 159, 196
Pope, Alexander 53
prodigal son, parable of 8, 43, 45, 49, 72, 103–104, 106, 113, 149, 159, 183–184
Protestant Reformers 40, 98, 105, 158
Puritans 63, 178, 189

R

Rambach, Johann Jakob 39, 104, 179
Rapp, George 163
rationalism 75, 151, 164
resignation (*Gelassenheit*) 106–109, 164, 182, 184, 191
Roman Catholics 38, 98, 158

S

sanctification 33, 38, 82, 83, 85, 102, 121, 157, 163, 179, 182, 184, 192
Satan 27, 43, 45, 74, 118, 136, 140, 157, 164, 191
Schaefer, Absalom B. 26–28, 57, 62, 64, 86, 154, 174
Scheidler, Monroe Lincoln 5, 8, 10, 16–17, 19, 23–26, 31–32, 37, 39, 43, 49, 51, 54, 60–63, 72, 77–78, 89, 100, 102, 108, 109, 111, 121, 123, 128, 130, 142–43, 149, 155, 165, 168, 173, 177, 184, 185
Schwenkfeld, Caspar 40
shout, the 107, 111
Showers 31, 61
social consciousness 147, 148
South Bend, Indiana 138
Spayth, Henry 78
Spreng, Bishop Samuel P. 10, 11, 17, 20, 29, 46, 53, 55, 56, 62, 64, 79, 86, 91, 101, 102, 111, 121, 142–3, 154–5, 157, 166–7, 171, 174–5, 182, 188–9
suffering 97–98, 108, 161, 173

T

Tauler, Johann 39, 40, 104, 106, 110, 111, 141, 143, 148
Tersteegen, Gerhard 39, 40, 104, 125, 130
theology 32, 35, 40, 58, 68, 81–83, 94, 104, 114, 120, 134, 138, 148, 154, 166, 181–182, 184
Tuttle, Robert G. 10, 34

U

United Brethren in Christ, Church 9, 29, 40, 73, 79, 126, 154, 167, 179, 188, 196, 201
United Methodist Book of Discipline 11, 121, 177, 181
United Methodists 7, 20–21, 28, 32, 51, 65, 74, 88, 96, 100, 103, 123, 153, 181, 183, 185, 187

W

Walter, John 37, 39, 78, 125, 129, 131, 143, 152–3, 161, 165, 167
Warren, Pennsylvania 95, 164

Wesley, Charles 54–55, 126, 164
Wesley, John 7, 32, 39, 40, 63, 75, 101, 110, 126, 143, 148, 159, 166, 183
Winebrenner, John 76
Wisconsin 67, 155, 173
Wissler, Benjamin F. 10, 26–29
witnessing 89, 155, 160, 171
Word of God 34, 38–39, 57, 74, 87, 96, 110, 119, 150, 153, 158, 166

Y

Yeakel, Bishop Reuben 10, 63–64, 78–79, 81, 85–86, 88, 91, 111, 121, 143, 155, 166, 167–8, 174–5, 182, 188–9
Yoder, Professor Don 66, 68–69, 78, 101–102, 110, 123, 128, 130–1, 142, 154–5, 167, 181–2, 201

Z

Zinzendorf, Count Nicholas von 82–83, 152

About the Author

Stephen O'Malley received his B.A. degree from Indiana Central University, 1964; B.D. degree from Yale University Divinity School, 1967; Ph.D. degree from The Graduate School of Drew University, 1970. He has taught church history and historical theology for more than thirty five years. His distinguished professorial career has included stints at five different institutions: Drew University (1968-70; visiting professor, fall 1999), the University of Indianapolis (1970-72), the Graduate Seminary of Phillips University (1972-77), the School of Theology of Oral Roberts University (1977-85) and Asbury Seminary (1985-present). He was installed into the John T. Seamands Chair of Methodist Holiness History in March 1994.

An ordained minister in the United Methodist Church, Steve has preached and lectured throughout the United States and Europe, and has served as pastor of a United Methodist congregation in Graz, Austria. He has earned recognition for his research and publications in post-Reformation and modern Church history, with special emphasis upon Pietism, German-American evangelicalism and the Holiness movement.

He is the author of the definitive study of the Otterbeins' theology, *Pilgrimage of Faith: The Legacy of the Otterbeins*, and a study entitled *Theology and German-American Evangelicalism: Sources in Discipleship and Sanctification*. He has edited more than twenty volumes in the Pietist and Wesleyan Studies series for Scarecrow and is the author of one volume in the series on the History of United Methodist Missions. Recent scholarship includes *Living Grace* (a study in Wesleyan systematic theology translated from German, Abingdon Press), and a position paper to be presented by the General Board of Higher Education and Ministry, to the 2008 General Conference of the United Methodist Church

Steve currently serves as director of the Center for the Study of World Christian Revitaization Movements as Asbury Seminary, and is general editor of the Revitatlization Studies Series, published by the Center. He is married to the former Angeline Gommel, who earned the Ph.D. in family relations-child development at Oklahoma State University. The O'Malleys have jointly conducted workshops in family life at numerous sites, including Fuller Seminary. Angie was a member of the Asbury College faculty from 1986 to 1993 and has also taught at Capella University and the University of Maryland. The O'Malleys have two daughters: Sarah and Karen.

www.ingramcontent.com/pod-product-compliance
Lightning Source LLC
Chambersburg PA
CBHW021142230426
43667CB00005B/216